Computer Games

Computer Games

Text, Narrative and Play

Diane Carr, David Buckingham, Andrew Burn and
Gareth Schott

polity

The right of Diane Carr, David Buckingham, Andrew Burn and Gareth Schott
to be identified as Authors of this Work has been asserted in
accordance with the UK Copyright, Designs and Patents Act 1988.

First published in 2006 by Polity Press

Polity Press
65 Bridge Street
Cambridge CB2 1UR, UK

Polity Press
350 Main Street
Malden, MA 02148, USA

ISBN-10: 0-7456-3400-1
ISBN-10: 0-7456-3401-X (pb)
ISBN-13: 978-0-7456-3400-1
ISBN-13: 978-0-7456-3401-X (pb)

A catalogue record for this book is available from the British Library.

Typeset in 10.5 on 13 pt Swift
by Servis Filmsetting Ltd, Manchester
Printed and bound in Great Britain by T.J. International Ltd, Padstow, Cornwall.

The publisher has used its best endeavours to ensure that the URLs for external
websites referred to in this book are correct and active at the time of going to press.
However, the publisher has no responsibility for the websites and can make no
guarantee that a site will remain live or that the content is or will remain appropriate.

Every effort has been made to trace all copyright holders, but if any have been
inadvertently overlooked the publishers will be pleased to include any necessary
credits in any subsequent reprint or edition.

For further information on Polity, visit our website: www.polity.co.uk

Contents

List of Illustrations

Acknowledgements

This book emerged from a research project called 'The Textuality of Video Games', funded by the UK Arts and Humanities Research Board (grant B/RG/AN8023/APN12462). The project ran from September 2001 to December 2003, and was based at the Centre for the Study of Children, Youth and Media at the Institute of Education, London University. David Buckingham and Andrew Burn co-directed the project, and Diane Carr was the lead researcher; Gareth Schott subsequently joined us from the Psychology Department as a research associate.

Although this was a collaborative project, we have assigned individual or joint authorship to each of the chapters in this book. David Buckingham was responsible for overall editing, and Diane Carr also contributed fine-tuning to each chapter.

An early version of chapter 5 was published as 'Play Dead: Genre and Affect in *Silent Hill* and *Planescape Torment*' in *Game Studies*, 3 (1) (Carr). An early version of chapter 6 appeared as 'Heavy Hero or Digital Dummy: Multimodal Player-Avatar Relations in *Final Fantasy VII*' (Burn and Schott), *Visual Communication*, 3 (3), October 2004. Chapter 9 was first published as 'Moving Between a Spectral and Material Plane: Interactivity in Social Play with Computer Games' (Schott and Kambouri), *Convergence*, 9 (3), 41–55. An early version of chapter 8 appeared as 'Signs from a Strange Planet: Role play and Social Performance in *Anarchy Online*' (Burn and Carr), conference proceedings, COSIGN 2003, 3rd conference on Computational Semiotics for Games and New Media, 10–12 September 2003, University of Teesside, UK, pp. 14–21. Chapter 12 draws on research undertaken with the support of the Eduserv Foundation.

We would like to thank all those who read and critiqued early drafts of our work, especially Simon Egenfeldt-Nielsen, Caroline Pelletier, Julian Kücklich and Siobhan Thomas, and the games industry professionals we interviewed in the course of our research. Diane would like to thank Paul. Thanks also to Liza Chan, and to all the players who answered our questions, especially Pete Katsiaounis, and Barney Oram and his students at Long Road VIth Form College, Cambridge.

Studying Computer Games

David Buckingham

COMPUTER games have existed in some form for almost half a century and have been a mass-market commercial phenomenon for more than twenty-five years. They are a regular part of life for millions of people. Given the current scale, significance and popularity of computer games, the reasons *why* we should study them might seem self-evident. Yet what is less obvious, even to computer games academics, is *how* we should study them. Deciding on the constituents or defining qualities of computer games has also proven rather problematic. How we distinguish computer games from other forms of media might have various ramifications, and different interest groups are naturally motivated to highlight those aspects of computer games that best reflect their own speciality, preoccupations or agenda.

Why study computer games?

Economically, games are one of the most rapidly expanding sectors of the cultural industries. For example, the US Entertainment Software Association claims that, in 2002, 221 million games were sold, and that the industry's annual income in that year of almost $7 billion had more than doubled over the preceding six years.[1] The European Leisure Software Association similarly estimates revenues in Europe of $5.5 billion, of which $3.5 billion were from the UK (which is the largest games market in Europe)[2] and there are alleged to be over 100 million games consoles in use worldwide. In Britain, the games market is twice the size of the market for video rentals and 1.4 times greater than that for cinema admissions,[3] while sales of games in the US exceed those of books (although the latter are in fact also growing). Industry forecasts project continuing expansion: one influential estimate suggests that the worldwide market will grow from $20 billion in 2002 to $30 billion by 2007, with revenues from online gaming growing more than fivefold.[4] The oft-repeated claim that the games

1

industry is 'bigger than Hollywood' may be misleading in some respects, but it is clearly not far from the truth.

Reliable recent statistics on the scale of gameplaying are rather more difficult to obtain. Research conducted in the late 1990s in Britain and the USA suggested that, on average, children were spending between twenty-five and forty-five minutes a day playing computer games (Livingstone and Bovill, 1999; Roberts and Foehr, 2004), although these figures have almost certainly increased since that time. However, it should be pointed out that children are not the sole or even the main market for games. The US Entertainment Software Association asserts that the average age of gameplayers is twenty-nine, and that 41 per cent of the most frequent PC gameplayers are over thirty-five. There are now growing numbers of gamers over the age of sixty.[5] Meanwhile, the market is also diversifying in terms of gender: according to recent figures from ELSPA[6] 39 per cent of gamers in the US are women; nearly 37 per cent in Japan are women; around 70 per cent in Korea; and 25 per cent in Western Europe. What these figures do not reveal, however, is the diversity of games that all these various people are playing. Many women, for instance, play online puzzle or card games, rather than the mainstream titles advertised on television or lining the shelves of computer games retailers. By contrast, the games that we focus on in this book are high-profile games with massive production budgets. Such games, especially those developed with consoles in mind, continue to be aggressively marketed at youthful, male consumers.

Despite these figures, the majority of new computer games lose money, and the costs of entry to the market are rising dramatically; and this inevitably leads to a form of conservatism, since it is safer to reproduce existing successes than to risk innovation (Zimmerman, 2002). The old view of games production as a creative 'cottage industry' is belied by the increasing concentration of the industry in the hands of a small number of large corporations. Likewise, there are significant 'digital divides' in terms of access to gaming, particularly when it comes to forms of online gaming that require subscriptions and broadband access; and, despite the industry's interest in attracting a female market, gameplaying continues to be perceived as a heavily male-dominated activity. Computer gaming is undeniably a mass phenomenon, but it has yet to approach the universal reach of television or video.

These qualifications aside, the sheer scale of computer gaming would suggest that it is worthy of study. Yet we also need to take account of more qualitative claims about the cultural significance of games, and about their effects. Despite their increasing popularity, computer games continue to be denigrated by critics and commentators of many persuasions: they are frequently condemned as a vehicle for sexism and

mindless violence, as antisocial and anti-educational, or alternatively as just a pointless waste of time. As Kurt Squire (2002) and others have pointed out, these kinds of criticisms have recurred with the advent of every new medium – and, as with debates about the effects of television, the evidence for such claims is often equally inconclusive (see Buckingham, 2002).

On the other hand, the popularity of computer games frequently reinforces a generational rhetoric that is characteristic of popular discussions of young people and new media (Buckingham, 2000). Young people are routinely described as a generation of cyborgs, whose relationship with technology has produced new orientations to learning, to play and to social interaction that are radically different from those of their parents. Thus, Jon Katz (2003) argues that gaming has produced a cultural 'chasm' between the generations, and that traditional forms of culture are 'declining and endangered' – although his arguments have generated some equally forthright abuse, even from self-professed gamers.[7] As with the claims about the negative influence of computer games, the evidence here is decidedly limited (Goldstein, 2001); it also tends to ignore the considerable continuities between older forms of gaming and those provided by new technology.

Some games researchers have sought to counter the widespread condemnation of computer games by defining them as a form of 'art'. Henry Jenkins and Kurt Squire (2002), for example, claim that games are one of the 'lively' or popular arts of the modern era. They raise important questions about the aesthetic qualities of games – their origins in other artistic forms, their ways of managing space, their unique approaches to creating mood and stimulating the engagement of players, and their use of texture, colour and light. Steven Poole (2000) likewise explores games using well-established concepts from art and literary criticism, such as genre, narrative and character. We will be drawing on and developing some of these approaches in this book, although we suspect that the claim for games as 'art' raises some rather awkward questions about the category of 'art' itself.

Yet, whether or not they are 'art', computer games are now an established cultural form, with their own history and their own place in the broader landscape of modern culture. While most claim that *Spacewar*, created by Steve Russell at Massachusetts Institute of Technology in the early 1960s, was the first computer game, some British scholars argue that the honour should go to A. S. Douglas, a Ph.D. student at Cambridge, who created a computer version of noughts and crosses (tic tac toe) in 1952.[8] There are now numerous scholarly and encyclopaedic histories of computer games (e.g. Herz, 1997; Kent, 2001; Kline et al., 2003; Sellers, 2001), although most of these are US-centric.

Furthermore, today's games are deeply enmeshed in the 'convergence' that characterizes modern media: books are made into films which are made into games (and vice versa), which in turn generate a myriad of other texts and commodities. Television programmes increasingly purport to be interactive, incorporating specific game-like elements; and the graphic styles and structures of games are taken up by musicians and visual artists in their work. It could even be argued that much contemporary media culture – from *The Matrix* (1999) to *Big Brother* (2000–) – is increasingly aspiring to the condition of the computer game.

Games are also a key factor in the globalization of the media industries. A phenomenon like the recent children's craze *Pokémon* illustrates both the convergence of media and the ways in which games are crucial to building global markets. *Pokémon* began life as a video game, designed for Nintendo's handheld GameBoy console, and subsequently 'span off' into television, movies, trading cards and a whole range of other merchandise. This process of globalization was decidedly double-edged: through a complex web of local franchises, Nintendo sought to 'deodorize' the potentially alienating Japanese aspects of the game, while simultaneously maximizing its Japanese 'cool' (Tobin, 2004). As we shall see, similar processes of cultural appropriation and exchange are at work in Role Playing Games targeted at a much older market, such as the *Final Fantasy* series discussed in chapters 6 and 7.

The current enthusiasm for using computer games in education is also indicative of this broader significance. Many educators are now looking to games as a potential means of re-engaging disaffected learners and of exploiting the apparent benefits of 'interactive' technology. Evidence thus far points to rather limited success – not least because of the limited nature of much 'edutainment' software (Buckingham and Scanlon, 2003). Some researchers have argued that the way forward here is for educators to pay closer attention to the nature of learning in apparently 'non-educational' games, such as those we consider in this book (Gee, 2003).

The reasons why we should study computer games are thus, we hope, fairly self-evident. The more difficult questions are to do with *what* we might study, and *how*.

What is a game?

This book is called 'Computer Games' rather than 'Video Games' (or 'Computer *and* Video Games') simply because it is a more inclusive term – in the UK, games are called 'computer games' irrespective of whether they are played on a PC or on a dedicated games console such as a Playstation or an XBox (and we use the PC to mean 'personal computer' whether it uses a Windows, Linux, or Macintosh operating system). Some games theorists have made a great deal of this distinction. Keith Feinstein (1999), for example, argues that 'computer games' (played on a PC) are more cerebral and strategic in their approach than 'video games' (played on a console or an arcade machine), which are more emotional, and focused on immediacy and action. He also argues that computer games are a solitary pursuit, while video games are more sociable. Others (e.g. Wolf and Perron, 2003a) argue that computer games are less likely to rely on the visual dimension than video games.

It is still possible to identify some differences between console games and those played on a PC, yet the prevalence of cross-platform games (that is, games that can be played on both PCs and consoles) would complicate any attempt to distinguish absolutely between the two. Ultimately, while PCs and consoles are different in important respects, and while certain kinds of games are more associated with one platform than the other, the differences are not sufficient or consistent enough to justify a fundamental schism. Thus, in the context of this book, when we say 'computer games' we refer to games that can be played on a PC or on a console (we have not included analysis of games played on portable or handheld gaming devices).

As we have noted, computer games draw on other media forms including, for example, science-fiction writing, fantasy novels and gangster movies. Computer games, in their turn, infiltrate wider popular culture. Yet, despite this two-way influence, it is of primary importance that computer games are recognized and studied as *games* (Eskelinen, 2001) and not simply as a new form of hypertext, literature, drama or cinema. Several credible and comprehensive definitions of 'game' have been suggested. For example, the games designer Celia Pearce (2002: 113) defines games as follows:

> A game is a structured framework for spontaneous play consisting of:
> - A goal (and a variety of related sub-goals)
> - Obstacles (designed to prevent you from obtaining your goal)
> - Resources (to assist you in obtaining your goal)
> - Rewards (for progress in the game, often in the form of resources)
> - Penalties (for failing to overcome obstacles, often in the form of more obstacles)
> - Information
>   - Known to all players and the game
>   - Known to individual players (e.g. a hand of cards)
>   - Known only to the game
>   - Progressive information (moves from one state of knowledge to another, e.g. Chance cards in *Monopoly*)

The first sentence of Pearce's definition points out the fundamental difference between games and other kinds of cultural texts: games are *played*, and the rules of the game provide a framework for play. Thus a computer game is not as self-contained as a book or a film, and games involve a different type and level of participation from that of reading a novel or watching a movie. For instance, in many (though not all) games, we effectively 'become' a character in the game – we assume the identity of an 'avatar' – and play the game from their perspective. Thus, Pearce argues, rather than simply 'getting to know' characters, players can play a part in actively defining and directing them. Furthermore, players do these things in different ways: in a game, players spontaneously generate variable sequences of action, which are never exactly the same each time (see Eskelinen and Tronstad, 2003).

Jesper Juul (2003) provides a model of what he calls 'gameness' – that is, the essentially game-like characteristics of games. Like Pearce, his primary focus is on computer games, but he attempts to locate them within a broader account of games in general. Juul argues that games can be defined by six common features, as follows:

1. Games are based on rules.
2. Games have variable, quantifiable outcomes.
3. Different values (positive or negative) are assigned to these outcomes.
4. The player invests effort to achieve the desired outcome.
5. The player is emotionally 'attached' to the outcome.
6. Games have negotiable consequences for real life.

Juul's definition clearly distinguishes between games and play. All games must be played, but not all play takes the form of a game. Games entail rules. It is rules that give meaning to players' actions (for example, by defining the different consequences that follow from them). In order to function, rules must be unambiguous: there must be at least some limits on how far they can be changed or renegotiated. Yet, as Juul himself points out, there are well-known games that fail to conform to his definition. *The Sims* (2000), for instance, has no particular outcome, while the rules of a table-top Role Playing Game like *Dungeons & Dragons* (1974) are, in practice, actually negotiable – and these games also have no particular outcome. The computer Role Playing Games (or RPGs), that we examine in this book have relatively quantifiable outcomes, and less negotiable rule sets, but other aspects of table-top RPGs, especially a concern with role, characterization and storytelling, are still evident.

There is a further general quality of games that is only implicit in the definitions we have considered thus far. This relates to the essentially *fictional* nature of games – that is, the idea that games are fundamentally set apart from 'ordinary life'. This argument was proposed by much earlier theorists of play, such as Johan Huizinga (1938/1955) and Roger Caillois (1958/1979). However emotionally 'attached' players may be to the outcome of a game, they nevertheless recognize on some level that it is 'just a game'. This applies even though, as Juul suggests, games can be assigned real-life consequences by players (for example, if they bet on the outcome). As Salen and Zimmerman (2003) put it, the game takes place within a 'magic circle', a frame that marks it off from reality, both spatially (in that the game world is distinct from the real world) and temporally (in that play must begin and end). In play, we can use our knowledge of real life, as well as our knowledge of other games (and indeed of other media or genres). Ultimately, it is the rules that apply within the magic circle that define what things mean – and, in many cases, there are significant differences between what things mean in games (or in different games) and what they mean in real life. We would argue that this applies even in cases like *The Sims* that make strong claims to resemble real life (and that possess what in semiotic terms is called 'high modality').

Distinguishing between games

The attempt to identify an essential 'gameness' of computer games may encourage us to recognize what games such as *Tetris* (1988) and *Final Fantasy X* (2001) have in common; but what they have in common may in fact be rather less interesting or important than the ways in which they differ. Of course, there are several fairly obvious distinctions we might make between computer games. We can distinguish between games in terms of the point of view players adopt (first person, third person or 'god'); between games with single or multiple players or teams; between games with defined levels of difficulty or progress and those without; between games that are based on completing tasks within a given time, and those that are not; between games that encourage exploration and those that require us to follow a linear path; and so on. As all this indicates, the differences between computer games are not simply about the manner in which they represent settings or narratives or characters – in other words, about those elements that apply to other media or cultural forms (which may in fact be more or less superficial). They are also about the ways in which games are *played*.

For example, Pearce's definition (above) draws attention to the different *economies* of games – their balance of rewards and penalties. Thus, we might make distinctions between the economies of games in terms of their diversity and complexity, and the degree of control that they afford to players (for example, through permitting 'trading' of one form of 'currency' or resource for another). Likewise, Juul alerts us to the fact that games differ in terms of the balance between elements of chance and elements of strategy. Indeed, it is essentially because of the element of chance that a game *must* be different each time it is played. A slightly broader way of looking at this is to say that there is a balance between elements that can be controlled by the player, and those that cannot be. Mark Wolf identifies four necessary 'elements' of games as follows:

> those indicating the player's presence in the game (the player-character); those indicating the computer's presence in the game (computer-controlled characters); objects that can be manipulated or used by game characters; and the background environment that generally serves as the setting and is not manipulated or altered by any of the characters during the game. (2003: 50)

Obviously, in the context of a single game, these elements would have to exist in some kind of coherent relationship. This recalls Salen and Zimmerman's definition of games, which stresses that games are systems: 'a set of parts that interrelate to form a complex whole' (2004: 55).

Another key element specific to games is that of *rules*. For example, Aki Jarvinen (2003) outlines a taxonomy of different types of game rules, as follows:

1. Components. These are rules relating to the properties of objects within the game (such as tools, avatars or resources) that define their number, status or value.
2. Procedures. These relate to the actions that players perform in order to play and to advance towards their goal. Thus, it may be that procedures have to be performed in a certain order, using certain components, or at certain points in the game.
3. Environments. This is the physical space of play, which may be more or less abstract. Environments typically contain objects or paths that permit or constrain movement, and define the boundaries of the game world.
4. Themes. Themes are the 'content' of the game – for example, puzzle-solving or driving or fighting or escaping to safety. They may be more or less abstract, and can enable players to use knowledge drawn from other areas of media or of real life (such as sport).
5. The interface. This refers to our means of access to the game, for example a board or a pack of cards or a computer screen. The interface may be more or less complex, but it is this that governs how we gain access to the game world.

Jarvinen suggests that these different types of rules may be combined in different ways, and prioritized or marginalized in different games or game genres. They may apply in different ways in different locations (or levels) of a particular game, or at different times, and they can be mutually interdependent or not.

Another significant component here is that of *obstacles* – or what Aarseth (1997) refers to as the 'aporias' or 'gaps' that effectively provoke the 'work' that is required to play the game. Markku Eskelinen and Ragnhild Tronstad (2003) provide a useful categorization of these gaps in gameplay, as follows:

1. Gaps can be either static or dynamic. Static gaps are always present and must always be overcome; dynamic gaps can be avoided and the goal can still be reached.
2. Gaps may be determinate or indeterminate: that is, they may or may not function in the same way each time.
3. Gaps may be transient or intransient: we may have to overcome them in a fixed (limited) time, or not.
4. Personal gaps are specific to a particular character (that is, to the avatar we play during the game); impersonal gaps apply to all characters.
5. Controlled gaps may appear depending on the player's progress and skills, whereas random gaps can appear at any time.
6. Linked gaps are connected to (and dependent upon) other gaps, while unlinked ones are not.

Taxonomies of this kind provide some ways of exploring the differences between games, which readers might wish to apply to their own chosen examples. (There are several others now emerging within the academic literature: see, for example, the various contributions to Wolf and Perron, 2003b; and Goldstein and Raessens, 2004.) On one level, they alert us to the diverse characteristics of games as structured frameworks for play (to use Pearce's terms), or as rule-governed systems (to use Salen and Zimmerman's). Clearly, these differences have significant implications for the experience of players. They determine how challenging a game appears to be, how much control it appears to give us, and how it seeks to motivate us to continue playing. The sense of engagement or frustration or immersion or boredom – the pleasure or displeasure – we experience in playing a game is thus at least partly determined by its 'gameness', or what might be called its ludic qualities (the term 'ludic' derives from the Latin word *ludus*, meaning 'game').

While such definitions and typologies are valuable, considering computer games in these terms by no means wholly explains the nature of gameplay. The experience of play also depends upon how we interpret and use these various elements of the game, and how they relate to our own existing enthusiasms and preoccupations. What players and reviewers call 'playability' is certainly an important dimension of games, and we can begin to define it in terms of some of the dimensions noted above. Yet what attracts and motivates players may also be the visual spectacle of the game, the storytelling, the emotional appeal of the characters, the use of humour, the sense that the game is somehow relevant to their own lives, and so on. In other words, games have a *representational* dimension that may be crucial to their appeal – and it is a dimension that we ignore at our peril.

Meanwhile, of course, gaming is also a *social* activity. This is literally the case if we choose to play with others; but even if we play alone, the wider culture of gaming involves a considerable amount of interpersonal interaction, both face-to-face and virtual. These elements are frequently emphasized in the research on gameplayers, particularly in relation to children (see Buckingham, 2002; Ermi and Mayra, 2003; Jessen, 1999), although they are often neglected by those who focus mainly on game 'texts'. Yet this too is a crucial dimension of the study of games.

Given this diversity, there are definite limits to the value of a generalized theory of games. For this reason, in this book we have chosen to focus on a specific genre or genres, rather than on computer games as a whole. The games that we discuss are computer Role Playing Games (or RPGs) and, to a lesser extent, action adventure games. We are particularly interested in these genres, because such games celebrate their relationships to other media forms (cinema or comics, for instance), and clearly rely, in terms of their appeal, on the creation of complex worlds, intriguing characters and twisting narratives. When analysing RPGs we have no wish to ignore their 'gameness' – but neither do we wish to ignore their obvious commitment to their representational aspects, or the social dimensions of play. In fact, it is the relationship between the game as system – its representational factors – and the social dimensions of play, that is of particular interest to us.

Who studies 'Game Studies'?

The question of how games relate to (and differ from) other kinds of cultural texts is not a purely academic concern. On one level, it is a legal issue, which relates to anxieties about media effects and the need for regulation. Thus, if we were to prove that players 'identify' with the protagonist of a first-person shooter game in a much more direct and powerful way than they do with the protagonist of an action movie, the case for censoring such games might become stronger (see The St Louis Court Brief, 2003; and Kline, 2003). It is also a cultural issue and an economic issue, which relates to the growing convergence of the media industries. If computer games are positioned primarily as 'spin-offs' from other media (such as the game versions of feature films or popular television quiz shows), then there are significant questions raised about the potential sources of innovation within the industry.

As Marinka Copier (2003) observes, the process of defining what a game is (and is not) also entails defining what game studies is (and is not). The attempt to define 'gameness', or the essential qualities of games, is thus intimately related to this struggle to establish computer games studies as an independent discipline. So, even within the academy, the question of how we define a game is tied up with the operation of institutional power, and has been subject to ongoing territorial claims and counterclaims. Computer games studies is a new field and, inevitably, most of those involved are refugees from other disciplines. An anthology such as Routledge's *Video Game Theory Reader* (Wolf and Perron, 2003b), for example, features contributions drawing from literary reception theory, psychoanalysis, art history, postmodernism and cognitive psychology.

For some, this disciplinary promiscuity is a problem. To establish computer games studies as a new humanities discipline, it is necessary to demonstrate that the topic of research is not sufficiently served, appreciated or understood. Thus, in July 2001, Espen Aarseth launched the first issue of a new online journal, *Game Studies*, with an editorial declaring it to be 'Computer game studies, year one', in which he firmly divorced the study of games from related disciplines such as film and media studies, literary studies and other aspects of new media. Others see the emergence of game studies not only as a matter of establishing a new discipline, but also as a challenge to established disciplines. Frans Mayra (2003), for example, argues that the genie of 'interactivity', once released from its bottle, will result in established theories of art, culture and learning (and the rest) having to be rewritten; although other games theorists (such as Aarseth (1997) and – even more strongly – Newman (2002)) dismiss the very notion of 'interactivity' as imprecise and meaningless. Others argue that the study of games should revolutionize existing disciplines, while still somehow preserving them: Julian Kücklich (2003), for example, argues that computer games are the ultimate fulfilment of postmodernist literary theory, and that all texts can ultimately be seen as games. Others seek merely to apply well-established theoretical approaches from literary or film studies (see, respectively, Rockwell, 1999, or Rehak, 2003), with rather less revolutionary intentions. Meanwhile, yet others argue for the relevance of theories of drama and performance (Eskelinen and Tronstad, 2003).

Theory developed especially for computer games is certainly useful (as the typologies and definitions used in this chapter demonstrate). Yet we would argue that theories drawn from narrative theory, film studies, social semiotic theory, sociology and audience research are also applicable – albeit not without thoughtful adaptation. Often what is interesting is not what such theories tell us about games, but rather the manner in which a game's playability complicates or challenges the theories themselves.

In this book we analyse games and game genres that foreground their associations to other kinds of texts. We recognize their distinctive identity as games, at the same time as we acknowledge their associations with other forms of popular culture. This emphasis is due in part, no doubt, to the fact that we teach and write from within a media studies tradition. This means that we are not primarily concerned with technical or aesthetic questions of game design, although we do address these in chapter 11, and in passing throughout the book. Our primary aim is to develop a set of critical 'tools' that will enable students of popular culture to engage with the unique characteristics of a relatively new cultural form.

The study of computer games involves revisiting a dilemma that media studies scholars have long (and perhaps quixotically) contended with: if we focus on analysing the structure of texts, do we risk underestimating the social and cultural specifics of the audience, and the degree to which such factors might alter their 'reading' of the same material? If, on the other hand, we focus on the audience, and ignore the specifics of the particular text they are engaging with, do we risk misunderstanding the audience's experience? This tension between textual analysis (commonly associated with the humanities) and audience-based research (generally associated with the social sciences) is impossible to ignore in the context of computer games and gaming culture, precisely because the game text is playable: it is only realized through play, and play is a lived, social and culturally situated experience. Hence the relationship between the text and the player is central to the structure of this book.

Accordingly, we begin by focusing on games as 'texts'. To call a game a text is not to deny that it involves play, mutability, chance, interactivity or change. Being a text does not mean that something has to have materiality; nor is it limited to things that are written down, as texts might well incorporate a variety of communicative modes (speech, song, sound, writing, visual design). A text is composed for some kind of purpose beyond the everyday, the disposable or the ephemeral. What matters is that it is recognizable and that (in some broad sense) it is replicable. So, for our purposes, the fact that computer games are only fully realized when they are played does not exempt them from being 'texts'.

In chapters 2–5 we look at the textual characteristics of games, their playable systems and their representational factors. More to the point, we examine the ways that playability and representation interrelate. We look in turn at genre, narrative, gameplay, space and navigation. Our analysis in these early chapters is largely based on our own experiences as players. The advantage of this approach is that it enables us to engage directly and in some detail with the games themselves. However, the limitations are obvious: the analysis will inevitably reflect the perspective of a particular player/author.

As the book proceeds, then, the focus progressively shifts from the game to the player's relationship with the game – to the avatar and the 'roles' available to players (in chapter 6) and to the manifestations of that relationship in fan art (in chapter 7). In these chapters we begin to draw more on interviews and email dialogues with other players. We focus on the ways that games combine different 'communicative modes' (that they are, in fact, 'multimodal') and analyse the ways in which players respond to, and manipulate, these various modes when interpreting a game, or designing their own experience of play. Finally, we turn our attention more towards social aspects of gaming, and to relationships between players. Thus, in chapter 8 we examine an online multiplayer game, while in chapter 9 we look at co-playing in a domestic setting on a games console, and in chapter 10 we consider the degrees of agency enjoyed by gamers, both in the act of play and in the context of fan culture. In chapter 11 we ask how the issues we have discussed have relevance to professional games developers, while chapter 12 focuses specifically on gender, looking across the different dimensions of gaming that we have addressed in the book as a whole.

There are many important issues that we have not addressed in the course of this book. We have focused on a limited selection of graphically rendered commercial games, and on specific genres. As such, we cannot hope to do justice to the full diversity of contemporary games. We have also largely bracketed off the 'political economy' of games – that is, the commercial dimensions of the global games industry, the marketing and promotion of games, and the patterns of ownership and control that significantly determine the kinds of games that are produced. There are also omissions that are the result of our own disciplinary leanings: we do not focus in any detail on issues of hardware, games programming or cognition, for example. These are all important issues; and, as the study of computer games continues to develop, new research in these areas is emerging all the time.

Another point worth noting is that, at the time of writing, the games that we are analysing are already several years old. We recognize that no matter how up-to-date we attempted to be in our selection of games, they would be passé by the time the book was published. For this reason we have focused on games that are widely known and played, and that might be regarded in some sense as representative. Our aim is to explore a series of key issues in debates about games in relation to these specific case studies; and, in the process, to offer some models or strategies that readers might use in analysing games of their own choice.

CHAPTER 02

Defining Game Genres

Andrew Burn and Diane Carr

MANY computer games could be said to offer degrees of role play, but not all games that do so are categorized as Role Playing Games (RPGs). So what is an RPG? To ask this question is to invoke the complex set of practices by which computer games are described and classified by a range of groups, with a variety of interests – from developers to marketing departments, reviewers to fans, cult audiences to academics. In some ways these categorizing practices are a continuation of the ways that the idea of genre has been used in literature, film, art and music. There are, however, important differences. In order to describe these differences, and prior to examining what differentiates RPGs from other game genres, it is necessary to review the theory and practice of genre classification itself.

What is genre?

The term 'genre' is used in everyday language, but it is also used in a more specialized or technical sense within literary, film and media theory. Genre theory belongs to a tradition of classification often traced back to Aristotle who, in about 335 BC, laid out systematic criteria for the analysis of epic poetry, tragedy and comedy. For Aristotle poetry was, above all, representation, or *mimesis* – and this serves as one basis of his classification: how do different fictions *represent* the world in different ways? He was also concerned with *form* as another basis for distinguishing between various kinds of poetry, and with *medium* (voice, flute or lyre). This balance between content, form and medium continues in genre theory to the present day.

The most influential modern theory of genres is that of Mikhail Bakhtin, a Russian cultural and literary theorist who saw genres as a form of *social action*. According to Bakhtin, genres are the conventional uses of language by social groups, and range from the 'little speech genres' (or everyday uses of language) discussed by his colleague Volosinov (1973) to the major genres of the novel analysed by Bakhtin himself (1981). The founding characteristic of language in Bakhtin's view is *dialogue*: genres are forged in the ceaseless exchange between speaker and listener.

Bakhtin's work, then, adds four new ideas to the Aristotelian model. First, genres are not to be found only in artistic texts, but in all uses of language – from the job interview to the political speech. Second, genre is not only found in the text, but also in the social context that produces it. Third, genre is not a fixed set of properties, but is fluid: it is constantly remade in a dialogic (from 'dialogue') process in order to suit the needs of the social groups who produce, define and contest its structures. Finally, genres are resources for both the production and the reception of texts. This means that they exist as patterns that cannot be ignored by makers of texts, however much they may seek to transform them. It also means that they serve as resources for the social use and the interpretation of texts by their audiences.

To give a brief example: later in this chapter we explore how the RPG genre was received and transformed by Japanese computer game designers in the 1980s. Games such as *Final Fantasy VII* hark back to earlier sets of generic characteristics (that themselves reflect the social interests of particular games communities), but these new games were designed to address the needs and interests of a different community, which was reared on the popular narratives of post-war Japan. These new RPGs were wedded to a different technology (games consoles) and, while they borrowed from pre-existing RPGs, they held no particular commitment to retain or duplicate their structures. Thus the genre evolved to accommodate itself to new social uses and new resources, both cultural and technological.

According to Bakhtin, this process of generic change is characteristic of language in general. Language, he argues, is naturally fluid and diverse; it contains many dialects and accents. However, there are also powerful forces that attempt to limit this diversity; that seek to pull language towards a unifying, standardized form. Similarly, genres could be regarded as ideological straitjackets that control how texts represent the world, and how we engage with them; or they can be regarded as structures whose patterns help us to navigate through and beyond existing representations of reality, and to find communities of like-minded readers, viewers and players.

The idea of genre as a form of social practice has been further developed in the field of film studies. Early film theorists tended to define genres in terms of more or less fixed sets of characteristics, for example, particular narrative devices, settings or character types. However, Steve Neale (1980) argued that genres were not simply about the qualities of film texts, but 'sets of expectations, orientations and conventions' that were shared between film-makers, the film industry and audiences. The industry might seek to fix or stabilize the characteristics of a genre in the hope of capitalizing on earlier successes, but it is also bound to encourage change (for example through the creation of new, hybrid genres), in the hope that it might reach new audiences. Neale's more recent work (2000, 2002) has tended to focus on the economic dimensions of this process – in effect, on how the industry attempts to use genre to regulate audience behaviour in order to generate profit. Yet genres are not solely defined by the industry: what 'counts' as a romance or an action movie, for example, is also debated by critics and filmgoers. Genre, then, is a matter of the dynamic relationships between producers, audiences and texts.

A further development of the idea of genre can be found in social semiotic theory, which we use in analysing some of the games in this book (see chapters 6, 7 and 8). Social semiotic theorist Gunther Kress (2003) writes that genres seek to establish particular kinds of interactions between producers, readers and texts. For example, his analyses of scientific texts suggest that in some cases science is defined as a set of objective facts that the reader is expected to learn. In other cases, it is offered as a more subjective narrative with which the reader is invited to engage in an active and questioning way. Likewise, we might classify games according to the way in which they establish the terms of the player's interaction. These terms might be multiple and simultaneous, however; so, while this form of classification is relevant, it might not be the most useful place to begin when classifying a game.

We could prioritize one aspect of a computer game in order to simplify or expedite its generic classification, but in truth these games are hybrid forms, and thus they invite compound classifications. As we noted in the previous chapter, computer games are played on various platforms, they incorporate different rules, outcomes, and obstacles, and they represent their worlds, themes and inhabitants in different ways. Generic classification that foregrounds any one of these factors would be valid, yet, taken in isolation, each would be (to varying degrees) partial. Thus, a game can simultaneously be classified according to the platform on which it is played (PC, mobile phone, XBox), the style of play it affords (multiplayer, networked, or single user, for instance), the manner in which it positions the player in relation to the game world (first person, third person, 'god'), the kind of rules and goals that make up its gameplay (racing game, action adventure), or its representational aspects (science fiction, high fantasy, urban realism). All these possibilities for classification coexist in games, and none are irrelevant, but we would argue that the *style of gameplay* on offer is of fundamental significance.

Game genres

We cited various theorists in chapter 1, including Salen and Zimmerman (2003), and Celia Pearce (2002), in order to argue that games are, first and foremost, rule-based systems, or structures for play. Games involve rules, and a game's genre is (to a large degree) determined by its rules.[1] Computer RPGs owe their rules to earlier table-top RPGs like *Dungeons & Dragons*. The rules govern timing and turn taking, combat outcomes, character creation, and the kinds of weapons and magic on offer to different character types. While table-top RPGs are open-ended (with negotiable rule sets), offline computer RPGs tend to have set outcomes – to 'win' is to complete the quest and defeat the archvillain. However, an emphasis on exploration, story-telling and characterization does mean that these games are relatively non-linear. Action adventure games like *Tomb Raider* (1996), on the other hand, tend to set specific goals that must be attained in a particular order before the player can progress. Rules are likely to concern the ways that resources need to be rationed or used up, the combination of commands that are necessary to get the avatar successfully past a spatial obstacle or the kind of error that will have them plunging to a (temporary) death.

Meanwhile, in those sports simulation games that mimic the experience of a single physical activity, such as car racing or skateboarding, the rules and objectives of the game are likely to relate directly to these activities. Alongside this will be the *economies* related to the competitive dimensions of such activities, such as rival drivers. A strategy game, by contrast, will typically be based on territorial objectives, and rules that are orientated towards the marshalling and management of available resources, whether these are armies, weapons, labour or geographical features. Even open-ended simulation games like *Sim City* or *The Sims* have rules that determine how characters and locations are constructed, and what can then be done with them.

When it comes to genre designation, gameplay is of crucial import, but it is still only part of the story. Our research with players suggests that, while expertise in and loyalties to particular kinds of gaming does matter, players also select and value particular games for their representational aspects. As we explore more in later chapters, online fan communities value these factors to the extent that they will invest enormous effort in expanding on these features, writing poems about characters in *Final Fantasy*, producing concept drawings for new characters in *Oddworld: Abe's Oddysee*, or inventing complicated personal lives for their characters in *Anarchy Online*.

Genre in practice

The idea of genre is very much an everyday part of gaming. It is key to how games are produced and marketed, and central to their evaluation by critics and players. The online game magazine *Videogame Review* (<www.pcgamereview.com>), for instance, organizes its player-submitted reviews by genre ('game type'). Their classifications seem fairly straightforward to begin with, and include adventure, puzzle, racing, simulation, sports, strategy and role playing. The local diversities buried beneath these classifications only become apparent within the text of the reviews. Here, for example, three, reviewers of *Final Fantasy VII* assess the game.[2]

> There's no describing how this game makes you feel, the story grabs ahold of you and never lets go . . . The gameplay is the best in any rpg I've ever played . . . The materia system was beautiful and the magic spells and summon materia were magnificently animated. (Review submitted by OmegaReaper777, 1 August 2004)

> Final fantasy 7 is . . . possibly the best RPG of all. For it's time, FFVII's graphics were stunning and brilliant . . . The storyline is very deep and you feel as if you personally know the characters. The music wraps you up in the emotions and makes you feel as if you are there (Review submitted by Eliza Kyo, 6 October 2002)

> I might not mind the 'random battles' (also known as 'every three steps you fight') if the storyline was any good. However, that isn't even the case. The storyline is this: Follow Sephiroth around until you finally, at the end of this mess of a game, kill him. Woo-hoo. Frankly, when Aeris died, I didn't care. I mean, Aeris had no personality. Or maybe she did, if you consider 'stereotypical giggling girls' to be a personality type. (Review submitted by Seifer, 3 December 2001)

These reviews reflect the approaches to genre that we have discussed. For one thing, different aspects of the game are identified and assessed, some of which (music, characterization, narrative) relate to the game's representational 'dressing', while others relate more to gameplay. These reviews are located in a specific context, and produced by a particular set of gamers. The reviews fall within the umbrella category of RPGs, but contributors make fine distinctions within that magazine's community, and different aspects of various games are prioritized and prized by different players. For instance, the reviewers tended to compare *Final Fantasy* to other Japanese RPGs, while games from the *Baldur's Gate* franchise were more frequently compared to table-top RPGs. In accordance with Kress's arguments, the conventions of genre serve here to express these players' relations both to other participants in the play culture, and to the text itself. These reviews also illustrate the notion that genre is dialogic (in Bakhtin's terms): reviewers make comparisons, and thus respond to the history of the genre, as well as to a specific game text, while directly addressing the reader, as a fellow-player and as 'you'.

Another online magazine, *Gamespot* (<www.gamespot.com>), attempts a much more complex system of classification. It allows readers to 'browse by genre'. Again, the list seems fairly straightforward at first glance, and very similar to the genres listed in *Videogame Review*: Action, Adventure, Driving, Puzzle, RPG, Simulations, Sports, Strategy. However, once individual games are selected, the genre description is broken down into a series of more detailed units. *Gran Turismo 4* becomes 'Driving > Racing > GT/Street'. *The Sims* is described as 'Miscellaneous > Virtual Life'. *Silent Hill 4* is 'Action Adventure > Horror'. *Mafia* is 'Action > Shooter > Third-Person > Historic'. *Baldur's Gate: Dark Alliance II* is 'Roleplaying > Action RPG'. And finally, *Final Fantasy XI* is 'Roleplaying > Massively Multiplayer Online > Fantasy'.

These complex genre distinctions illustrate the hybrid nature of game texts. They acknowledge the mix of game systems (Driving; RPG; Shooter), the social experiences offered by the games (Street; Virtual Life; Massively Multiplayer Online), the characteristic point-of-view options (third person; first person), as well those representational features that are closer to the familiar genres of literature and film (horror; historical; fantasy). There are yet finer distinctions that can be made: between *Dungeons & Dragons*-derived RPGs played on PCs, and Japanese RPGs played on consoles; between offline and online RPGs; and so on.

As this suggests, it is important to understand game genres both in terms of the *social practices* of those who produce and those who play games, and in terms of the *textual characteristics* of games themselves – both the representational dimensions and the forms of play that are on offer. Genres bear the different motivations of these various social groups: from the marketing intentions of game distributors, to the fan commentaries of player communities, from the aesthetic intentions of the independent game developer, to the analytical intentions of critics and academics. Genre classifications represent an expression by each of these groups of their relation to each other, and to the text – and so genres will evolve to express competing interpretive commentaries, marketing drives, player tastes and so on. Genres are dynamic, dialogic and historical; they build on the relatively settled conventions of the past, and adapt to the needs of the future.

RPGs: Some distinguishing features

Many computer games offer the player the chance to assume or play a role, whether it is as a hyperactive marsupial, a hapless alien worker, a soldier or a secret agent. There are, however, marked differences between this kind of implicit role play, and the deliberate role playing at the heart of RPGs. According to most accounts computer 'Role playing games really owe it all to *Dungeons & Dragons*.[3] Created by TSR (Tactical Studies Rules), *Dungeons & Dragons* was a game that allowed people to role play a fantasy character created on paper by rolling dice' (Waine, 2001: 98). In these (non-computer) games, Role Players create a character that 'levels up' as they accumulate skills and experience points. They collaborate, acting 'in role' with others to play out scenarios under the direction of a referee of sorts, the 'Game Master' or 'Dungeon Master'.[4] The earliest text-based action adventure games playable on a computer (such as *Adventure*, made in the mid-seventies),[5] also borrowed elements from *Dungeons & Dragons*-style games (mazes, treasure, monsters and magic). Contemporary action adventure games and computer RPGs continue to share key characteristics. At this point, a brief comparison of the two will help to outline the generic tendencies of each.

In action adventure games such as *Tomb Raider* or *Oddworld: Abe's Oddysee* (1997) the avatar is provided by the game. He or she is characterized by the game's backstory, and their physical capabilities (strength or speed, for example) are, to a large extent, predetermined. The hero or heroine might detour to rescue others, but by and large he/she tends to travel alone – although, as games such as *Ico* (2001) and *Primal* (2003) prove, this is not always the case. The avatar's path through the game world is generally quite pre-set: a particular set of puzzles or obstacles need to be confronted and overcome, in a given order. Aside from gradually acquiring bigger weapons, the avatar does not necessarily alter through the game: thus, it is the player's strategic acquisition of skills that matters. Obstacles tend to have a single solution, there is relatively little dialogue or on-screen text, the menu options are quite straightforward, and the 'economies' of the game relate to easily quantifiable properties, such as the character's health status, and the amount of ammunition that he or she is carrying. Confrontations tend to occur in 'real time', with success allowing for onward progression, and failure resulting in injury or death. In an action adventure game, the goals are usually clearly proposed and unambiguous, and there is an emphasis on spectacle, pace and accuracy. For these reasons such games are often pleasurable to co-play with companions, watching and playing in turn.

In contrast to this, in a computer RPG the protagonist (more generally called a 'character' than an 'avatar') is likely to be constructed or at least developed by the player. The player may have a choice about the kind of protagonist he or she will use: it may be possible, for example, to play the same game as an ambitious fighter, or a wise negotiator, or an inept thief. As the player moves through the game, the protagonist acquires experience points that translate into specialist skills. One outcome of this character specialization is that the protagonist tends to survive longer, and progress faster, if they are supported by a team of diversely skilled companions: a thief character to disarm traps and pick locks, a magic user for protection and healing, a fighter for defence. This is true even in stand-alone RPGs with a single user. In such cases, the player might construct the central character and lead a team of computer-generated teammates. RPGs tend to feature multiple quests and long, journey-based narratives set within detailed and crowded worlds. The player mulls over various strategic options, manages sets of skills, distributes experience points and shuffles loaded inventories, all of which means that RPGs tend to prioritize reflection, reading and strategy over pace or spectacle.

We would argue that in order to be considered an RPG, a game would need to offer (to a greater or lesser degree) the ludic characteristics we have outlined here. This would hold true whether the game's representational aspect evoked a futuristic alien planet, a suburban neighbourhood or a world of orcs and elves. In this sense, it is the characteristics of the *game*, rather than the way that the game world is *represented*, that define its generic status. However, it does not follow that these representational qualities should be ignored. When it comes to the preferences of users, gameplay and representational factors are often entwined. As we shall argue in more detail in the following chapters, neither of these two elements has absolute priority: in the case of RPGs, the interaction between them is a crucial part of the gaming experience.

In the remainder of this chapter we introduce three particular RPGs, each of which is explored in more detail in the chapters that follow. These games are played on different platforms, and each represents a very different game world, but they are all RPGs. The first game, *Baldur's Gate*, is an obvious candidate for analysis: this PC game features all the characteristic gameplay elements of an RPG, and it also celebrates the most conventional of RPG game worlds (high fantasy, elf and orc infested). Second we consider *Final Fantasy VII*, from the massively successful Japanese franchise. The *Final Fantasy* games were designed primarily for consoles, and they rework generic elements to a degree (players do not construct the central protagonist from scratch, for example). However, the *Final Fantasy* games feature team play, inventory management and skills, and so are clearly RPGs. Finally, we look at a more recent online multiplayer game, *Anarchy Online*. While this game transposes the action to a faraway alien planet, it too features a familiar set of elements (character construction and specialization, for instance) that we see as characteristic of the genre.

Baldur's Gate

Baldur's Gate is a 'classic' example of an RPG in that it is directly adapted from the table-top game *Dungeons & Dragons*.[6] As we have noted, table-top RPGs are elaborate and open-ended. The emphasis is on developing an interesting protagonist while acting 'in role'. Games are hosted and adjudicated by a Game Master who, to a greater or lesser degree, follows a handbook of rules, and throws dice to provide an element of chance. Fantasy games such as *Dungeons & Dragons* themselves evolved from earlier game forms. According to Fine (1983: 8–12) fantasy Role Playing Games evolved from War Gaming (and War Games have been played in one form or another for thousands of years). War Gaming involves the accurate re-creation of a historic battle or conflict, and the player does not take on the character of a participant. In fantasy RPGs, however, players do situate themselves as characters within the scenario, and traditional military units and technologies are replaced by orcs and mages.

As we have noted, an RPG could be set in 1940s Paris, seventeenth-century Japan or on board a Klingon freighter: it is not the setting that determines its generic designation. Nevertheless, when Role Playing Games made the move to computers, certain conventions were brought along. *Baldur's Gate* celebrates the most obvious of these: the sword and sorcery, dragons and orcs of high fantasy. *Baldur's Gate* is set in 'The Forgotten Realms' – an *Advanced Dungeons & Dragons* campaign setting that strongly resembles Tolkien's Middle Earth. The Forgotten Realms in their turn feature in a series of fantasy books commissioned by *Advanced Dungeons & Dragons'* publishers (such as *Canticle*, by R. A Salvatore, first published by TSR in 1991).

The *Baldur's Gate* franchise is part of a family of PC games that began to emerge from BioWare, Black Isle Studios and Interplay during the 1990s. The games share a game engine that was developed specifically to deal with the complexities of *Advanced Dungeons & Dragons'* rules. The series could be said to have ended with the release of *Neverwinter Nights* in 2002. This game dropped the look and the interface of the earlier games, and it was sold with a toolset, meaning that players could conceivably build their own game scenarios and landscapes, and host multiplayer events while operating as Game Master. Alternatively, the series could be seen as ending with the release of *Baldur's Gate: Dark Alliance* (2001). This was developed specifically for console gaming and as a consequence, the menus and rules are simplified, and the perspective (or 'camera') modified. Some players of *Baldur's Gate* meet online to join networked versions of the game (with up to six participants). Other associated online activities include sharing character biographies and player-built chapters or new characters. While *Baldur's*

Gate succeeded as an offline single-player mainstream commercial game, these online activities affirm the game's status as an RPG, by highlighting its relationship to previous Role Playing forms.

Baldur's Gate was far from being the first (or last) computer game to draw on Tolkien's work. There are numerous examples of RPGs (on every format and platform, from text-based MUDS (Multi-User Dimensions), to graphically rendered online persistent worlds) that directly or indirectly draw on *The Hobbit* (first published 1937) and the *Lord of the Rings* trilogy (first published 1954–5). Tolkien's work lends itself to gaming – and the reasons for this are not difficult to identify. Through his phenomenally popular novels Tolkien presents a huge, detailed and varied world, populated by species with different traits and distinct cultures. In addition to this, his narratives hinge on fellowships of diversely skilled individuals, undertaking missions, fighting monsters and uncovering treasure. Maps, navigation and travel are pivotal to his stories and, as computer games theorists have noted, these are also central to many computer games, especially those that feature episodic scenarios set in vast and explorable worlds (Fuller and Jenkins, 1995).

The inhabitants, flora and fauna of Middle Earth arrived in *Baldur's Gate* via *Dungeons & Dragons*. Other, perhaps less obvious, elements of Tolkien's work also appear to have survived the move from novel to game, and to computer game. In *Baldur's Gate*, characters become fatigued and ineffective if they do not get regular sleep. Sleeping for '8 hours' (which takes a few seconds of the player's time) restores the team's health and heals any injuries. These temporal factors recall Tolkien's novels – especially a pattern identified and described by Jenny Turner, in 'Reasons for Liking Tolkien'.

> To read *The Lord of The Rings* is to find oneself gently rocked between bleakness and luxury, the sublime and the cosy. Scary, safe again. Scary, safe again. Scary, safe again. This is the compulsively repetitive rhythm Freud writes about in *Beyond the Pleasure Principle* (1920), and which he links to the 'death instinct', the desire to be free of all tension for ever . . . This rhythm was fundamental to Tolkien's imagination: the subtitle of *The Hobbit* was 'There and Back Again'. (2001: 22)

This motion between danger and safety, progression and recoil, is also reflected in *Baldur's Gate*'s game mechanics, especially in the antithetical relationship between the tumult of real-time peril, and the sudden relief afforded by the pause button. *Baldur's Gate* has a modified turn-based system, which means that it mixes real-time action with turn taking. Playing the game alone means manipulating and managing a team of up to six characters at a time. Combat is frequent (exactly how frequent is up to the player), and assailants also tend to be in groups. At any point the player can freeze everything on-screen with the pause button. He or she is then at leisure to assign suitable weapons, spells and directives to the entire troupe, one character at a time. Once all are readied, the player can hit the space bar again and restart time. As one player-reviewer writes of combat in *Baldur's Gate*: 'what makes it great is the "pause" option. By pressing space you'll pause the game while you assign actions to your party. This is essential in larger battles, as it's real easy to loose track of things' (Faceless, 2000). This switching between real-time mayhem, and paused preparation, echoes the 'safe, scary, safe, scary' rhythm identified in Tolkien by Turner.

Visually, the *Baldur's Gate* series borrows from the *Dungeons & Dragons'* 'house style', which in turn harvests traditions of fantasy pulp, comic and poster art (artist Frank Frazetta, for example) and fantasy illustration (such as the work of Alan Lee). The characters tend to have big muscles, big hair and skimpy clothes, and they accessorize on the go, stocking up their inventories via monster slaughter and dungeon plundering. Besides arms, they accumulate gems and rings, necklaces, gloves, gauntlets, girdles, magic boots, cloaks and tunics. This emphasis on collectables recalls hobby-gaming miniatures, and cult or subculture practices in general, as well as fantasy's generic tendency to revel in detail.

Final Fantasy

Final Fantasy is another 'classic' representative of a different RPG tradition, that which emerged with Japanese console game systems during the late 1980s and 1990s. While this tradition is quite different from that of the Western RPG, the two are historically connected. Quite how the RPG arrived in Japan is unclear, although table-top role playing of the *Advanced Dungeons & Dragons* variety was established as a minority, niche activity by the 1980s. Andy Kitkowski (2002), in a series of articles on role playing in Japan, describes his experience of playing TRPG (what he calls 'Table-Talk RPG') while working as a teacher in Japan. He notes that the console RPG tradition began with the 1986 release of Enix's *Dragon Quest* for the Nintendo Famicom, and describes how this led to an explosive obsession with console RPG gaming. The extent of this obsession is legendary among American players, who frequently refer to stories of Japanese legislation limiting the release of *Dragon Quest* titles to Sundays so that schoolchildren would not be encouraged to play truant.

Dragon Quest derived both game system features and narrative elements from the Western tradition. The game challenges were based around quests and combat with monsters, with appropriate economies determining the power of weapons, spells, characters and so on.

The settings and images were equally generic, featuring medieval towns, knights, dungeons, castles, dragons and the rest. However, the new game added two importantly different sets of characteristics. In terms of the game structure, it introduced the possibility of upgrading weapons and armour, hit points and magic points, a turn-based combat system and a number of other innovative features (Bub, 2002). In terms of the iconography, it introduced a distinctively Japanese style through its designer Akira Toriyama, the artist of *Dragonball Z*, whose work was firmly located within the manga tradition of Japanese comic books.[7]

The *Final Fantasy* series, which was eventually responsible for the mass popularity of console RPGs in the USA, began the following year, 1987. The first title of the series (produced by Squaresoft, now merged with Enix), similarly combined traditional RPG structures, characters and settings with a distinctly manga-influenced visual style. As the series progresses, however, these influences recede, and the importance of traditional Japanese patterns of legend and folk tale are becoming more apparent. At the same time, these are combined with images, dialogue styles and themes from contemporary American popular culture, partly to appeal to domestic interest in this imported culture, and partly to extend the global reach of the series. *Final Fantasy VII*, the game we focus on in chapters 6 and 7, moved the series in several different directions, using a new artist more firmly rooted in a popular manga tradition, scrapping some important elements of the traditional RPG system such as the character classes, and, perhaps most importantly in economic terms, dissolving the company's partnership with Nintendo in favour of Sony and its Playstation console. The game broke all sales records in Japan and, on its release in the USA, became the first massively popular console RPG there.

The game system of *Final Fantasy VII* is, then, both connected to and distinctly different from the Western *Dungeons & Dragons* tradition. In both traditions, the challenges of the game are based around complex quest structures; the player controls teams of characters, and one avatar in particular; the character acquires experience points, magic, weapons and currency; the battles involve the strategic deployment of available resources. The differences are marked, however. The characters in *Final Fantasy* are not constructed by the player – there is no distribution of attributes, and the system of character classes, used in the previous games of the series, is abandoned. Nor do the characters evolve in the same way – they remain much the same throughout the game, at least in terms of their function in the game system, if not in terms of its narrative, which is profound and complex. The battles, in spite of requiring deployment of resources in the same way as *Dungeons & Dragons*-based games, are differently structured as turn-based, choreographed sequences. And, finally, as players often remark, *Final Fantasy VII* is a linear game – in spite of some choice about the order of events and the subquests embarked on, there is little option but to follow the tracks set out for the central character.

There are also some interesting differences in terms of the game's representational features. Like the Tolkienesque worlds of the *Dungeons & Dragons*-based games, the worlds of the *Final Fantasy* series are extensive, self-contained fantasy lands, accessible to the player at various levels from eye-level views to elaborate world maps. However, the themes, narratives, images and visual style of the Japanese games descend directly from, and continue to be implicated with, the distinctive traditions of manga (comics) and *anime* (animation). These traditions often blend traditional Japanese motifs with contemporary ones (Iwamura, 1994; Izawa, 2000); and much of this converges around the tragic axis of the Second World War. In *Final Fantasy VII*, the hero/avatar, Cloud Strife, is both samurai maverick and modern eco-warrior; his enemy the faceless corporation and their toxic nuclear plant. There is a profound ambiguity in the imagery of this game, which (as we shall see in chapter 7) gives considerable scope to the interpretive work of players.

Anarchy Online

Anarchy Online represents a later, additional development of the genre. *Anarchy Online* is an RPG, in that players construct and develop their protagonist, join teams (if they choose) and 'level up' in specialist skills. Where *Anarchy Online* differs from the games previously discussed is that it is played online. In fact, it is a Massively Multiplayer Online Role Playing Game (MMORPG), which means that players collectively inhabit and shape the events of a persistent, shared game world. Players open an account with the game's providers, after which they have access to the game for as long as they continue to pay a monthly subscription. Developed and published by Funcom, a Norwegian company, in 2001, *Anarchy Online* (<www.anarchyonline.com>) was the first science-fiction MMORPG. It is set 30,000 years in the future, on Rubi-Ka, a distant planet where a mining corporation is locked in a violent struggle with anarchist rebel clans over the control of a valuable natural resource.

Anarchy Online suffered serious technical problems on its release. The game's developers apparently 'underestimated the challenge of publishing online gaming worlds' (<www.funcom.com>). According to various commentators, the game was saved from oblivion by consultants who advised Funcom to (among other things) improve the game's introductory and training levels for inexperienced players, and to heighten the appeal of the game by launching a four-year story arc (animated instalments are available to players at the game's website). The developers implemented these changes, and within a year of its release the game was accruing industry awards. The number of subscriber accounts has since steadied at around 40,000. This means that *Anarchy Online* has a small player population compared with other online games, such as *Final Fantasy XI* (280,000 players) or *EverQuest* (in the region of 450,000), or *Lineage* (a Korean game that has millions of subscribers). These figures are estimates, however: accurately ascertaining subscriber numbers in online games is complicated by secretive corporative policy on the one hand, and by press and marketing hyperbole on the other (Woodcock, 2003).

While the inhabitants, townships, technologies and wildlife of Rubi-Ka are alien, the game system incorporates generic structures that will be familiar to veterans of stand-alone computer RPGs (or, indeed, table-top RPGs). Just as in *Baldur's Gate*, the first step for the new player is a character generation phase. Players build their protagonist by selecting from various options (relating to gender, species, physicality and profession). During gameplay, mission completion and success in combat lead to the accumulation of points and loot and, gradually, the character levels up in skills and experience. In order to progress, it is necessary to specialize – to invest points in particular skills and faculties rather than others. This counterbalancing of specialized strength with vulnerability functions as a ploy to stimulate team play.

The game world is vast, and professions such as 'adventurer' offer players the opportunity to create relatively self-sufficient and independent character types, suitable for lone exploration. *Anarchy Online* offers players the option of solo missions, and arenas for player vs. player combat. For a significant proportion of subscribers, the whole point of *Anarchy Online* is that it functions as a colourful stage for collaborative, dramatic play. These self-described Role Players (or RP'ers) meet in virtual bars, attend in-game social events, interact with other players and go on missions while in character (IC). Role players form guilds and clans, create and distribute scenarios, and invent fictional biographies that go far beyond the basic character templates or mission briefs offered by the game itself. In short, the game offers players the opportunity to embrace, or to avoid, full Role Play. Thus *Anarchy Online* is open to a degree of generic reworking by players, who can choose to align themselves with various player communities, according to their preferred style of gaming. Some players seek to undertake Role Play in its fullest sense, while others prefer to ignore the Role Playing aspects of the game as much as possible.

As we explore in a later chapter, players bring expectations about genre and gaming with them when they sign on to *Anarchy Online*, and these expectations shape the ways in which the game's generic qualities are muted, or made manifest. For example, three (adolescent male) friends whom we studied initially rejected outright the Role Play potentials of the game. Instead, they researched the game's manual in order to build characters that would enable them to play solo and carry a sniper gun, and thus to replicate their past experiences playing First Person Shooter (FPS) games. Despite this, once one of the boys began to play, he found an online 'Elvish' translator and used it to generate his character's name. As this suggests, certain generic associations (especially the genre's high fantasy connotations) have survived the move to deep space.

Changing genres

While there are significant differences within the genre, RPGs clearly share defining characteristics that set them apart from other types of computer game. As we have noted, these are primarily to do with a game's playability and structure. However, there are also representational aspects of the genre – the 'typical' settings, iconography, narratives and character types that have evolved in tandem with these ludic qualities, and that cannot easily be separated from them.

As the above examples show, the characteristics of this genre are a mobile, mutable set of social resources for players on the one hand, and game designers on the other. If cultish gamers desire to construct detailed characters, and to negotiate and engage with complex rules and economies, the genre will develop to accommodate their appetites. If mass audiences desire something that prioritizes storytelling while enshrining imagery of popular pleasure and anxiety, then the genre twists in that direction. There will always be audiences who can't get enough of elves and orcs, and new Tolkien-themed games will emerge to cater for them. For those players for whom one more elf is an elf too many, other versions of the genre will generate the heroes of urban dystopia that games like *Final Fantasy* provide.

The genre pulls towards the past, as well as the future, seeking to reach new audiences who may be restless with existing formulae. Similarly, we can expect the oscillation between cultish hobby-gaming and mass adventure enthusiasts to continue to shift, and the games to shift with it, one moment hurrying to keep up, the next prompting new tastes with a surprise innovation. This evolution does not reflect, however, an equal exchange between players as autonomous social agents and games as entirely benign structures for their dramatic or ludic pleasure. The history of the genre reveals other economic and cultural forces at work, not least a pattern of global cultural export, as the products of North America and Japan struggle for footholds in each other's territory. The indebtedness of one to the other is apparent in the fascination of early Japanese animators with Disney, and the inverse fascination of cult manga audiences in the US; in the borrowing of the RPG by the Japanese games industry, and their return export of it as a mass popular form to America (for further discussion of this dimension, see chapter 7). This global cultural and economic sparring, swapping, theft and adaptation has resulted in texts of extraordinary richness and complexity. Players, through their inventive uses of these labyrinthine structures, continue to make sense of a genre that evolves and mutates, as it strives to combine the reassuringly familiar with the spectacularly new.

03 Games and Narrative

Diane Carr

I like RPG's because they (normally) have a good strong story, and are normally fantasy or science fiction based, which I enjoy. Sometimes a good RPG can be like an interactive storybook. (Player interview, AP)

I think [the appeal of RPGs] is about being part of a story with a beginning and end that doesn't just tally all the people you have killed. I like the story element and interacting verbally (or in computer speak) with other characters at will . . . I hope this makes sense, but it's kinda like being part of an interactive film . . . (Player interview, JC)

THE computer RPG *Baldur's Gate* is full of characters that spin tales, libraries scattered with readable books, cutscenes that relate dreams and memories, and scrolls telling of things that have 'come to pass'. The game's forests, trails and caves invite exploration, while its combat sequences and inventories involve improvisation, repetition and playful experimentation. In other words, *Baldur's Gate* insists on storytelling – but it also incorporates things that have little to do with traditional narrative.

Computer games theorists have approached the issue of narrative from different perspectives. Jenkins (2004), for instance, has looked at the creation of narrative via spatial exploration and episodic play.[1] Murray (2000) has considered the player's generation of sequential events in terms of 'procedural authorship', while Salen and Zimmerman (2004) have distinguished between emergent and embedded narrative material and Grodal (2003) has called for an embodied, experiential understanding of narrative. For an overview of the narrative in games debate, see Frasca (2003) and for more on the application of literary theory to games, see Kücklich (2003).

According to Espen Aarseth (1997: 4–5), to 'claim that there is no difference between games and narratives is to ignore essential quali-ties of both categories. And yet . . . the difference is not clear-cut, and there is significant overlap between the two.' Narrative structures and spontaneous gameplay are entangled in *Baldur's Gate* – so precise, specific tools are needed to prise them apart. The literary narrative theory of Seymour Chatman (1978) and Gerard Genette (1980) has proven useful to games analysts who are interested in clarifying the differences between games and narratives, including Juul in 'Games Telling Stories?' (2001), Eskelinen in 'The Gaming Situation' (2001), and Aarseth in *Cybertext* (1997). Narrative theory can help to specify the ways in which computer games are 'not narrative' and in the process, somewhat paradoxically, narrative theory proves its relevance to computer games studies.

This chapter investigates *Baldur's Gate* as it is experienced when played offline, by a single user. The narratives that might be generated when players describe events after a game session, or those that are produced and shared by fans are not under consideration. Here the focus is on the ways in which narrative is offered to players as they read, explore, navigate, wander, hack and slash their way through *Baldur's Gate*.

Baldur's Gate

Playing *Baldur's Gate* involves the real time manipulation of character-ized components, according to a set of rules, in order to achieve particular goals. These ludic[2] attributes have not prevented the game from incorporating narrative material. Torill Mortensen (2002) wrote of role playing gamers that: 'the reader is part of the player, but the player is not limited to the reader'. Similarly, in *Baldur's Gate*, storytelling is part of the game, but the game is not limited to a narrative. In some computer games, the storytelling is non-existent; in others, it is merely peripheral. In *Baldur's Gate*, the story matters, even if it remains secondary to the pleasures, activities and demands of gameplay.

Much of the storytelling in *Baldur's Gate* is related to the player via the direct 'you' of second-person address. So, if the player chooses a thief as his or her protagonist, the game will announce that because of 'your foster father's colourful tales of rogues and scoundrels, you have spent your childhood yearning for intrigue'. If, on the other hand, the player opts to play as a fighter, the game relates that thanks to 'your foster father's loving tales, you have always dreamt of living the life of an adventurer, travelling the land by your wits'. Either way, according to *Baldur's Gate*, you (to adopt the address of the game) are an orphan. You have recently come of age, yet you know little about your birth family. You were raised and schooled at Candlekeep, a fortified religious community. Your foster-father, Gorion, is wise and loving, but 'lately, Gorion has been growing distant from you, as if some grave matter weighs heavily on his heart . . . you cannot help but feel that something is terribly wrong'. He instructs you to prepare for a journey, but he refuses to elaborate: 'you must trust me . . . Hurry, for there is no time to tarry!' Preparing for the journey constitutes a training level where you learn how to move within the game world, how to 'converse' with characters, how to fight, as well as how to buy, sell and use objects.

The player is taught to 'click' on bystanders to generate dialogue, and then reply using the options supplied by the game. In the process information is related about the game world. An old man in a bar, for instance, mutters that with 'this iron crisis upon us, the trip from Beregost was more hazardous that I care to relate . . . You're Gorion's ward, aren't you? My, you have come into your own.' Other Non-Player Characters (NPCs) urge you (the protagonist and the player) to buy provisions and practise fighting with a team. Minor characters offer gossip and advice, and then remind you to meet Gorion. It is time to leave Candlekeep.

Once the journey is under way a cutscene (animated insert) begins, during which a mysterious villain attacks and murders Gorion. The protagonist is left desolate and vulnerable: ' "Hand over your ward," the armoured fiend had said. He was after you and you alone, but why . . . now you are alone and lost.' There is no way for the player to interfere with these events as Gorion dies during a cutscene. According to the stern, male voice that then reads from an on-screen scroll, 'You awake with the realization that you have not been having some horrible dream. Ambushed, you saw Gorion cut down before your eyes, and even his powerful magic could not stop the onslaught.' The game hints that the protagonist won't survive on his or her own for very long. A scroll (a text on-screen) bearing advice that Gorion dispensed before his death, prompts the player to make for a rendezvous at The Friendly Inn.

As play continues, the game offers the protagonist and player a number of computer-generated companions (the player can accrue and direct up to six teammates at a time). The first is Imoen: 'When asked about her past, Imoen slaps your shoulder playfully' (to quote from her character biography screen). These fictional teammates have their own motives and personalities. They compliment you when they approve ('Gorion would be proud!') and complain when they don't. They moan when they are tired, flirt with each other and grumble when they are bored. Meanwhile, an iron shortage is continuing to cause upheaval in the region. Somehow the mines have been poisoned. The troupe is urged to track down those behind the conspiracy. Every so often, reference is made to the mystery of your birth: dreams hint (via the on-screen text box) that your character's fate hangs in the balance, and that he or she has inherited a tendency towards despotism and homicide. The quest continues and eventually leads to the city of Baldur's Gate where (after extrication from treacherous plots, intrigue and false imprisonment) the truth of the protagonist's paternity is revealed. Your blood-father is an evil deity – which means that Saravok (the archvillain, and Gorion's murderer) is your brother! It was the ruthless Saravok who orchestrated the iron shortage, and various other nefarious schemes to gain power in the region. Eventually you confront Saravok and his henchmen in his lair. Once he is defeated, the game is over. A final cutscene sweeps you to a subterranean pantheon, where Saravok's statue crumbles to dust.

As this demonstrates, when playing *Baldur's Gate*, 'you' sometimes means a fictional character while at other times (on other screens), 'you' refers directly and solely to the player. At yet other times, 'you' are a curious blend of fictional avatar and actual player. The player is approached, urged, ordered or invited by different characters to undertake missions or quests. Thus, some of the game's goals and objectives are delivered in a narrative guise, while other goals (such as gaining experience points to level up) are not. Events that have already occurred are constantly being related to the protagonist (and player) through dialogue, on scrolls, letters, in journal entries and in cutscenes. Yet the player will also instigate, avoid or repeat events themselves. The game world is graphically rendered while written text appears on various prompts, menus, boxes and menu screens. There are audible fragments of spoken dialogue, and a music soundtrack. Places, actions and personalities are related to the player through the visual and audio representation of the setting, and via the words and actions of the figures on-screen. These factors all contribute towards the storytelling in *Baldur's Gate*.

From Gorion's ambush to Saravok's demise, the series of events outlined above will be familiar to anyone who has played *Baldur's Gate* to completion. Different players will adopt different fighting styles, build a different central character, or select different team members. One player might explore the game world at length, while another might take the most direct route possible. Either way, Gorion will be murdered, and Saravok will poison the iron mines. In order to discuss with any clarity how this storytelling coexists with the playable nature of the game, it is helpful to take a closer look at narrative theory.

What is narrative?

Narrative theory is concerned with the ways in which a narrative text communicates events, settings, characters and perspectives. In narrative

Illustration 1 A screenshot from *Baldur's Gate* showing the isometric perspective and dialogue between characters. The team is portrayed down the right of the screen. Links to the team's inventories are on the left, and the available actions along the base. Published by Black Isle Studios/Interplay.

Illustration 2 A player-character's statistics, *Baldur's Gate*. Published by Black Isle Studios/Interplay.

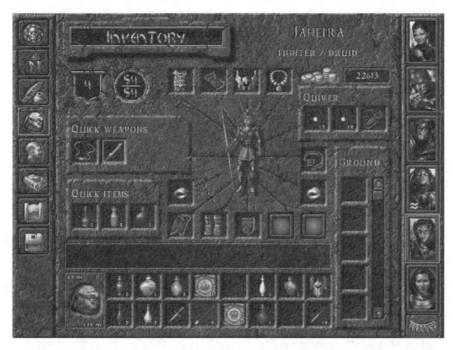

Illustration 3 The inventory screen for Jaheira in *Baldur's Gate*. Published by Black Isle Studios/Interplay.

theory, terms like 'story' have a specific meaning. In *Story and Discourse: Narrative Structure in Fiction and Film*, Seymour Chatman writes that:

> each narrative has two parts: a story (*histoire*), the content or chain of events (actions, happenings), plus what may be called the existents (characters, items of setting); and a discourse (*discours*), that is, the expression, the means by which the content is communicated. In simple terms, the story is the *what* in a narrative that is depicted, discourse the *how*. (1978: 19)

The 'what' is the raw material of the story events, and the 'how' is the re-presentation of these events in the narrative discourse. Story events are sequenced, arranged in time and space: plotted. The same set of story events can be plotted in many different ways. Thus, the same 'story' can give rise to many different narratives, each of which would accentuate, exclude or emphasize different things. Additionally, narrative involves the relating or communication of these events. Narrative theorist Gerard Genette has described story (content), narrative (the statement or discourse itself) and narrating as the 'three aspects of narrative reality' (1980: 27).

Rather than applying these terms directly to a game, it would be useful to explore them first in greater detail using an example: the fairy tale of *Cinderella* involves a set of story events, and there are different ways that these story events could be made available to a reader or viewer. Imagine a clichéd film version. The first scene shows us a girl sitting alone by the hearth in a dismal kitchen. The screen fades, sad music swells and we are shown a flashback. We understand, thanks to our familiarity with the conventions of cinema, that we are seeing events from Cinderella's childhood: her father's second marriage; her banishment to the kitchen. The flashback ends, we are in the kitchen again and back in the 'narrative now'. The fairy godmother arrives, waves her wand and Cinderella is off to the ball. Her journey to the palace is abbreviated to a single shot of the coach rushing along a road. When she dances with Prince Charming, the film switches to slow motion (and we understand that this is indicative of the protagonist's emotional state, and not the result of a bizarre temporal accident). The clock strikes midnight; she runs away; her slipper is left behind. The screen fades (indicating that time has passed) and a montage shows that Cinderella's life as domestic drudge has been resumed, until (back to the narrative now) there is a knock at the door. Prince Charming is on the doorstep with the slipper. The film jumps forward to the couple's lavish wedding feast. The newly-weds embrace, and the credits roll.

The same set of story events, differently arranged (plotted) could produce a very different narrative. The first twenty minutes of another film version might show the prince bored at the ball. Suddenly his face lights up – he's seen Cinderella. They dance, the clock strikes twelve, she escapes and he's left clutching her slipper. Broken-hearted, he wanders around the castle muttering. Weeks pass. After much prompting from his family, the prince decides to track down the slipper's owner. For the next fifty minutes of the film, the prince and his entourage argue with each other and moan about the weather as they trek around the kingdom through an entire winter, seeking the slipper's owner. Finally, by accident, they end up at Cinderella's door. After an ugly scene with the stepsisters, in which the details of Cinderella's troubled life emerge, the prince finds Cinderella in the kitchen and throws himself at her feet. He proposes, she accepts, they embrace and the screen fades.

In the first hypothetical film version, the prince's search is implied, rather than portrayed. In the second, Cinderella's domestic duties are mentioned only in passing, whereas they are more fully described in the first, as is the couple's wedding. In each case, some story events are shown in normal time, or as flashbacks, while others are elongated, or abbreviated, or merely implied. According to Gerard Genette (1980), this is a key element of narration: when story events are plotted, and thus emerge in discourse, their duration, frequency or order is manipulated.

For Genette, narrative analysis also involves asking questions about perspective: through whose eyes do we witness these events? Whose voice is telling us about the characters and their actions? (1980: 186). Imagine yet another version of these same story events, this time described from the perspective of a particular narrator, a neighbour named Mr Good. Perhaps Mr Good looks at Cinderella and regards her as an angel, or as an idiot, or a brat. Depending on how his subjective account of events is communicated to us and how he himself is portrayed, we will regard Mr Good as a reliable witness and narrator, or not. Perhaps there is more than one narrator, each offering different accounts of the same events, in which case it is likely that clues in the discourse will signal that one account is more reliable (or misguided, or naive) than the other. Then, according to Chatman's account of narrative structure, if Mr Good is relating his version of events to another character within his reality (his wife Mrs Good, say) then the narrative discourse is said to have a narratee, as well as a narrator.[3]

Pulling the strings, as it were, of this narrator and narratee, and influencing the veracity with which we regard their version of events, is the implied author: the structural entity that establishes 'the norms of the narrative' (1978: 149) – and note that it is a structural entity, an organizing principle within the text that Chatman is describing, not the actual flesh-and-blood author. The narrator might be covert, disembodied and closely aligned with the implied author, but this does not mean that the two roles are interchangeable, because:

> the implied author is not the narrator, but rather the principle that invented the narrator along with everything else in the narrative, that stacked the cards in this particular way, had these things happen to these characters, in these words or images . . . it has no voice, no direct means of communicating. It instructs us silently, through the design of the whole, with all the voices, by all the means it has chosen to let us learn. (Chatman, 1978: 148)

The implied author occupies a controlling, 'sending position' within the narrative text. Then, at the receiving end, is the implied reader: the target of the message being transmitted and 'the audience presupposed by the narrative itself' (150). Throughout the narrative there are clues and signposts signalling to this implied reader how they should regard what they are being told. For example, the narratee is 'one device by which the implied author informs the real reader how to perform as the implied reader' (1978: 150). Thus, the narratee (Mrs Good, in our example) might be depicted as wise or drunk; she might be angered, or amused by the things her husband tells her. Of course, the actual real-life reader might well reject the subjective responses suggested by the implied author to the implied reader in this way.

To summarize: according to narrative theory, story events are only available or perceptible to us once they have been plotted out and arranged in a narrative discourse. This narrative discourse is a form of transmission, from implied author to implied reader. It was necessary to introduce these terms in some detail, because it is through these concepts that the differences between games and narratives can be shown.

Narrative theory and *Baldur's Gate*

Computer games, even those that contain substantial amounts of story-telling, do not reside comfortably within existing models of narrative. It would be nonsensical to disregard the parts of *Baldur's Gate* that make it a game, in order to have it conform to a model of narrative structure. On the other hand, it would be counterproductive to ignore the game's narrative qualities, in order to have it obey a preconception about what games (and hence the study of games) should be about. Understanding the coexistence of these elements might eventually require us to rethink what we mean by narrative in general. In the meantime, we can examine how the different aspects of *Baldur's Gate* incorporate, complicate or elude classic models of narrative.

1 Story events and play

As noted, narrative involves events on a story or content plane that are re-presented on a discourse or narrative plane. In the move from story plane to discourse plane, the temporal features of these story events are manipulated. They could be stretched, shrunk, reordered, reversed, repeated or abbreviated. *Baldur's Gate* is a game; it is played, so it involves real time activity and the generation of new events that are orchestrated or plotted by the user.[4] Yet *Baldur's Gate* also incorporates past events – events already arranged in time and space that are recounted to the user.

Baldur's Gate insists on storytelling. Under the fluctuating layers of played, saved, replayed and played-over events, there is a baseline of conventionally structured narrative that retains its plotted order, regardless of the player's actions. For example, while exploring a village that the player has been directed to, the team comes across a character named Minsc. This character will join the team if the player (in the guise of the protagonist) agrees to help him rescue 'his witch' Dinheira. Poor Dinheira is being held captive in an orc fortress. Minsc and Dinheira have a relationship that pre-exists the player's arrival. Their situation, personal histories and personalities are recounted to the player, and cannot be altered. Likewise, the location of the orc fortress, its architecture and its population involve events and exist-ents (things that exist) that are arranged in time and space, prior to their being communicated to the player. These elements conform to, or at least strongly resemble, conventional narration.

However, it is the player who chooses or rejects Minsc as a teammate, and who decides whether to undertake Dinheira's rescue or not. The player arranges the journey to the fortress, choosing a direct or a more exploratory route (that might generate more or different events). The player invents or experiments with strategies for the infiltration of the fortress when he or she arrives. In other words, the player deter-mines if certain events will occur at all, and how they will unfold if they do: at such times the player is the one doing the plotting. This means that these events cannot be considered narrative in its strictest sense.

There are other aspects of *Baldur's Gate* that cross the line between narrative and gameplay. For instance, events generated during play are immediately described or 'told back' to the player, via the settings and the actions of the animated figures on-screen. The game also has a text box where on-screen acts, events, scores and dialogue are recounted to the player. In this example, the player's character 'Bad Joan' attacks a hapless nobleman, who promptly dies:

> Bad Joan – Attacks Nobleman
> Nobleman – Damage Taken (5)
> Nobleman – Death
> The Party's Reputation Has Decreased 2
> The Party Has Gained Experience 15

This running commentary resembles what Genette has described as simultaneous narrative. Simultaneous narration, as distinct from the 'classical position of the past tense narrative' is narration that is 'contemporaneous with the action' (1980: 217). Genette cites sports commentary as an example, describing it as 'the most perfectly live form of this kind of narrative' (216). This aspect of the game certainly resembles narrative, but, again, it does not fully obey traditional models of narrative, because the player is pulling the strings and plot-ting events. Yet the player is not designing these events with a free hand. All the acts and happenings are shaped by their context: by the game, its physics and rules. It is the game that decides the identity of the archvillain and the game that disallows the protagonist from saving Gorion or joining forces with Saravok. It is the game that decides that a character can use magic boots, or trans-dimensional portals, but not aeroplanes or motorcycles.

In short, there are different kinds of events in *Baldur's Gate*. Some fit quite snugly into classic narrative formula (plotted events, recounted to a user). Others only fit the formula in part (such as simultaneous narrating); while still other events – those that occur in real time only to be discarded or played over, for instance – have little or nothing in common with conventional narrative.

2 Senders and (mixed) messages

According to Chatman, narrative discourse is a communicative transmission. Within a narrative text, this transmission goes from a sending position (the implied author) to a receiving position (the implied reader). The implied author shapes the overall intent of the communication and directs it to the implied reader, perhaps using narrators and narratees in the process.

In his book *Cybertext*, Espen Aarseth adapts Chatman's model in order to apply it to a text-based action adventure game, called *Deadline*. Aarseth notes that, unlike in conventional narratives, the player has a hand in plotting events and determining the action, and so he replaces Chatman's 'story' and 'narration' with the term 'intrigue', which is borrowed from drama theory.

> Instead of a narrated plot, cybertext produces a sequence of oscillating activities effectuated . . . by the user. But there is nevertheless a structuring element in these texts, which in some way does the controlling or at least motivates it. As a new term for this element I propose intrigue, to suggest a secret plot in which the user is the innocent, but voluntary, target. (1997: 112)

Aarseth then proposes various 'sending positions' and 'receiving positions' within the intrigue: the 'intrigant' (sending) and the 'intriguee' (receiving). The intrigant is a combination of Chatman's implied author and narrator. Aarseth describes the intrigant as 'the intrigue's alternative to the narrative's narrator' and writes that the intrigant, 'as the architect of the intrigue, might instead be compared to an implied author, the mastermind who is ultimately responsible for events and existents' (1997: 114). Aarseth also proposes an inclusive receiving position: 'The target of the intrigue might be called the intriguee and is a parallel to the narratee, to the implied reader of the narratologists, as well as to the main character (or "puppet")' (1997: 113).

However, *Baldur's Gate* is very different from a text-based game like *Deadline*, and in the case of this graphically rendered RPG it is not helpful to bundle various sending and receiving positions under collective, umbrella terms. Collapsing these positions together in order to have the game fit within Chatman's model, or Aarseth's version of Chatman's model, might conceal more than it explains.

When relating the 'story' of *Baldur's Gate* it is difficult to avoid conflating the protagonist with the player, but that does not mean that they are equivalent, or irrevocably joined, or that the position of the player is fixed or constant. Note that the player discussed here is an *implied* player (like Chatman's implied reader) and therefore is not an actual person – it is a textual construct, the point in the game where the actual player encounters the possibilities of the game text (and so describing the implied player is different from predicting or prescribing the actions of any actual player).

Sometimes the game addresses the player and the protagonist with a single inclusive 'you', at which points the player and the main character could feasibly be grouped within a single designation. Yet, elsewhere (on the statistics screen, for instance), any fictional pretence is dropped, and 'you' only means the player who, for the moment, is directly addressed and is empowered to make strategic decisions about pausing the game, distributing resources or sorting out experience points. Similarly, at times the protagonist is told of events by other characters and thus, for the moment, acts as a narratee. Yet, at other times, the protagonist performs as the narrator – such as when speaking in the first person in his or her journal entries, or when events are subjectively related from his or her perspective. Sometimes events on-screen are triggered by the presence of the lead character, yet at other times the player views events in the game world from other perspectives (through a secondary character or a character biography screen, for example) – and at such times the player is accessing information that does not rely on the protagonist acting as narrator. Sometimes the player is told of events, at which point they are in a position equivalent to the implied reader. Yet, at other times, the player instigates and orchestrates events, or determines a character's traits, at which point they assume a position closer to that of the implied author. All these possibilities are offered by the game. At times these offers exist simultaneously, but at other times (or on other screens) they exist in a singular, isolated manner.

This suggests that rather than conflating the various sender and receiver positions within the game text under encompassing designations, it is more productive to regard them as a set of distinct, multiple positions, any of which might be offered to or imposed on the player by various aspects of the game, at different times. In other words, the player is not confined to a particular location equivalent to either Chatman's sender or receiver positions: the implied player is mobile, and not just in the sense that they explore the game world. They are also mobile in that they move between the various offers, possibilities and varying perspectives offered by *Baldur's Gate*. It is possible, in fact, that this mobility – this ability to shift between different positions in the text – is one of the reasons that computer games like *Baldur's Gate* are so absorbing.

Chatman's and Aarseth's models do help to explain what is going on when we play *Baldur's Gate*, but (as discussed in the previous chapter) *Baldur's Gate* is the computerized version of a table-top RPG. For this reason, it is arguable that there is already an 'implied sender' designation that offers itself more readily, and with greater descriptive capacity, than either Aarseth's 'intrigant' or Chatman's 'implied author'. Classic RPGs are conducted by a Game Master, or GM. The real-life GM uses narrative to set the scene, weaving scenarios for their players (and incorporating the player's input). The GM also uses dice and game manuals to judge the outcomes of an event or confrontation (granting rewards, points, injury, death or advancement). In the computer adaptation it could be argued that the Game Master, its scene-setting and storytelling, dice, and umpiring, are incorporated into a single textual construct: the *implied Game Master*. Admittedly this implied GM is less negotiable and less variable than the original flesh-and-blood version, and so the analogy is provisional. This means that the implied GM is not a robust enough model to import to other games indiscriminately, but it is a useful concept through which to examine structure in *Baldur's Gate*.

In Chatman's model, the narrator is a conduit for the implied author, but the narrator does not have the same power over the implied author. Like the implied author, our implied GM has the power to transmit different messages via different conduits. The implied GM has various delegates at its disposal, and these agents perform different functions: some communicate ludic (game-orientated) information, while others deliver narrative (and representational) material. These agents are not in conflict: on the contrary, they work together – they are in cahoots. This multiplicity is answered by the potential activities of the transmission's receiver (who is, by turns, a reader, a viewer and a player). These two broad categories of address are then replicated outside of the game in the two most common forms of fan writing: walkthroughs (ludic orientation, imperative address) and fan fiction (narrative emphasis, indicative and descriptive address), as we explore further in chapters 6 and 7. As Burn (2003) has pointed out, games have a tendency to address their players using imperatives ('Do this! Go there!'), while here the notion of narrative as being indicative or descriptive is drawn from Genette's *Narrative Discourse* (1980: 161): 'Since the function of narrative is not to give an order, express a wish, state a condition, etc., but simply to tell a story, and therefore to "report" facts (real or fictive), its one mood, or at least its characteristic mood, strictly speaking, can be only the indicative.'

The implied GM directs various communicative agents within the game text. Thus, the implied GM occupies a sending position, one that is reasonably parallel to Chatman's implied author. In relation to *Baldur's Gate*, the advantage of the implied GM over Chatman's implied author, is that the implied GM can issue ludic as well as narrative transmissions. The advantage of the implied GM over Aarseth's sending position (the intrigant) is that the implied GM is easier to distinguish from the other agents in the text. This is important, because while the implied player does jump to the authorial, sending position occupied by the GM – when instigating events or characterizing the protagonist, for instance – it does not follow that the implied player remains there, or that they take on a fully fledged 'authorial' role. This is because events instigated, plotted and orchestrated by the player must still conform to the parameters of the game text (unless they cheat, which only means importing a new set of conditions), and these conditions remain the jurisdiction of the implied GM.

The limits of narrative

Narrative theory asks questions about the perspective from which story events are described. Through whose eyes do we witness the events of the narrative, and whose voice is relating the information? (Genette 1980: 186). When investigating narrative in games, it is also necessary to ask who instigates events. Who determines their duration, frequency or order?

There are straightforward narrative elements in *Baldur's Gate*, in the form of events that elude manipulation by the player. These events are plotted (arranged in time and space) and then related to the player in cutscenes, in the testimony of NPCs, or in character biographies. Through these means the player learns about the protagonist's sheltered youth in Candlekeep, and his or her relationship with Gorion. This narrative material establishes the identity of the archvillain, Saravok, the mystery of the protagonist's paternity, the histories of places and the traits of their inhabitants. Much of this narration is indeed arranged in 'the classical position of the past-tense narrative' (Genette, 1980: 217), and this portion of the game could quite satisfactorily be expressed in a different medium. In line with narrative theory, it is 'independent of the techniques that bear it along. It may be transposed from one to another medium without losing its essential properties: the subject of a story may serve as argument for a ballet, that of a novel can be transposed to stage or screen' (Bremond, cited by Chatman, 1978: 20).

The real-time events of play, on the other hand, unfold act by act, as the player manipulates the game components in order to win (or lose, or repeat) a fight, or cross a mountain, or swap swords with a merchant. Resources are accumulated or used up, goals attained, battles fought, and strategy tested. Teammates are killed off and resurrected, or replaced. Some of these play-generated events are simultaneously narrated to the player as they occur, or once they have occurred, in the game's text box, in much the same way that a commentator at a sports event will narrate the game to an audience. Yet, despite the resemblances, this material does not comfortably sit within the structure of narrative discourse as proposed by classic narrative theory. For one thing, these events might be saved, or not. For another, at least to a degree, the player plots these events. Ultimately these elements do not obey or conform to classic models of narrative – and, given that *Baldur's Gate* is a game, there is no reason to expect that they should.

Players might not finish *Baldur's Gate*, or they might skip as much of the storytelling as possible. One player might read all the text that the game offers, check all of their teammates' character biographies, and open (click on) all of the books scattered through the game world's libraries. Another player might ignore the storytelling, kill all potential teammates, and be happy crossing and recrossing the same piece of map and slaughtering the respawning monsters, unconcerned about resolution. One player's trail through the game's world may vary considerably from another's. One player's character might favour negotiation and subterfuge, while another's might opt for ruthless necromancy, and yet another for a path of brute force. Yet no matter how well we play, Gorion will be ambushed and killed, and no matter how pathological we decide our protagonist is, the game will still tell us that after Gorion's death he or she is shocked and grieving.

While it is possible to distinguish between gameplay and the narrative offers and events in *Baldur's Gate*, in practice the two are interwoven. Once the game is under way, each saved point reflects a long chain of chance, player action, setting and narrative content, all worked together. Each time the game is loaded, the characters are in a particular location, facing a set of circumstances, and subject to conditions that reflect a complex combination of accumulated gameplay, plot and player choice. The game invites various kinds of participation (reading, listening, watching, playing). It incorporates static parameters and structures, as well as space for inventive manipulation. As this implies, *Baldur's Gate* offers the player a myriad of positions to explore, occupy and move between. The mobility that this affords is explored in the next chapter.

Play and Pleasure

Diane Carr

*B*ALDUR's *Gate* is a game. It has rules, conflict, components to be manipulated, goals, chance and quantified outcomes. *Baldur's Gate* also incorporates representational elements, including characterization, narrative material, and a detailed and decorative game world. It is difficult, perhaps even artificial, to separate these aspects of the game. While *Baldur's Gate* might not appeal to everyone many players find the game deeply engrossing. Various attentive states have been associated with the absorbing pleasures of games, including immersion, engagement and flow. These potential states do not rely solely on either the game's playable qualities or its representational assets. On the contrary, it is the combination of these attributes, and the player's motion between such varied offers, that makes the game a compelling experience.

As previously noted, computer RPGs have their roots in table-top games. *Baldur's Gate* owes its setting and combat system, its rules and its character-generation templates to *Dungeons & Dragons*.[1] The player begins by making a series of choices about the appearance and capabilities of the central character. *Baldur's Gate* then supplies the player and this lead character with a team of companions. Levelling up (upgrading in skills through the accruing of experience points) is key to gameplay. Members of the troupe each carry an inventory, and through combat, exploration and shopping they can acquire magical items, jewellery, enchanted cloaks and boots, talismans, amulets, arms, spells and potions. As this implies, the management of the team's weaponry, luggage, skills and experience points might consume a significant amount of the player's time and attention.

During battle the various combatants' statistics, arms and armour are taken into account by the game engine, the computer rolls the internal equivalent of dice, and immediately delivers a verdict as to the amount of damage received and inflicted. This simplification of *Baldur's Gate*'s rules gives some indication of the number of variables that a player might be taking into account if formulating a strategy. For some players, these rules might be second nature due to a familiarity with table-top gaming. For others, they might remain opaque or peripheral. Yet even a novice skimming through the game is likely to notice that the numbers attached to armour, strength or dexterity have ramifications. As the player learns, they become more effective, and as the player and their team level up, the game spawns bigger monsters and more powerful enemies.

It is possible to enjoy *Baldur's Gate* without investing too heavily in the intricacies of levelling and character generation, but to understand RPGs as a genre, and the pleasures that these games offer, it is necessary to have a sense of these processes. Players constantly face options, and most are of strategic import. How any individual player exploits or ignores, enjoys or is irritated by these choices is, of course, a matter of personal preference. The ways in which a particular player might realize these potentials would depend on mood, expectations, expertise and taste. It would certainly be valid to explore the different selections made by actual players, and the various cultural, social or psychological factors that might be said to inform their choices. In this chapter, however, the focus remains on *what the game invites players to do*, rather than on what actual players might do in response.

Generating character

Many of the choices presented to players of *Baldur's Gate* involve the central character and his or her playable companions. Before the main game gets under way, the player compiles the protagonist during a 'character generation' process. The easiest way to explain this part of the game is with a condensed 'walkthrough' of the procedure.

A new game of *Baldur's Gate* begins with the character-generation screen. Down the left-hand side of the screen (as if etched into dark stone) is a list of eight categories. 'Click' on any category and an explanation appears, and more guidance is available in the game's manual. The first category on the list is gender. The player has to choose male or female, but this 'is an aesthetic choice and will not affect your attributes in any fashion'. The next step is choosing an image from the portrait selection. The available faces vary considerably in their features and colouring (yet there are more to choose from if building a male and/or white character). The images are generically appropriate, and run the high fantasy gamut. They are heavy with explicit traits: elven or dwarvish, wily, noble, sultry or scary.[2] Due to the game's 'top down' (or isometric) perspective, the actual figures on-screen during the game are quite small, and it is not possible to make out their faces. However, the portrait selected by the player will appear on the right of the screen during the game, representing the character and acting as an interface short cut.

Having chosen a face, the player moves on to selecting the 'race' of their character. Race approximates species in this essentialist, 'Tolkienistic' cosmos, and there are six to choose from: human, dwarf, elf, gnome, halfling (a hobbit) or half-elf (part elf, part human). At this point the player's choices begin to have strategic ramifications. As a scroll states: 'The race of your character will determine what their base abilities can be, as well as assign possible intrinsic talents such as infravision.' These are factors to bear in mind when considering the next category, 'class'. Class refers to the profession in which the character has served an apprenticeship. Each class has different special powers – druids perform certain forms of magic, bards are charismatic and manipulative, while thieves can pick locks. The game offers eight initial choices, although that number expands to twenty-six once multi-class, dual-class and specialist classes are taken into account.

If a player decides, for instance, to construct an elf character, certain professions will suit its base abilities, while others will not be an option. The player with a specific profession in mind can select the species that offers appropriate talents, because the prime requisite of each class can be matched to the bonus attributes of the various races. Having nominated to play as an elf (elves are granted bonus dexterity), the player might opt to play as a thief (dexterity is the prime requisite of thieves). Players are also free to go 'against the grain'. Gnomes, for example, have high intelligence scores, balanced by low wisdom. Intelligence is the prime requisite of the mage; wisdom the prime requisite of the priest. So, to play as a gnome would be a sensible choice if intending to play a mage, and an interesting choice if intending to play as a priest.

The next category is 'alignment'. The game's manual describes alignment as 'a character's basic attitude toward society and the forces of the universe' (page 89). Each alignment is composed of two elements: one element (good, neutral, evil) is the character's moral outlook, while the second (lawful, neutral, chaotic) refers to how consistently the character adheres to the first. Next is the 'abilities' screen. Here the player makes choices about the protagonist's mental traits (intelligence, wisdom and charisma) and physical traits (strength, constitution and dexterity). Ability scores are then given by the game, and 'calculated as if you rolled three 6-sided dice for each ability, adjusted for character race' (game manual, page 9). The player has the option to alter these scores to a degree. The choices made at the abilities screen will then affect the ratio of points at the player's disposal on the 'skills' screen. Here players invest points in skills that are appropriate to their new character's profession. After skills, the game directs the player to choose the weapons that the character will wield most effectively. The player then makes choices concerning the character's appearance. Palettes are offered for skin, clothes and hair (and selections are not required to match the portrait chosen earlier). Next, the player chooses a voice for his or her character from those on offer. Finally, the player invents and enters the name of their creation.

Using the above templates and options, for example, it was possible to create a character called Lottie. She is an elf, and a thief. Lottie is intelligent and charismatic; she is good at opening locks and sneaking, but hopeless at detecting traps. This means that she is a persuasive leader, but she is liable to lead her team into lethal situations. Lottie's moral alignment is 'Chaotic Good', so she is likely to behave well, when it suits her. She has a high dexterity rating, but she is not very strong. This will affect her ability to absorb or inflict damage, and it will limit the weight she is able to carry. Being a thief, she is not allowed to wear metallic armour, and this will add to her vulnerability in battle. In compensation for this, she is stealthy, and skilled with long-range weapons, plus her proficiency with small swords means that she will be able to quietly stab unsuspecting foes in the back. In addition to these fundamentals, the game calculates a set of ratings for magic or missile resistance, morale and reputation, all of which are explained in the game's manual, to be ignored or investigated as a player sees fit. The small figure of Lottie appears on-screen as the game begins, blue-faced, green-haired and attired in mauve. An alternative set of choices would have resulted in a completely different protagonist.

Characters, traits and play

As Lottie demonstrates, constructed characters are the culmination of a series of choices, some of which apparently hinge on ludic or strategic considerations (thief, mage or fighter, bow or sword) and some of which reflect aesthetic or representational considerations – such as name, voice, colouring or outfit. In actuality, however, these choices blur ludic and representational agendas. The choice to play as an attractive elf or a gnarled gnome, for example, would involve aesthetic or storytelling preferences, as well as strategic ramifications.[3] As noted, this central character is subsequently joined by game-generated teammates.[4] When discussing these characters, players rate them in terms of their strategic value, as well as in terms of their personality traits and relationships, as this fan posting suggests:

> Okay, okay, so she does occasionally use words like 'buffle-headed', but that doesn't compete with her effectiveness in a fight. Who gets the most kills in the coal mines? Imoen. Who is usually responsible for battles

that end without a drop of friendly blood? Imoen. She's fantastic with
that bow of hers, and her relationship to the main character makes her
your best friend, at least at the beginning of the BG story. My hat's off to
Imoen, and she'd be welcome in my party any day. (Booje, 2001)[5]

According to Seymour Chatman's summary (1978: 111) literary theorists have tended to analyse characterization in terms of the relationship between a particular character's traits and the actions that they
perform. Within a narrative text, traits such as loyalty, gullibility,
cowardice or clumsiness are what set one figure apart from another.
If a character possesses the trait of being foolhardy or cautious, for
example, the trait would express itself in how he or she performs an
action – when gambling or driving, for instance (Chatman, 1978: 138).
If a character has only a few traits, and performs in predictable ways,
he or she can be described as 'flat', whereas a more rounded character
takes a wider set of traits, and acts in a less predictable manner.

Another literary theorist, Tzetan Todorov (1977), has argued that
different kinds of narratives will establish the links between trait and
act in particular ways. He goes on to suggest that what is significant is
not just the link between trait and action – but the temporal gap
between the identification of a trait, and its expression in an act, and
the extent of the range of the possible acts that might occur as a result
of that trait. It is possible to apply Todorov's distinction to different
computer-game genres. Avatars, for instance, that have a few, very dominant traits (they are hungry, they like to eat berries), that are expressed
immediately in a single, monomaniacal activity (for example, they eat
as many berries as possible), would be at the other end of the scale from
avatars who have a host of traits (from bravery to kleptomania, say) that
may be expressed, or not, when they perform a varied set of actions
while undertaking a range of possible tasks. In RPGs like *Baldur's Gate*,
the characters – or at least the playable characters – would fall into the
second category.

Literary theories of character might apply to avatars to some degree,
but game characters are not characters in the traditional sense,
because they are directed, and potentially misdirected, by their oper-
ators; the player's choices will influence the way that the avatar will
behave. A character trait described within the text (whether it is bravery, dexterity or charisma) may be very pronounced in one person's
style of play, and barely discernible in another's. This is true whether
an avatar is supplied by the game or compiled by the user. It is also true
for avatars in other genres. For one player of the action adventure
game *Tomb Raider*, for instance, the avatar Lara Croft might hurtle
through temples at high speed with her guns out, acquisitive and
aggressive. For another player, Lara might walk the entire route,
cautious and inquisitive, hunting in every nook and cranny for secrets.

In either case the avatar has the same menu of possible acts and traits, but the style and preferences of the player determine how that potential is made apparent, or kept dormant. Yet the player only has influence within certain parameters. Lara Croft would have stayed at home had she not been quite so ruthless or adventurous, and, if an avatar is not programmed to sing or juggle, she won't. Often in 3-D action adventure games, physical traits (how an avatar can move, leap, sprint, swing, clamber or carry) are intimately linked with the game world's geography. A cliff face or a chasm calls for particular actions – and thus the avatar is provoked into demonstrating particular attributes. In the action adventure game *Ico*, for instance, the eponymous child hero has to escape from a castle. He scales great heights, and wobbles over chasms in his sandals. His character traits, such as his persistence and bravery, are 'told' in part by the setting.

Characterization is differently communicated in the isometric *Baldur's Gate*, not least because the team have a more limited set of real time movements. The characters can't jump, climb or run, for example, although they can find magical boots that make them walk faster. The protagonist is described by the game itself, in text (as youthful, rash or doomed) and through the dialogue of other characters. Spatial agility is exchanged for variability in skills, and the complexities of inventory management and levelling up. As in other computer games, a character's actions will reflect their traits, as long as the player has decided to play 'in role'. A player might choose to construct a mild, pious druid as a protagonist, only to have the cautious cleric perform the role of an aggressive public menace during the game.

In computer games, then, the play between the user's input and the game's supplied characterization will potentially give rise to unpredictable behaviours that would contradict the apparent flatness of a character. Because of this, it would be a mistake to describe an avatar or character solely on the basis of its stated attributes or traits. No matter how limited, flat, clichéd or archaic game characters may seem, the player's input will mean that they are, at least to an extent, unpredictable creatures.[6] The player's apparent freedom to intervene between trait and act is, of course, only a matter of degree: it is possible to play Lara Croft as a harmless person who doesn't shoot people or steal things, but she won't survive for long in *Tomb Raider* unless she gets her guns out. Similarly, I can reject all the potential teammates in *Baldur's Gate* and play my character as a lone-wolf pacifist, but I am unlikely to progress through the game world, or level up in experience, unless I assemble a team with mixed skills and specializations, and kill at least some of my assailants.

In the world of *Baldur's Gate*, monks are knowledgeable and lurk in libraries; dwarves are gruff; elves are handsome; and orcs are

unreasonable. Yet the flexibility of the protagonist means that any evaluative designation can be faced from a variety of perspectives: a crafty
assassin might be an ally or an evil to be wiped off the face of the earth,
depending on the alignment of the central character. A Non-Player
Character might offer to collaborate or attack on sight, depending on
the protagonist's own reputation. Meanwhile, according to the preferences of a player, young Imoen (a teammate supplied by the game)
might be a loyal and useful comrade, or an irritant to be dispatched as
rapidly and violently as possible. Thus, in a sense, the power to assign
traits to characters within *Baldur's Gate* is a continuing collaboration
between game and player. The player decides on the protagonist's identity from a menu of possibilities, which means that the traits of the
central character are implicitly acknowledged as arbitrary. In short,
character itself is played with.

This apparent flexibility has its limits. If the player does attempt to
play as a 'baddie', for example, it quickly becomes clear that *Baldur's
Gate* makes certain traits and acts necessary to scoring and progress,
and that the game will veto more extreme behaviour. A player and fan
related such findings, when asked if he had ever played as a villain:

> Only briefly. It became completely impractical playing a character who
> was working against [the game] because you are constantly under
> attack from the city guard. In all honesty, I think this was a flaw in the
> game design. Given the fact that you were playing a descendant of the
> Lord of Murder, it seemed ironic to try and play it nicely . . . I fairly
> quickly reloaded the game and carried on with my fixed 'goodie' char-
> acter as per usual. (player SD, email)

I tested the limits of the game by playing as 'Bad Joan', a homicidal
ingrate, and found myself thwarted almost immediately. Playing out
the first chapter of *Baldur's Gate* bent on evil did little to alter the
game's plan. If I persisted in trying to kill the 'wrong' person, my character would be obliterated by a much more powerful game character.
Limits are also imposed by the dialogue options, because they are
supplied by the game. In most conversations there is an obliging or
curious option, a noble response, and a rude or villainous retort. If my
protagonist is too rude, or too violent, none of the game's other characters will help her. The only effective way to play Bad Joan as a real
villain is to have her obey and conform where expedient – for her to
manipulate others via an affectation of virtue. Obviously this would
mean that she was nasty, but it would also mean that her dominant
trait (evil) would reside solely in the perceptions of her user.

Furthermore, the game imposed limits on Bad Joan's psychosis: it
was not possible to turn patricidal. If Bad Joan attempted to slay her
guardian, Gorion, he blew her up in self-defence. As outlined in the
previous chapter, the game's narrative plan requires Gorion to be

slaughtered early on by the archvillain, Saravok, in an ambush near Candlekeep. It is impossible to side with Saravok, and, because the fatal ambush happens in a cutscene, it is not possible to intervene. Once Gorion is dead the screen switches to the image of a scroll that tells of Bad Joan's shock and grievous loss – even if she had spent the previous hour attempting to kill Gorion or elope with his murderer.

In terms of characterization *Baldur's Gate* offers its players both fixed conditions and numerous, interconnecting variables. Some of these variables involve ludic considerations (statistics, skills), while others are more representational. A trait such as politeness may appear to be limited to the representational or narrative sphere, but actually it will have gameplay consequences, because it will shape the manner in which other characters relate to (and assist, or repel) the protagonist. The characters in *Baldur's Gate* epitomize the game's interweaving of ludic and representational factors. Furthermore, both ludic and representational aspects of *Baldur's Gate* are crucial to its ability to enthral a player.

Immersion, engagement and 'flow'

Baldur's Gate has a long and twisted narrative, colourful dialogue options, rambunctious foes, querulous teammates and complex inventories. The game makes varied demands on its players; and it is compelling because of these demands, not despite them. Different games elicit different pleasures, and there is no point pretending that *Baldur's Gate* will suit the tastes of all gamers, or that all fans enjoy the game for the same reasons.

In his essay 'Semiotics of *Sim City*' Ted Friedman writes about gameplay identification in terms of location and mobility:

> We could see playing *Sim City*, then, as a constant shifting of identifications, depending on whether you're buying land, organizing the police force, paving roads, or whatever. This, I think, is part of what's going on. But this model suggests a level of disjunction – jumping back and forth from one role to the next – belied by the smooth, almost trance-like state of gameplay. Overarching these functional shifts, I think, is a more general state of identification: with the city as a whole, as a single system. (1999: 5)

Despite the differences between the two games, the kind of general focus proposed by Friedman is also partially appropriate to *Baldur's Gate*. The player attends to the system as a whole, but in the case of *Baldur's Gate*, the player also telescopes in to manage a series of subsystems: the characters (their acts, arms, inventories and skills). Thus, the game invites the player to move 'in' and 'out' at different points, and for different reasons. In the regular course of play, a player might peruse the game world from an isometric vantage point, directing the events unfolding on-screen. They might dive into a team member's backpack, open and read a letter or diary, and pull out again to review the immediate locality, or the entire game world on a map screen. The player might skim through a book discovered in a monk's cell, or pore over the statistics screen of a particular character. During combat it is standard procedure to pause the game, zoom in to each teammate's inventory, arm them appropriately, and restock spells and healing or empowering potions. Because the game has a well-designed interface the experienced player might flick between gameplay, inventory, journal entry and map screen without much in the way of conscious effort. The new player, on the other hand, faces a considerable learning curve.

Despite these repeated shifts in perspective, the player becomes absorbed: 'time flies'. This absorption is not compromised by the game's isometric perspective, or disrupted by the mechanistic 'point, click, point' of the game's keyboard commands. Players are mobile: they explore the game world, and they also move between different menus, screens, variables and statistics, without necessarily experiencing a sense of discontinuity. In other words, a player's engrossment does not rely on the game offering a 'realistic' 3-D space. Nor does the player's attentive state necessarily shift in response to moves between the game's ludic and representational aspects. Furthermore, the factors that trigger these attentive states are not consistent because they will alter as the player learns the game and develops greater fluency.

It is possible to further examine the player's potential absorption in *Baldur's Gate* using theories of *immersion*, *engagement* and *flow*. The term immersion covers a range of meditative and non-conscious states involving the sensation of being transported or submerged within a text (Murray, 2000: 98). Immersion, as a concept, implies different things, depending on whether it is borrowed from literary theory, Virtual Reality analysis or presence theory. Presence theory addresses the sense of 'being there' that various technologies (from the telephone to virtual reality) are able to evoke in their users. According to Lombard and Ditton, such technologies 'are designed to provide media users with an illusion that a mediated experience is not mediated' (1997: 1). Lombard and Ditton identify immersion as one of the ways in which presence has been conceptualized, and they go on to divide immersion into two categories: perceptual, and psychological.[7]

Perceptual immersion involves the degree to which a technology or experience monopolizes the senses of a user. In a movie theatre, for instance, the lights are turned down, and the audience is expected to be quiet. In Virtual Reality experiences, the ears, eyes and hands of the participant might be covered. Psychological immersion, on the other hand, involves the player's 'mental absorption in the world' (McMahan, 2003: 77). The player is slowly drawn into the game world via his or her imaginative investment. *Baldur's Gate* is played on a personal computer, not in a VR environment. The game is presented to the player in an isometric perspective, and not in 3-D. Additionally, playing the game involves digesting a large amount of information and manipulating numerous variables (ludic and/or representational). For all these reasons, in the case of *Baldur's Gate*, psychological immersion appears the more pertinent form, even though the game's audio and visual detailing simultaneously inspire degrees of sensory or perceptual immersion. The distinction between psychological and perceptual immersion may make it possible to theorize the varied ways that different genres of game engross their users. Here, however, the aim is to look at user pleasure and attentive states within a single game – to examine the relationship between psychological, imaginative immersion and engagement within *Baldur's Gate*. A model proposed by Douglas and Hargadon (2000, 2001) makes this possible.

Douglas and Hargadon have examined the concept of immersion from another perspective, relying on literary studies, and schema theory (in turn adapted from cognitive psychology). Within literary studies, immersion refers to the non-critical absorption enjoyed by readers of undemanding or generic fiction. Douglas and Hargadon define schemas as follows:

> Schemas enable us to perceive objects and occurrences around us and to make efficient sense of them by consulting our readymade store of similar occurrences and understandings, which we gain from reading, personal experience and even advice we receive from others. (Douglas and Hargadon, 2001: 154, citing Beaugrande)

According to Douglas and Hargadon, within a text 'the aesthetic remains largely (one of) immersion as long as the story, setting and interface adhere to a single schema' (2001: 158). When reading a generic novel, for instance, the reader may slip into a pleasurable, trance-like state of absorption. By keeping to a few, or a single schema, these novels are able to deeply immerse their readers.

Engagement, as the word suggests, is a more deliberate, critical mode of participation. Engagement happens when less familiar or more difficult material makes demands on the user, who is driven to reread or otherwise reconsider information in an attempt to make sense of it. Engagement involves those portions of a text where extra effort or interpretive skills are called for, where external referents are sought. With the experience of engagement, 'the cognitive demands of grappling with the text tend to be discontinuous, involving shuttling between competing schemas, prospecting and retrospecting through the text, and pausing over obscure passages' (Douglas and Hargadon, 2001: 156). Engagement involves the consideration of multiple schemas, whether from within or beyond the text itself. Douglas and Hargadon have summarized the two states as follows:

> The pleasures of immersion stem from our being completely absorbed within the ebb and flow of a familiar narrative schema. The pleasures of engagement tend to come from our ability to recognize a work's overturning or conjoining conflicting schemas from a perspective outside the text. (2000: 2)

In *Baldur's Gate* some ludic elements entail engagement – a relatively distanced, strategic stance, while other gameplay factors invite an immersed mulling and pondering, clicking and pointing. Likewise, some representational elements evoke immersion: enjoying the scenery, changing a character's clothes or following a descriptive piece of dialogue. Yet others will require the player's engagement – as when a new plot twist or the reappearance of a particular character calls for interpretation, memory, filling 'gaps' of various kinds. The game thoroughly entangles its game system with its representational 'dressing', and they are complicit in the facilitation of immersive and engaged states. Players of *Baldur's Gate* slip between immersed, close absorption and an engaged, critical distance. Thus it would not make sense to value engagement over immersion or vice versa; the two states are complementary. The game is compelling, not because of its capacity to evoke either immersion *or* engagement in the player, but because it allows the player to constantly move between the two.

Immersion is fostered when the on-screen situation invites an immediate, localized response: ponder, gaze, read, hit, explore, shuffle, tinker, poke, march or blast. Engagement is demanded when a failure to surmount the problem at hand makes the player hesitate, rethink, reconsider, or seek solutions at an increasing distance (temporal, cognitive or otherwise) from the on-screen action. The impasse might involve a forgotten name or code word, a character's traits (alignment or morale for example), a lost path or a powerful enemy.[8] Seeking a solution might initially mean having the team pause or repeat a particular action, or retrace their steps. If that does not help, the player might move away from the game screen to check a map screen, reread a letter, retrieve information from the avatar's journal or reload from an earlier save-point. If still stuck, a player might consult the manual, ask a friend's advice or refer to an online walk-through guide or website. The following query, for example, was found at an online forum.

I left Durlag's Tower by way of that ghost on the 5th floor, but I need to get back down. I can't seem to figure out how to get past the 3rd floor, because the helmet that triggers the 2 doors to open in the room where 3 dopplegangers show up is no longer there . . . How do you get them to open – or is there another way?[9]

Clearly, by this point, the player is regarding the game's events from 'outside', and consulting resources altogether external to the game itself. The game's mouse-clicking repetition, inventory rearranging, pastoral landscapes (complete with birdsong) and descriptive story-telling are immersive, while its plot twists, mutating characters and increasingly lethal monsters call for a more engaged style of attentiveness. In *Baldur's Gate* the two potential attentive states are mutually dependent, rather than exclusive or counteractive. The player's slide between more and less conscious modes of attention underlies the pleasures of play. The shifting between the two states enriches the satisfactions of each.

The fluidity and ease with which players move around the interface and the game world shape the experience of play. Thus the experience offered by *Baldur's Gate* will alter as the player comes to grips with the keyboard controls, levelling up, navigation and resource management. As players learn and gain familiarity with the game, the amount of conscious effort required in order to perform routine actions will change. As Steven Poole (2002: 182) has observed, in a well-designed computer game 'one of the reasons you feel so fluidly involved is that your muscle memory has taken over the mechanical business of operating buttons, joysticks, trigger or foot-pedals'. Yet progressing through *Baldur's Gate* requires more than the gradual attainment of improved accuracy or reaction times, because levelling up in an RPG involves the acquisition and application of relevant *information*: this is a cognitive process, not just a sensori-motor process. However initially baffling the multiple options concerning character or magic spells (for instance) appear, they also move via a learning curve into the interpretive, cognitive equivalent of 'muscle memory', demanding less and less of the player's conscious attention. As the player comes to know the game thoroughly, his or her relationship to the game's offers will shift. Certain aspects of *Baldur's Gate*'s setting, narrative and gameplay will begin to require less deliberate effort, and thus may move from being engaging to being immersive. At the same time, the game counterbalances this shift, by continually confronting the player with new twists and increased challenges, bigger monsters, and more complex situations, so that the potential for engagement is constantly renewed.

The game matches the player's new competency with increased difficulty and harder (yet still feasible) goals. These are also the preconditions of *flow*. Players often report a sensation of being 'in the groove'

(Poole, 2000: 182) or 'in the zone' (Jarvinen et al., 2002: 22) and these feelings have been linked to theories of flow (Csikszentmihalyi, 2002). The flow state is possible when an activity involves escalating yet manageable challenges, options, decisions, risk, feedback and achievable goals. It is an intensely pleasurable, optimum state, incorporating focus, euphoria and high levels of motivation. Flow states have been associated with a variety of activities, including computer games (Bryce and Rutter, 2001; Myers, 1992). Douglas and Hargadon have discussed flow in relation to immersion and engagement, in order to argue that 'Since flow involves extending our skills to cope with challenges, a sense that we are performing both well and effortlessly, it hovers on the continuum between immersion and engagement, drawing on the characteristics of both simultaneously' (2000: 6). Many computer games, including *Baldur's Gate*, appear conducive to flow, and once evoked and associated with a particular context, the flow state can even be experienced in preparatory, peripheral or associated situations (Marr, 2001). This may help explain the pleasure that some players take in game-related activities, including the production of online fan sites, art and fiction.

Ideas of immersion, engagement and flow may help to explain some of the pleasures involved in playing a game. Yet, while it is possible in theory to associate various aspects of the game text with these sensations or states, in practice it would be difficult to *prove* that these states happen, or that particular aspects of the game generate them. As this suggests, theorizing the pleasures of play raises a methodological conundrum. If analysts refuse to shed their critical distance, their experience of the game will remain partial. Yet relying on other approaches, such as the observation of players, or the interviewing of players after a gaming session, will not resolve this dilemma. All accounts of gameplay are partial or reductive, because the process of documenting or articulating any lived experience is inevitably selective.

Conclusion

Playing *Baldur's Gate* involves manipulating a set of evolving characters according to certain conditions (rules, interface commands and limited options). The protagonist is described by the 'stats screen', characterized by fictional cohorts, and manoeuvred by the player. At the same time, the player exercises their prerogative to ignore, resist or respect the character's biographic attributes.

The management of strategic variables and the incremental challenges of the game world invite different states of attention. Players slip from engrossed immersion to a more deliberate or calculating engagement. Because computer games offer an immersive, participatory environment, as well as feedback, incremental and engaging challenges and contextualized goals, they may potentially evoke a flow response in their users. As this suggests, no single textual factor (whether ludic or representational) is accountable for the pleasures of *Baldur's Gate*. On the contrary, it is the combining of potentials, the player's motion *between* possibilities, and the playful relay between the fixed and the variable, the automatic and the calculated, and the easy and the difficult, that makes the time fly.

Space, Navigation and Affect

Diane Carr

P<small>LAYERS</small> are invited to navigate and explore their way through game worlds in different ways, and this has ramifications for the emotional or affective experience of play. In this chapter these issues will be explored by means of an analysis of two contrasting games: *Planescape Torment* (Interplay, 1999) and *Silent Hill* (Konami, 1999). There are some superficial similarities between the games: both feature zombie assailants, violent confrontation, exploration, peril and death. However, *Planescape Torment* and *Silent Hill* belong to different genres, and they employ different strategies in their bid to generate generically appropriate affect.

   Planescape Torment is an RPG, and the game's meandering structure reflects its generic roots. *Silent Hill* might be described as an action adventure game – or perhaps more specifically as a 3-D survival horror game.[1] While *Planescape Torment* fosters the kind of contemplation and exploration that we have described as characteristic of RPGs in general, the success of the *Silent Hill* series depends directly on the game's capacity to frighten its users. Each of the games invites a form of navigation that aids and abets its generic intent; and each proposes gameplay that nurtures a particular affect. The avatars, Harry in *Silent Hill*, and The Nameless One in *Planescape Torment*, perform differently for their players, and the relationship of each avatar to the worlds they infiltrate on our behalf is another factor to consider in relation to the games' generic intentions.

Planescape Torment and *Silent Hill*

Planescape Torment has much in common with *Baldur's Gate*. The games were both developed by Black Isle Studios, and they share a publisher (Interplay), as well as a games engine (BioWare's Infinity Engine).[2] *Planescape Torment* opens as the protagonist character, The Nameless One, regains consciousness in a grim mortuary. Zombie morticians lurch from slab to slab carving up corpses and trailing dirty bandages.

It looks like a scene from a horror movie. However, *Planescape Torment* sets out to intrigue, rather than to frighten. The central aim of the game is to solve the riddle of the protagonist's identity. The Nameless One is a mutilated, immortal amnesiac. The first clues about his identity are read to him from the tattoos on his own back, by a floating skull named Mort. Although the player does not build the protagonist from scratch, the game still makes a feature of character construction, in that the player will make decisions concerning The Nameless One's alignment, inventory and professional skills.

Planescape Torment is set in Sigil, the City of Doors, where unpredictable portals link to multiple worlds. Its monsters are grotesque rather than scary, and it revels in the strange and smelly. It is a freak show, a long story, a zoo and a cabinet of talkative curiosities. Progress through the game is reflective and responsive, and the player is sent on cyclical, scenic detours. Even letting the avatar get 'killed' is a valid strategy. He is immortal, but the shock can shake loose new fragments of memory and, as long as he is not incinerated or eaten, he just wakes up back at the mortuary. Quests and subquests are so numerous that the avatar carries a journal that is automatically updated to help the player keep track. Game-generated teammates join The Nameless One, and each carries an inventory bulging with unpredictable and complicated artefacts. Tools can be identified, magic tattoos purchased and charms deciphered.

By contrast, *Silent Hill* is tense, sparse and linear. The protagonist, Harry, wakes up after a car crash in a small North American town, to find that his young daughter Cheryl has disappeared from the passenger seat. He sets off into the fog, calling for her. He stumbles across bloodstained alleys, zombie bats, skinless dogs and chasms where the road out of town used to be. Cheryl is missing and presumed to be in some kind of horrible danger. Most of the town's inhabitants have already been either wiped out or changed into groaning, homicidal undead.

Whereas *Planescape Torment* features 'adventuring' music, *Silent Hill* uses suggestive and worrisome noises like footsteps, wings and bad plumbing. Harry carries a disconcerting radio that crackles with squeaky static when monsters are around. As Jonathan Ree has pointed out, spooky noises are an excellent way to give us the creeps, because 'the spatial indeterminacy of sound means that auditory illusions can be even more disconcerting than either optical or visual ones' (Ree, 1999: 46). *Silent Hill* wants its players to be frightened, and the discomforting sounds move out of the game world to infiltrate our own space.

Silent Hill is sequential; its goals are clear: stay alive, fight off assailants, penetrate the next space and locate Cheryl. While the game space is available to the user in three dimensions, the clues, keys and puzzles all lead the player in a particular direction: forward. There is not

Illustration 4   *Planescape Torment's* The Nameless One in conversation. Published by Interplay.

Illustration 5   The avatar Harry in *Silent Hill*. Reproduced by kind permission of the publisher, Konami Corp.

much dialogue, and what there is, happens in cutscenes. There is little on-screen text. The menu is simple, and resources such as medicine and ammunition are self-explanatory and rationed. The avatar, Harry, is ready-made. He accumulates some accessories and weapons, but because he does not really grow in strength or experience it is up to the player to accumulate skills. *Silent Hill* favours causality over description: it presents the player with a chain of puzzle-solving and conditional progression, and this linearity enables it to instigate and maintain pace and tension. One online reviewer described it as 'one of the most enjoyable, and truly frightening, games to have come out in a long time'.[3]

Navigation: maze, rhizome and labyrinth

In *Hamlet on the Holodeck*, Janet Murray describes two models of spatial navigation in interactive texts: the maze and the rhizome (Murray, 2000: 130). The concept of the rhizome is drawn from the philosophy of Deleuze and Guattari (1988) and describes the kind of tuber root system that, like a potato, can sprout in any direction. Murray suggests that adventuring in the maze involves the conditional progression towards a single exit or resolution, whereas in the rhizomic environment no particular direction would be marked as more desirable than any other. The disadvantage of the maze is that the user is steered towards a single outcome in a predetermined manner, while the drawback of the rhizome is its lack of structure. Hence, according to Murray:

> Both the overdetermined form of the single-path maze adventure and the underdetermined form of rhizome fiction work against the interactor's pleasure in navigation. The potential of the labyrinth as a participatory narrative form would seem to lie somewhere between the two, in stories that are goal driven enough to guide navigation but open-ended enough to allow free exploration. (Murray, 2000: 135)

The labyrinth, then, incorporates the best aspects of the maze, with the freedom of the rhizome. It follows that different versions of the labyrinth might be more maze-like, or more rhizomic, and that these qualities could be incorporated in varying degrees, in order to generate different experiences for their users. If this is the case, then *Planescape Torment* could be said to reside at the rhizomic end of the scale, while *Silent Hill* is relatively maze-like. The two games belong to different genres; they seek to generate different affect; and they effectively exploit different styles of navigation in order to achieve that end.

In *Silent Hill*, players are directed to proceed to particular locations, in a certain order, to solve puzzles and unlock the next phase of the game. Progress is conditional on success at earlier stages, and incidents are overtly sequential. Paths may branch (there is more than one possible ending), but the drive towards resolution maintains a tidal pull on the player. The game aims for intensity, tension and fright, and its ability to generate such affect is fuelled by its more directed gameplay. *Planescape Torment* also has conditional progression, but it mixes and accumulates goals in a less orderly fashion. It sends its multitasking players in rhizomic circles, deviations and side-quests in search of lost memories and fragmented histories. One player's route through the game could differ quite dramatically from that taken by another.

Silent Hill does feature characters other than Harry, but *Planescape Torment* is crowded by comparison, and each new face 'invariably involves . . . a new story, the one which explains the "now I am here" of the new character' (Todorov, 1977: 70). Meeting an NPC in *Planescape Torment* often involves reading a description of their eyes, their fingers, what they are wearing, where they come from or how they smell. Details are so prevalent that they act as a kind of magnification. This magnification underlines *Planescape Torment*'s concern with the invented and the fantastic, with perceptual alteration and with strangeness for its own sake. Moving forward through the game leads to further revelations about The Nameless One's past. The amount of dialogue from the game's inhabitants makes it difficult to empty any space of its potential for novelty, and undertaking quests will send players repeatedly into locations that keep altering. Players are thus encouraged by the game to examine and then re-examine its places and inhabitants.

The overarching quest of *Planescape Torment* involves solving the mystery of the amnesiac protagonist's past identity, but this goal can only be attained via any number of smaller quests. One outcome of this is that players are distracted from any single directive. Subquests might mean that players run about in circles, but all the missions accomplished make possible the accumulation of experience points that will alter the characters' abilities and powers as they level up. Progress through the space of the game is concurrent with progress in terms of the 'level' of the central character, and the two patterns of accumulation remain intimately linked. This tendency is characteristic of the genre. In most action adventure games (such as *Silent Hill*), to ask someone what level they are on is to ask them what location they have reached. In an RPG, to ask someone what level they are on is to ask what their character's experience rating is. Experience is a strategic, indexed commodity.

In *Silent Hill* it is reaction times and accuracy that count. Confrontations happen in real time and Harry has to fight or flee, just to survive. To save a game, the player must position the avatar in front of clipboard folders that are found on registration desks or in hallways in different buildings. The locating of save-points within the game world, as objects, pins time to specific points in space. Temporality is thus ordered, just as onward spatial progress is conditional. These features limit the openness of the 3-D game space. *Silent Hill*'s mobile 'camera' and long corridors associate access with progress and penetration, and while a player could endlessly run round and round the same block, the location would soon be emptied of its potential to divert or surprise. If Harry meets other characters in *Silent Hill*, their dialogue happens in cutscenes, and their conversation is outside the player's control. Once the monsters have been killed, the locks opened or the puzzles solved, there is nobody to talk to and not a lot to see. Players are urged to keep moving.

In *Silent Hill*, the game world fills the screen, whereas in *Planescape Torment* the screen is framed by icons and menu short cuts. In *Silent Hill*, spaces scope around Harry. As a player you can enter a room, but you can't see it all at once: it feels like somewhere you could become trapped; somewhere that something could sneak up behind you. By contrast, the stable, isometric (top-down) perspective of *Planescape Torment* has arguably less emotive charge, but this perspective lends itself to observation and rummaging about. The game world lies open to the player's gaze. In *Planescape Torment* a player does not have to arrive at any particular location to save their game, and pausing a game in order to sort out a strategy, mid-confrontation, is par for the course.

In *Silent Hill* Harry hits his assailants when the player hits their action button, whereas in *Planescape Torment* the 'click and point' action of the player triggers 'rounds' of action during a combat sequence. Combat in *Planescape Torment* is not just about survival; it can have various profitable outcomes. A team will gain experience points and booty if they prevail. As the team earns experience points, they are moved through levels of subsequent rank. Their various powers and skills are augmented, and the game world alters in return, heightening the ferocity, tenacity or might of the opposition. Meeting with a game-generated character in *Planescape Torment* involves being presented with a range of dialogue options, from which the player can select a reply according to strategy, or whim, or curiosity. The choice of reply will move the dialogue, and any subsequent action, in a particular direction. The Non-Player Character might respond by attacking the avatar, or by offering useful advice; he/she may reward or initiate a quest, or teach the avatar a particular profession.

Silent Hill's tight, maze-like structure fuels its ability to frighten its users. The game maintains tension (more or less) throughout because it refuses to be diverted or slowed by elucidation. *Silent Hill* emotively loads scenes and incidents using trans-textual shorthand. The limited justification for the town's trauma is provided in cutscene flashbacks that rely on film references and horror movie conventions to make their point. This keeps gameplay pared down and fast paced. In one empty domestic interior, for instance, the soundtrack features a child pleading with her strange and abusive mother. The pair seem trapped replaying a past that sounds part *Psycho* (Hitchcock, 1960) and part *Sybil* (Petrie, first aired 1977). The game is set in everyday places – cafes and gas stations, schools and hospitals – and this ordinariness makes it all the more disturbing when things turn nasty.

As Robin Wood (1997: 190) has argued, generic horror regularly employs 'a simple and obvious basic formula . . . normality is threatened by the Monster' – although normality, the monster, and the frequently ambivalent relationship between the two, are all variable. *Silent Hill* clearly fits Wood's horror formula. Normality is threatened, trashed, by the monstrous. The eponymous North American town looks commonplace, but, as Harry helpfully points out to other characters in a cutscene, 'something bizarre's going on'. The innocent are imperilled. Hell has eviscerated the town's school and hospital. Harry has to rescue his daughter and oppose evil. As Tanya Krzywinska (2002: 212) argues, 'Whatever players do in most horror-based games, they still have to occupy the position of an avatar of good. As a predetermined transcendent force, the moral occult is at work in the way these games channel the player through their labyrinths.' While there are degrees of ambiguity in *Silent Hill*, this basic antithesis of good and evil is never actually undermined.

Planescape Torment, on the other hand, is not set in a place where 'normality' has gone wrong – there was no normality to begin with. Its ghouls and zombies are not agents of perverse disruption or upheaval. Its monsters are indigenous. They are not intruders. The avatar and his teammates are not fated to restore a particular or dualistic moral order because *Planescape Torment* reflects *Dungeons & Dragons*' cosmology, and there is a double axis of 'alignment' along the *Dungeons & Dragons*' moral compass. The positions along one axis range from good to neutral to evil, while values on the other axis range from lawful, through neutral, to chaotic, and relate to the consistency with which a character acts.

Despite a shared preoccupation with zombies, death, loss and fleshy transformation, there are significant differences between *Planescape Torment* and *Silent Hill*. These differences reflect their generic status, and they are underpinned by dissimilarities in the games' navigational structures.

Text and the traversal function

Espen Aarseth has proposed a typology (a system of classification) for cybertexts, including computer games. He offers a broad definition of text, in which a text is an object that *relays information*. According to Aarseth, a text relays information in the form of 'a string of signs' (1997: 62). He argues that it is useful to 'distinguish between strings as they appear to readers and strings as they exist in the text, since they may not always be the same' (1997: 62). Strings as they appear to readers are called 'scriptons', while strings that appear in the text are 'textons'. To put this another way, textons are all the potentials offered by a game, and scriptons are the ways in which those potentials are played out, on-screen, by different users. The 'mechanism by which scriptons are revealed or generated from textons and presented to the user of the text' is named the *traversal function* (1997: 62).

The classifications of the traversal function proposed by Aarseth provide a useful 'toolset' with which to further investigate the different forms of navigation invited by *Silent Hill* and *Planescape Torment*. Aarseth lists seven variants of the traversal function, but for the sake of brevity we will be referring only to those modes where the two games under discussion appear to differ most obviously: the categories of dynamics, determinability, access and linking.

The *dynamics* of the traversal function relate to the number and constancy of the textons and scriptons present. In these terms, *Planescape Torment* is more dynamic and less static than *Silent Hill*, because of its greater number of goals and quests, and the fact that only some of them are compulsory, combined with the complexity of the team's inventory, mutating avatars and all the possible dialogue options. Both games offer the player choice and options and variables at the scriptonic level, but *Planescape Torment* has a lot more textons to begin with, and the range and number of potential scriptonic combinations increase exponentially.

The games also diverge on the question of determinability. Determinability, in Aarseth's definition:

> concerns the stability of the traversal function . . . In some adventure games, the same response to a given situation will always produce the same result. In other games, random functions (such as the use of dice) make the results unpredictable. (1997: 63)

This is difficult to quantify in relation to the games under consideration, but the two games do position themselves differently in relation to chance. *Planescape Torment* employs *Dungeons & Dragons'* rules, so there are virtual dice lurking somewhere in the game engine. The numbers that describe the team members on their statistics screen are odds, basically. In a confrontation, the strength, armour class and hit points of each opponent and their weapons are rated and the internal dice rolled to determine the outcome. *Silent Hill* no doubt features its own elements of chance and luck, but they are less overt and, generally speaking, a repeated action will tend to give the same result. Harry does not particularly change, except for the fact that he gets weaker if he is wounded, and stronger again if he gets medicine. *Planescape Torment* has a greater number of variables, and thus more opportunities for chance to play a part.

Aarseth's categories of *access* and *linking* also manifest differently in the two games. Access involves the ability of a user to enter a text at any point. Obviously this is controlled in both games (although you can always cheat or use a walkthrough) but, as mentioned above, you can save and reload at any point in *Planescape Torment*, while this is only possible at very specific places in *Silent Hill*. Links that connect spaces or segments of *Planescape Torment* are generated via dialogue options. Additionally, the use and manipulation of portals (doors from one place to another that defy distance) are important parts of the game. These function as links between different areas, and, while they are conditional, they are activated by various magic items, or by chance, as well as through actions or puzzle-solving. As such, they are more variable and less consistent than those that determine Harry's route through *Silent Hill*.

Aarseth's traversal categories and their variants therefore help to identify those factors in each game that shape their different spatial orientations. In each case, *Silent Hill* is more static, more controlled and more determined. These parameters shape the maze-like structure on which the game is based. By contrast, the relative openness of *Planescape Torment*'s traversal mode serves its rhizomic, expansive tendencies.

Body doubles

In both games the player's trajectory is influenced by promised rewards, goals, clues and diversions. *Silent Hill* intends to scare its players, and its controlling, maze-style parameters enable it to establish and maintain tension. *Planescape Torment* aims to provide its players with a sense that they are excavating a history (The Nameless One's forgotten past) while exploring, more or less at will, a vast and bizarre invention. Its rhizomic elements assist in this. In both games spatial and navigational factors facilitate a particular emotional affect, one that is aligned with the game's genre. In each case the spaces are accessed by means of an avatar. What follows is a speculative account of how elements within each game might influence or contribute to the relationship established between player and avatar. My aim is not to fully account for this relationship, but rather to suggest ways in which it might vary, from genre to genre.

Film theorists have used Sigmund Freud's account of the uncanny and the double to explore the carnal sensations generated when we watch bodies in motion on film. Lesley Stern (1997), for example, has described the feeling of corporeal empathy that might be evoked when we watch a figure falling, being thrown, or performing acrobatics on-screen. For an instant our bodies respond in recognition to this other body's movements with an imaginary symbiosis. This sensation is closely followed by a brief jarring, an uncanny discontinuity – triggered by the recognition that we are, after all, watching rather than performing the embodied motion. In the wake of this experience 'the effect persists, the fear and exhilaration, the frisson' (Stern, 1997).

Perhaps avatars, too, are capable of generating forms of uncanny resonance. The player hits a button – the avatar jumps, somersaults or flicks a switch. All players, surely, have found themselves flinching when an avatar bangs its head, have felt themselves lean over with pseudo-centrifugal forces or recoil when an avatar plunges over a cliff. Certain kinds of recognition or 'identification' – this would suggest – do exist between the player and avatar. Game analysts cannot explain such phenomena simply by applying models of cinematic identification. Theories of cinematic identification were developed using models drawn from psychoanalysis, and the film spectator's still-ness in front of the screen is a central premise. The player's relation-ship to on-screen events and bodies, by contrast, is dependent on the user taking action, and any theory of 'ergodic identification'[4] would have to allow for this. Additionally, games position and address their players through various perspectives, modes, channels, menus, inputs and outputs. This suggests that it would be a mistake to try and impose a single model on to all avatar–player relations.

Nevertheless, in *Planescape Torment* and *Silent Hill* the avatars are our emissaries in the game world and thus each is (to some degree) our double. The relationship between player and avatar in either game is differently framed and, as a result, the emotions generated via the player–avatar relationship may vary. It is possible to further speculate about the differences between Harry and The Nameless One by refer-ring again to Freud's work on the uncanny and the double. According to Freud, the 'double was originally an insurance against the extinc-tion of the self [. . .] and when this phase is surmounted, the meaning of the 'double' changes: having once been an assurance of immortal-ity, it becomes the uncanny harbinger of death' (Freud, 2003: 142).

Fortunately, we are not concerned with arguing about whether Freud was right or not. What is useful is that he has suggested two kinds of double: one that is reassuring; the other that is uncanny or disconcert-ing. Representations of both categories of double might manifest in figurative computer games (or at different times within the same game).

However, the games under consideration clearly set out to generate certain kinds of experiences for their users. *Silent Hill* is a horror game, so an uncanny double would best serve its agenda. While some of the doubling in *Planescape Torment* might be uncanny, it is arguable that the reassuring double-as-ally is the more serviceable in this case.

In the previous chapter it was noted that because *Baldur's Gate* is an information-laden, isometric RPG, it relies more on psychological immersion, and less on perceptual immersion. The same could be said of *Planescape Torment*. *Silent Hill*, on the other hand, is a 3-D action adventure game designed for the console. It features much less written text, and relies more on visuals and kinetics to immerse the player. As a result it is arguable that this game relies more on evoking perceptual immersion. To recap, immersion is involved in generating a sensation of presence – a sense of 'being there' in the game world (Lombard and Ditton, 1997). Immersion has been divided into two categories: perceptual immersion, which occurs when an experience monopolizes the senses of the participant, and psychological immersion, which involves the participant becoming engrossed through their imaginative or mental absorption. If these games do rely on different styles of immersion, this may impact on player-to-avatar relations.[5] Marie-Laure Ryan writes in a discussion of Virtual Reality (VR) that:

> a mind may conceive a world from the outside, [but] a body always experiences it from the inside. As a relation involving the body, the interactivity of VR immerses the user in a world already in place; as a process involving the mind, it turns the user's relation to this world into a creative membership. (1994: 34)

It would not make sense, of course, to categorically separate a player's mind from his or her body, yet it is possible that different games (and the manner of immersion they rely on) might position the player in a way that reflects either the 'inside' or the 'outside' referred to in Ryan's statement.

A game like *Planescape Torment* that generates layers of detailed information, multiple prompts and lengthy, written descriptions would favour psychological immersion, and would evoke a sense of 'creative membership' – to use Ryan's phrase. *Planescape Toment*'s complex interface shapes the nature of the link between the player and his or her on-screen agent. The isometric perspective and the assembled nature of the protagonist defuse direct (sensory or kinetic) symbiosis between player and avatar, and so the player may seem 'further' from the body on-screen. Yet the player becomes deeply immersed by another route: via the volume of descriptive text to be read, and the slow accumulation of detail involved in the manipulation of the protagonist, his team and their inventories.

Players manipulate The Nameless One's evolution and they are encouraged by the game to take responsibility for his growth and fate. Players must make choices about the protagonist's characterization: his profession, skills, memory and alignment. The manner in which he develops is designed to reflect the player's preferences – as the game's manual explains, 'throughout the game your character adapts to fit your own personal gaming style'.

The Nameless One gradually acquires a troupe of companions. These teammates will be selected from the (ready-made) candidates presented to the player as he or she progresses through the game. Once they join the player's team, they are under his or her control. Visually and demographically (that is, in terms of caste, profession, species) these team members may not resemble each other, but the player has access to all of their resources and will, as a strategic necessity, rifle through the various inventories of each, assigning and reassigning their stuff to other team members as he or she sees fit. Despite their apparent individuality, from the perspective of the inventory and statistics screens, these teammates resemble each other. Each is a bundle of variables manipulated by the player and honed to perform a specialized role within the team. Thus, the double (or the multiple) in RPGs is domesticated via the character menus. Each team member is partially assembled by the player, and thus is a known quantity, a resource, and each becomes further assurance against the in-game opposition.[6] Taken together, these aspects of the game suggest that any doubling between player and avatar in *Planescape Torment* (and similarly structured RPGs) is of the double-as-ally persuasion, rather than of the uncanny double variety. Furthermore, it suggests that the reassuring double is particularly compatible with psychological, imaginative immersion.

By contrast, the threatening or uncanny double seems to hold sway in 3-D games like *Silent Hill* – and this may be in part because the game relies more on sensory immersion, and less on imaginative or psychological immersion. In *Silent Hill* the world is explored in three dimensions, and a player's commands directly trigger Harry's movements (run, hit). The game evokes a higher degree of perceptual immersion because it drags the player through space tied behind a character who is running, shooting or bashing at monsters in real time and in direct response to the player's button tapping. Sensory or perceptual immersion implies a relationship between player and avatar that is more immediate, but less negotiable.

The sensory immersion that the atmospheric *Silent Hill* evokes works in combination with the linear gameplay to deliver a specific, intended affect: fear. The 3-D avatar has a particular relationship to the screen: as an embodied agent it actually penetrates into spaces on the player's behalf. As a by-product, it generates a greater degree of uncanny resonance. In RPGs players fiddle with the avatar's vital statistics, but the action adventure game avatar is typically less accessible (and thus less explicable). Perhaps it is the uncanny aspect of 3-D avatars that stimulates our appetite for their extreme physical capabilities. Their acrobatics expiate the anxiety aroused by the uncanny doubling that is generated by the relay between user and avatar.

However, not all 3-D games feature superpowered avatars, spring-loaded by uncanny fallout. *Silent Hill*'s Harry is resoundingly normal. He's a regular guy and an average shot. He doesn't know kung fu. He even trips over on his way downstairs. Perhaps this in turn means that the game recoups the uncanny frisson that Harry's manipulation generates, and employs it to maximize the creepiness of the game's hallways and streetscapes. The doubling between the player and avatar in *Silent Hill* is not channelled and purged via a superhuman avatar. It remains disconcertingly present; Freud's 'harbinger of death' shadows us, and stokes the game's dark vision.

Conclusion

Planescape Torment is so encyclopedic that the parameters of the game and its goals are relatively dispersed and vague. Players move from description to situation, to negotiation, and more description, rather than from kill to kill, or from space to new space. Its limits are elusive. Players level up, accumulating details, companions, journals, spell books and complicated charms. Even small choices have multiple and unpredictable results, leading the player to an incident or a confrontation, or to nothing much. The game resists resolution or even comprehension. A rambling text like *Planescape Torment* bounces when you try and nail it down; it evades totalization. It has its moments of 'rush' and of confrontation, but it wants to be savoured, wandered through, in the company of armed companions.

While *Planescape Torment* refuses to be hurried, the nerve-racking *Silent Hill* urges the player from point to point, puzzle to solution, and onwards to a resolution. It can be completed and charted, at least to a degree. *Silent Hill* aims at a particular intensity and pace. It wants to frighten its players, and it succeeds by maintaining a more directed, linear style of gameplay. *Planescape Torment* and *Silent Hill* have different intentions. Each game uses the model of spatial navigation (rhizome or maze, respectively) that serves its generic agenda, and each uses an avatar that responds to its world, and its players, in a manner that amplifies the game's own particular brand of pleasure.

CHAPTER
06
Playing Roles

Andrew Burn

SQUARESOFT's *Final Fantasy VII* (1997) is a hugely successful Japanese Role Playing Game. It sold to virtually all Japan's Playstation owners within the first forty-eight hours of its release in 1997, and was no less popular in the USA on its release there later that year.[1] In this chapter, we use *FFVII* as a case study to explore one of the key dimensions of Role Playing Games: the avatar.

'Avatar' is the Sanskrit word for 'descent', and refers to the embodiment of a god on earth. It is by means of the avatar that the player becomes embodied in the game, and performs the role of protagonist. Cloud Strife, the protagonist-avatar of *FFVII*, is a mysterious mercenary. Dressed in leather and big boots, he wields a sword as big as himself; but he has an oddly childish face, whimsically delineated in the 'deformed aesthetic' of manga, with enormous, glowing blue eyes, framed in cyberpunk blond spikes (Illustration 6).

This is how Rachel, a seventeen-year-old English player of *FFVII*, described Cloud in one of our research interviews:

> It's just basically you play this character who's in this like really cool like cityscape and you have to, er, and he finds out . . . and, er, he escapes because he finds out that, um, he's, because he starts having these flashbacks, and he escapes from this city because he's being pursued I think, and, um, he has to defeat this big corporation and try and – oh yeah, Sephiroth, he's this big military commander, and you have to go and try to stop him, 'cos he's trying to raise up all the beasts, and you do this by collecting materia, which you can use for magic and stuff, and you use your own weapons, and –

Rachel's phrase 'this character' evokes the conventional idea of the fictional character operating as a protagonist in a narrative. However, as well as being a protagonist in this conventional sense, Cloud is the player's embodiment in the game, the avatar. This chapter will explore how this dual function is constructed, how it is experienced by the player and why Rachel's words 'you play' indicate very precisely the relation between player and avatar.

Illustration 6   Cloud Strife – the avatar of *Final Fantasy VII*. Reproduced by kind permission of Square Enix UK.

In particular, we will consider how this dual function relates to the two fundamental elements of the game: what we have identified in earlier chapters as ludic and representational aspects of the game. We have proposed that games are systems that operate in terms of sets of rules, which in turn specify particular objectives, economies, obstacles and so on. In this chapter, we argue that representation is also a system; and we consider how it might mesh with the game system. The game system means the rule-based system of the game, which in computer games is produced by the procedural work of the game engine, while the representational system refers to how the game represents the world, and includes the visible and audible game world, the narrative and the characters overlaid on the system. As we shall explain, the avatar-protagonist operates in both systems, and understanding the avatar enables us to see how the two systems work together to produce the player's experience of the game. In this chapter, we will focus on the narrative system, which is part of the representational system. Specifically, we will concentrate on one important part of that system: the fundamental relation between the narrative function of the protagonist (that of hero) and the actions she or he performs. This system will be seen to interrelate with the game system, in which the protagonist is realized as a playable character, with programmed functions enabling the player to navigate the game.

A social semiotic approach

This chapter draws on some of the narrative theories we have used in earlier chapters, but it also brings a new perspective to bear: that of social semiotics. Within media studies, the use of semiotics generally draws on the work of writers who have analysed visual media, such as Roland Barthes and Christian Metz. However, social semiotics also employs ideas from the sociolinguistic theory of M. A. K. Halliday (1985). From a Hallidayan perspective, language is seen as a form of social behaviour, and the point of linguistic analysis is to reveal the *social functions* of elements such as lexis (vocabulary) and grammar. When social semiotics is applied to visual media (for instance by Kress and van Leeuwen, 1996), it proposes a 'grammar of images' which adapts Halliday's framework of three overarching functions of all language: *representational* (representing the world); *interactive* (allowing communication between the makers and readers of texts; but also between readers and imaginary characters in texts); and *organizational* (enabling elements of text to be cohesive and coherent – to stick together in ways which further realize the meanings they carry).

The first two of these have an obvious relation to the representational and ludic elements we have explored in earlier chapters. Thus, in terms of *representation*, we can look at the narrative of *Final Fantasy VII* (and, in this chapter, we look specifically at the central character as an element of that narrative). In terms of *interaction*, we can look at the game system and how it addresses and engages the player. We should expect that both these systems will operate very differently in game texts; and we will see whether social semiotic theory can help to conceptualize the relation between them.

A further development of social semiotics, *multimodality theory* (Kress and van Leeuwen, 2001), considers how texts combine different semiotic modes – such as speech, writing, sound and images – and how these relate to each other. Games are obviously multimodal, so we can ask how the three overarching functions referred to above are realized by combinations of communicative modes: animation, visual design, music, written text and sound.

In the case of the *representational* function, social semiotics would lead us to focus on the system which in language is called *transitivity*: how *Actors* perform *Actions* upon *Goals* – or, simply put, who does what to whom. This is the basic idea on which the narratologist Gerard Genette (1980) builds his theory, proposing that narrative is an expansion of the grammatical category of the verb: it is about *action*. In the first part of this book we looked at other aspects of Genette's theory of narrative discourse. Here we are focusing on a different aspect of his theory: how action works at the centre of narrative, and how it produces a semiotic system which in language is transitivity.

The grammatical structure of Rachel's account above suggests that the element of 'Actor' in the transitivity system of the game is divided. In parts of her account the Actor is, conventionally, Cloud, rendered in the third person ('*he* escapes'). Elsewhere, the pronoun representing the Actor changes to indicate the player ('*you* have to go . . .'). The pronouns here can be seen as important signifiers, naming the central character. On the one hand, Cloud is 'he', the term by which Oliver Twist or Robin Hood are most often named in their respective narratives. On the other hand, he is 'you', a name by which a central character in literature could never be known.[2] Rachel's account reveals, in its oscillation between 'he' and 'you', the grammatical yoking together of the traditional protagonist and the player.

The next step would be to ask: if Cloud is the Actor in two senses (conventional character and avatar), what Actions does he perform, and are they different in his two states? The answer to this latter question is 'yes', but we will return to this aspect of the representational function of the avatar later.

The next obvious question follows Genette's theory a little further. Having considered the verb as a basic building-block of narrative, Genette moves on to look at the system of mood in language, which is traditionally organized under three headings: *indicative* (making statements); *interrogative* (asking questions); and *imperative* (giving orders). Essentially, we are going to suggest that, if conventional narratives make statements, game narratives also ask questions and give orders. We will see this as part of the *interactive* function of the text: how a game establishes a relation between itself and the player.

As we noted in chapter 3, Genette suggests that the natural mood of the narrative is the *indicative* – narratives make *statements*. Rachel's account of Cloud, in its grammatical rendering of the avatar, makes it clear that, while in some parts of the narrative the hero is going about his business wrapped in the familiar indicative mood ('*he escapes* from this city because he's being pursued'), in other parts, the player has become the protagonist, and the game is manifestly in the *imperative* ('*you have* to go and try to stop [Sephiroth], 'cos he's trying to raise up all the beasts'). In terms of its interactive function, then, the game is not only offering a narrative statement but also telling the player to do something – in effect, telling the player to insert herself into the transitivity system of the game. Social semiotic theory would regard this as an aspect of the interactive function of the text because it is establishing a relation between text and audience, in this case a *demand* relation, where the text tells the player to do something. The difference between this and a conventional text is that the player will comply by taking an action which, in effect, poses a further command to the game, demanding that it respond in its turn. The other difference is that, in taking up this challenge, the interactive function and the representational function of the game become fused. This fusion points towards a social semiotic definition of *interactivity* – a definition that in our view is much more precise than is often the case.

Role Playing Games *do* offer narrative statements, then, as in Genette's classic model. We can ask some familiar questions about this. How is the protagonist constructed? What other texts or genres is she or he derived from? What kinds of narrative function will she or he perform? What ideas does she or he represent? On the other hand, RPGs, like all games, ask you questions and tell you to do things. If narrative requires a willing suspension of disbelief, games require a willing submission to rule-based systems. So we should go back to the question of *transitivity*, to ask how the player is involved in the actions the character performs, and back to the question of *mood*, to ask how the relations between the text and the player are invited and constructed. The next two sections will address the functions of the protagonist and the avatar respectively.

Cloud – heavy hero

Rachel's word 'character' points to Cloud's function as a protagonist, part of the representational system of the game. If the narrative is Genette's verb-writ-large, Cloud is the Actor who performs that verb. His narrative function (as a hero-mercenary who defies the ruthless Shinra Corporation and his nemesis, Sephiroth) is typical of hero roles in popular narrative, and, in many respects, of the formulaic character types of folk tales, analysed by Vladimir Propp (1970). An important aspect of Cloud as protagonist is determined by the structure of Japanese console RPGs in general, and the *Final Fantasy* series in particular: the characters are fixed givens, rather than compositional palettes offered to the player as for the avatars of *Baldur's Gate*, who (as we have seen) are constructed by the player from a kit of visual attributes, abilities and orientations. In this respect, Cloud is much more like a conventional media character, and he can be engaged with as such in fan cultures, as we will see in the following chapter.

As the folk tale analogy suggests, a character like Cloud does not spring out of nowhere to fulfil the needs of commodified mass entertainment in the twentieth century, but draws deeply on traditional forms of folk culture, oral narrative and popular romance. At least since the medieval period, these forms have provided fantasies which offer consolation, moral polemic and psychic testing grounds, through elaborate allegories, for the rites of passage and tribulations of everyday life. Eri Izawa (2000) describes how the characters of manga and *anime*, and of *Final Fantasy III*, draw on epic themes in Japanese folklore, on hero legends based on historic warlords, and on supernatural narratives informed by Shinto and Buddhism. Though the historical origins of the character of Cloud may be obscure for players – at least, most non-Japanese players – a recognition of the legendary quality of the narrative and its characters is evident in fan writing, as in this fan reconstruction of Cloud's backstory:

> Sephiroth had a power unseen and unrivalled by anyone at that time. To the people of Nibelheim, he was a living legend. All the children had dreams of becoming as powerful as the Great Sephiroth, but Cloud was the only one with the motivation to join SOLDIER. (Innocente, 2002)

Taking an even broader view, Janet Murray (2000) makes a suggestive link between computer-game characters and Homeric heroes, citing the early twentieth-century scholars who revealed the structures of the oral tradition. She points out that a game character might be formulaically constructed in similar ways to the Homeric poet's formulaic construction of Achilles – a comparison which radically shifts the ground on which conventional aesthetic objections to games are typically made.

In the protagonists of both oral narratives and games, there is a predictability about their appearance, the tools of their trade and their actions. The dynamic of the texts is to see how improvisatory flair on the part of the poet can stitch together and adapt the formulae; and, in the case of games, how the player can stitch together the given repertoires into the sequence that will gain the desired goal. This kind of improvisatory work can be seen in Rachel's account of how she explores the world of *Final Fantasy*, how she looks after Cloud when he's sick and how she fights the battles with him. In both game and oral narrative, the text is woven on the spot by the poet/player. Indeed, it might be better to use the term *text event*, to suggest the particular nexus of representation, narrative and affect that is experienced in a particular moment or version. The word *text*, as Walter Ong (2002) reminds us, derives from the Latin word to weave (*texere*); and he also invokes the idea of 'rhapsody' as a possible description of oral perform-ance, from the Greek *rhapsodein*, to stitch together.

A further useful point about the analogy with oral narrative is that it interposes another figure between the text and the reader: the performer. The poet who actually performs an oral text is not the author: the text already exists in the tradition. The poet-performer is on the one hand a real reader who actualizes the implied reader (as discussed in chapter 3). On the other hand, she or he is a mediator between text and audience, who is able in certain ways to adapt and rework the text. The implication for games is that players are both performer and audience: they have the ability to improvise upon the fixed elements of the text to some degree, whereas in other respects they also fulfil the function of audience, receiving and imaginatively interpreting the text.

Ong's (2002) analysis of the 'psychodynamics of oral narrative' points to several features which are arguably also characteristics of games; and some also apply more generally to modern popular narratives. These include, first, *heavy heroes*: oral narratives require larger-than-life, stereo-typical heroes who can be formulaically constructed, easily recognized and remembered by audiences, and made to represent one or two key characteristics. Second, oral narrative is *agonistically toned*: it revolves around conflict externalized in the form of physical or verbal combat. Third, it is *aggregative* rather than *analytic* – narrative sequences are added and stacked up, rather than organized hierarchically. This is related to a fourth point; that oral narrative is high in *redundancy*, and in what in rhetoric is termed *copia*: it repeats the same thing many times, in different ways, to give the listener the best chance of purchase on it, as well as buying time for compositional effort for the performer. And, finally, oral narrative is *empathetic* and *participatory*: the performer and audience are both immersed in the narrative, to such an extent that, in an example Ong gives from African narrative, the narrator slips from third to first person, his identification with the hero, Mwinde, completed in the grammar of the telling.

If we take up Murray's (2000) suggestion, and compare Cloud Strife to the Greek hero Achilles from Homer's *Iliad*, the resemblances are striking, and the ways in which both figures fit Ong's categories are clear. Cloud is formulaic: like Achilles, he always fights in the same way, always wears the same clothes and is partly controlled by gods (in the shape of players). Achilles is infused with strength by Apollo, nourished with nectar and honey by Athena, and given high-quality armour by the god Hephaistos. Cloud is infused with health points, and equipped with weapons, protective devices and magical properties by the player-as-god (and by the game system). He is a 'heavy hero': exaggeratedly attractive, good with his sword and equipped with a mysterious myth of origin, combining ordinary mortal and supernatural features, like Achilles. He operates agonistically: his problems are expressed in terms of physical combat or the overcoming of physical obstacles. He moves in a world replete with redundancy: the experience of playing him is to keep revisiting the same places again and again until familiarity shows us the next step; or fighting the same monsters over and over until we learn their weak points.

However, like Achilles, Cloud is not by any means a simple muscle-bound warrior. The appeal of Achilles is that he contains two powerful character traits, absolutely compatible in the culture of Ancient Greece: the powerful warrior and the beautiful lover (his lover, Patroklos, is with him at Troy). This combination of strength and beauty has plenty of modern counterparts; Cloud's androgynous good looks have often been commented on by players, and are developed in certain forms of fan art in explicitly homoerotic terms, as we shall see in chapter 7. One extremely perceptive review of *Final Fantasy VII* points out that Cloud is really role playing the action hero – that underneath he is actually an angst-ridden adolescent with a fantasy of himself as the warrior who saves the world (Moby, 2002). In a further twist, this editorial writer for the online magazine *RPG Dreamers* suggests that Cloud operates as a metaphor for the player, who is carried into the fantasy role play of the game through the mechanism of the role play that is modelled by the protagonist.

Of course, in certain important ways, games depart dramatically from traditions of oral narrative. The commodified, electronically mediated culture of games moves rapidly across and between global audiences, and is dependent on a wide range of particular skills and literate practices. Our argument is not that contemporary computer games are, in some simple way, a continuation of the oral tradition, but rather that they contain its residues, in terms both of narrative and character types, and of performative, improvisatory rhetorics. In this respect, they provide an instance of what Ong describes as the 'secondary orality' of high-technology societies – an evolution of the oral mindset in ways that are dependent on literate and technologically mediated culture.

Thus, we can also locate Cloud in a tradition of comic-strip heroes, specifically Japanese in this case, but belonging to a wider global tradition of popular media with its roots in the American comic strips of the early twentieth century. Here we find superheroes with dual identities that enable them to step outside the banality and anomie of urban life, in costumes which are the polar opposites of the suits worn by Clark Kent and Bruce Wayne, and in bodies with Renaissance musculatures offering aspirational ideals to those who in real life may sport only the skinny frame of Peter Parker. The post-war manga comic-strip superheroes, and their moving-image descendants in *anime* and live-action television and film, were directly influenced by the US tradition, borrowing the structures of aggrandized heroic powers and bodies, as well as dual identities, but adding specifically Japanese motifs such as martial arts skills and weapons, enemies composed of monsters and atomic power plants and eventually superhero teams (Allison, 2000). It is from this tradition that the *Final Fantasy* designers descend; and in fact *Final Fantasy VII* saw the arrival of a new designer from a popular mainstream manga tradition, Testuyo Nomura.

An important difference between the visual semiotic of comic strip and film and the oral narrative tradition is that the heroes become to some extent fixed in visual form. Nevertheless, they remain extremely visually versatile and adaptable. Variations on Batman and Superman over the years, for instance, retain key iconic attributes, but adapt to suit variations in aesthetic preferences, social concerns and audience demands in successive decades. The semiotic hybridity of games produces a more concentrated kind of variety. Cloud's appearance varies across a range of artistic and technical design contexts in *Final Fantasy VII* – for instance between cutscenes, game sequences and packaging. Furthermore, his design spills out into the fan cultures that adopt and develop the game, so that fan art produces further variations, which we explore in chapter 7.

As we have suggested, then, the game employs some of the immersive, agonistic, episodic, aggrandized structures of both traditional oral narratives and modern popular superhero narratives. Nevertheless, *Final Fantasy* is not only a narrative, but also a game. Although Cloud operates as a superhero protagonist within the representational system of the game, in the game system he embodies, like any RPG avatar, the symbolic and technical mechanisms through which the player performs actions within transitive sequences of the text. So how are these narrative elements fused with the rule-based system of the game?

Cloud – digital dummy?

The substance of Cloud, as a larger-than-life, highly specific protagonist within the representational system of the game, is overlaid on the character as an entity module in the game engine – a skeletal set of programmed repertoires within the game system. In this respect, as well as in all the ambiguities of his design, he is, like all RPG avatars, what Steven Poole has called 'a comparatively blank canvas' (Poole, 2002), on which the player can project imaginary structures of his or her own. He is a kind of puppet, and we pull his strings. When we press the Playstation buttons or PC keys, it is this programmed entity we engage with and control.

Cloud is thus a bundle of semiotic resources that facilitate the player's engagement with the game's system, equipping us to move through its links and nodes, landscapes and events. He is a set of economies: health points, hit points, experience points, weapons and magic with quantified capacity – the so-called *materia* system of the *Final Fantasy* series. He is a kinaesthetic grammar, with a limited set of actions for us to deploy – talk, walk, run, jump, get, fight. Our engagement with these actions is more direct in this, as in other console games: unlike the point-and-click procedure of *Baldur's Gate*, we control Cloud by pressing directional buttons on the Playstation (or on the PC keyboard, in the PC version). Cloud is a digital dummy, whom we manipulate at will – albeit within limits that are defined by the possibilities of the game engine.

Thus, Cloud is both heavy hero and digital dummy. Furthermore, the two roles, though presented here for the sake of contrast in a polarized way, are interdependent, and leak into each other, just as the representational system and the game system affect each other. The heavy hero, for instance, is the kind of protagonist ideally suited to being constructed by rules and formulae, being already predictable in his behaviour and formulaic in his nature. However, though it is tempting to regard a textual construct like Cloud as a fixed object, this would miss the point of the player–avatar relation, and perhaps of texts in general. The game is not so much an object as a series of processes. It begins, obviously, with the design and production of the text: this is itself a complex combination of different communicative modes, and it draws on images, sounds and narrative patterns from both recent and distant cultural histories, and on a constantly developing game engine common to the *Final Fantasy* series. Yet it is also the product of the meeting of text and reader, or, in this case, player. One reason for comparing the playing of a computer game with a performance of oral narrative is that it allows us to see the text as an event, rather than as a fixed object. Furthermore, the playing of games is iterative – it is many text events, all different, with a dynamic relation between the computer game as a textual resource or text *in potentia*. The player is a dynamic textual element, whose fingers and skills become no less part of the game system than the avatar's strings of machine code. And, as we shall see in more detail in chapter 7, the player is also a cultural resource, an interpreter, and an adapter of the game's resources in the production of fan art and writing.

Playing the avatar

Cloud as heavy hero and Cloud as digital dummy offer different sets of semiotic resources from which the player can experience the game. The heavy hero, in many respects derived from conventional narratives, and constructed through non-interactive modes (visual design, music, animation), is largely *read* by the player (along with the representational system in general). The digital dummy, mostly made up of interactive textual forms, is largely *played* by the player (along with the game system in general).

The sense in which the player both is, and is not, the avatar, is central to the experience of the game; and the pronoun slippage in Rachel's account of her experience of the game directly represents this ambiguous relation. This ambiguity extends to the symbolic and social meanings that might be attributed to gameplay. Cultural studies typically emphasizes *agency*, as a positive quality of 'active readership', and so we could argue that the degree of control we possess over the avatar's actions can be equated with a degree of more general cultural power. However, as Perry Anderson (1980) observes, agency has two opposed meanings: one in which we are autonomous, powerful social actors; and one in which we are merely the representative of another (as in FBI agent). Both meanings can be read into the player–avatar relation. On the one hand, we might choose to celebrate the unprecedented degree of participative agency allowed for the reader within the text, as for instance in Brenda Laurel's positive image of the audience moving on to the stage to become actors in the digital play (Laurel, 1991). Yet, on the other hand, there is a sense in which players merely accept and play out the roles determined for them by game texts devised by global corporations, dominated by patriarchal narratives and what Brian Sutton-Smith (1997) calls the male-dominated power rhetorics of combative play. The question of player agency in *Final Fantasy VII* is therefore quite ambiguous and debatable. (We return to the question of agency in more detail in chapter 10.)

As mentioned above, Walter Ong (2002) demonstrates the participatory nature of oral narrative by the pronoun slippage of the Mwinde narrator, suggesting a slide from objective oversight of the narrative to empathetic, performative identification with the protagonist. Similarly, Rachel's account of Cloud, as we have seen, is characterized by pronoun-switching. Cloud is 'he' when the representational system is most emphasized, and 'you' when the game system is most emphasized. The former is characterized by structures of offer (the indicative mood); the latter by structures of demand (the imperative mood).

The player's dual engagements with offer and demand structures inform each other, producing a sense of dynamic play and of identi-fication with a fictional character. As different moments in the game move more in the direction of offer or demand, however, it seems likely that the kind of engagement will change. The battle scenes, perhaps, are the most demand-dominated scenes, where the game system would seem to be all that matters, the economies of health, hits and magic become critical, and the temporal elasticity of the game shrinks to real time conflict.

Rachel's account of the battles gives some clues about how player agency is constituted here:

> R: Well you kind of get a choice of what to do in battles, and you have to learn how to defeat some monsters some ways and you have to learn how to defeat them this way and you have to learn what order to put the stuff in, and it just – it's really quite good when you've built up your character because for every battle you get – experience points – and so, um, after a while you've built up your character, and so you know how to use everything more efficiently – and it's – the camera angles are cool too –
>
> AB: In the battle scenes?
>
> R: Yeah.
>
> AB: How are the camera angles different?
>
> R: 'Cos they zoom – it zooms right into your character, and they have different angles – one sometimes looking up at the beast, or across, or down – it's – really spectacular.
>
> AB: How does it feel then, to be in that?
>
> R: Exciting! 'Cos it kind of, right – what the game does is, it has a little sequence where it actually spirals into the battle scenes, and the music changes and the tempo changes and it really kind of, actu-ally kind of gets you a bit more excited.

In the relations between player and game, the agency is clear here, reflecting Rachel's engagement with the demand of the game. In the first part of her account, the Actor – literally, the subject of the clauses she speaks – is the player ('you'), and the actions you are performing are represented as imperatives, as in the triple repetition of 'have to learn'. These transparently reflect her engagement with the game system. Yet, in the second part of her account, the subject becomes the text ('it'), and its actions are textual ones: it 'zooms', 'has different angles', 'has a little sequence', 'spirals'. The player becomes the Goal of these actions: 'it gets you a bit more excited'. This would seem to be more to do with offer – the actions of the text here are conventional cinematic ones, designed to position the spectator and to work for particular kinds of affective response.

Multimodal offers and demands

Although Rachel's account precisely represents the two-way interactive function of the game text – you do something to it, it does something to you – the demand/offer structures cannot be so simply separated. How do they work together; and how are they realized multimodally?

The demand exercised by the text is realized in different ways by the different modes combined within it. For instance, the music described by Rachel is specific to the battle scenes; and she describes it accurately – the tempo does change (it speeds up); and the rhythm changes to a regular 4/4 time, with the mix of midi voices including a martial snare drum (the music of the *Final Fantasy* series, all by Nobuo Umare, is a celebrated example of the composer's art in game design). The orientation of the music to the player, then, operates as a kind of musical imperative – a call-to-arms, as it were. At the same time, the swirling graphics which introduce the battle scene produce a giddy, disorientating sense, a feeling of risk, of danger, in combination with the music. As the battle scene appears on the screen (Illustration 7), the player sees the characters lined up against the enemy, with the battle statistics represented graphically at the bottom of the screen. The readiness of each character to attack is shown by a thermometer-style bar, which fills up. This specific graphic operates, again, as a form of visual demand, effectively instructing the player to wait, but get ready. When the bar fills up, a yellow triangle appears above the head of the character, indicating that it can attack – a visual imperative equivalent to 'Attack now!'.

In the representational system of the text, the method of attack is very like the composition of a clause, in strict sequential form. When the yellow arrow appears, clicking OK selects the character – the Actor. The next choice is the means of attack, a specifying of the process, which determines what the character will actually do – whether he will slash with a sword, fire a lightning bolt, or throw a grenade, for instance. Finally, a white hand appears, which can be moved by the player to select the enemy at whom the attack is aimed – the Goal. This particular sequence, then, is a transitive structure made up from a restricted set of elements, forming a classic 'restricted language' of a kind typical of many games (see Halliday, 1989).[3]

In terms of the player–avatar relation, the player here has a dual function. In one sense, the player fuses with the avatar: both of them are the Actor, both do the attacking. Yet, in another sense, the player is like a puppeteer, pulling the character's strings, or even a kind of

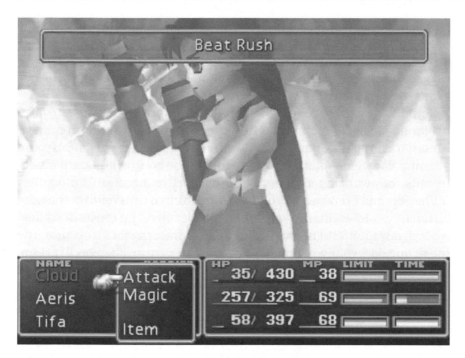

Illustration 7   The battle screen of *Final Fantasy VII*. Reproduced by kind permission of Square Enix UK.

author, composing a sequence within a restricted language as part of a rule-based structure of causality. As we argued earlier in this chapter, the availability of these textual elements to the player means that, while they are part of the representational system, they are also part of the game system: the two functions combine, and the player writes a sentence of the narrative, so to speak. It should be observed, however, that this piece of narrative is bounded: the battle scenes are structurally separated from the larger narrative of the game, and make no impact upon it.

The cinematic element also contributes to the interactive work of the text, positioning the player in particular ways in relation to the action and the characters (Burn and Parker, 2001). Whereas in the rest of the game we are usually positioned above the characters in a fixed position, here we are positioned much lower down, alongside the characters, as if fighting with them. At times, the swooping camera angles place us even lower than the characters. This feels as if you're fighting with them, helping them stock up health points, or recharge their weapons. Though this is an offer – it is distinct from the function of those parts of the text that demand specific actions – it fuses with our response to those demands, changing our sense of how we act. In effect, it mutes the sensation of being a puppeteer that the demand-response structures create. If we were given these powers and simultaneously placed high above the characters, the feeling of pulling strings from a distance would intensify. The low angles and close-ups bring the player closer to the avatar at exactly the moment when the demand structures are at their most urgent.

Beyond the battle scenes, where we follow Cloud through the dark urban spaces of the city of Midgard and its pastel-coloured rural hinterland, the feeling of offer rather than demand is reinforced multimodally. The music of these sequences is much less stark rhythmically, either using unmeasured rhythms or regular duple times muted beneath flowing melodies, which either chime with cheerful characters and locations, or evoke the kind of mysterious sorrow which Izawa notices in *Final Fantasy III* (Izawa, 2000). In any case, the music suggests that you're being offered an event and a mood; if there is any trace of demand, it is more of an enticement than an urgent command. This musical enticement, though part of the representational system of the game, operates in tandem with the game system, which invites you to make a move.

Similarly, you explore and progress through the game world in a fixed camera environment. Here, you are positioned isometrically above the action, with the avatar and other characters rendered as chunky, polygonal figures. This design distances them from the player; or, perhaps, during these parts of the game, makes them more puppet- or doll-like, developing a tamagotchi-like relationship in which the player trains and nurtures the avatar like a pet. The fixed-camera, high-angle position, by contrast, is a spatial and visual reinforcement of the offer mode. It detaches the player a little, and offers stability.

However, the sense that the exploration of the game world is characterized by a weaker form of demand – enticement rather than command – depends on player perception as much as on semiotic design. In terms of the distinction introduced in chapter 3, *Final Fantasy VII* seems to offer the potential for both maze-like and rhizomic navigation. Ben, one of our interviewees, points out that 'One of the problems with *Final Fantasy* is . . . it is really linear, but they make it seem like it's not.' In fact, he says, there is 'only one place you can go to' – so the appearance of a world where all experiences are causally related to the narrative is an illusion. This echoes a similar perception in a review of *FFVII*: 'As is typical of the Japanese RPG form, the game is extremely linear. You may not see the train tracks, but the feeling that you've been railroaded is unmistakable' (van Cleef, 1997). Rachel's experience of the game, by contrast, emphasizes the rhizomic qualities: 'it's fantastic 'cos you can just explore everywhere, and you just never get bored 'cos there's just so much stuff to look around and find out, basically'.

The modality of the game in this respect – and hence the degree of agency that it affords to the player – seems to be quite ambiguous. The requirement to explore the game could be seen as a form of demand – in effect, 'explore!' However, as noted above, it is a weakened demand, more of an enticement or plea, and may well be experienced by the player as accentuating, rather than diminishing, their sense of agency. Thus, Ben appears to read the game as an urgent demand, as puzzles demanding to be solved, while Rachel interprets it as a weak demand – a rhizomic world to be explored, the strong demand being kept for key moments of progression or battle.

The most direct responses to the demand structures of the game, then – to the battle scenes, or the nodes of the puzzle maze – are those when the player is most likely to report their experience in the second person. And these are the aspects of the game driven by the game system, where the avatar is most empty, most like a vehicle for the dynamic action of gameplay, most simple in their characterization, reduced to a sword or to the sliding economies of health and experience points.

However, this kind of involvement, most similar to the agonistic patterns Ong (2002) reports of the oral tradition, is set against the offer structures of the game's representational system, marked by the third person in the player's account. It is through the representational system that the character is filled out – when the declarative mood of the cutscene or interpolated dialogue fills out part of Cloud's history, his murky past, the uncertainty about his mercenary motives, his obscure love affairs and his ambivalent relationship with Sephiroth.

The experience of play would therefore seem to entail an oscillation between two contrasting ways of relating to the protagonist-avatar. At one moment, we are playing Cloud, while at another we are watching his story unfold. Yet, as Ben and Rachel's comments suggest, these different positions may be differently valued – or even differently 'occupied' – by different players. This is apparent, not only in how players engage with the game, or interpret its images and narratives, but also in how they imaginatively appropriate and remake them. In order to explore these issues further, it is now time to turn our attention more directly to the players themselves.

Reworking the Text: Online Fandom

Andrew Burn

Lᴵᴋᴇ many RPGs, *Final Fantasy VII* has an enormous global base of devoted players and fans. In the last chapter, we considered the experience of the player as he or she engages with the avatar during play, and how to analyse this process. But engagement with the game does not finish when the game session ends and the computer or console is switched off. Players continue to think about, imagine, even dream about, the events, landscapes and characters of the game; and particularly committed fans go further, joining online communities of fans, and contributing to message boards, art galleries, writing groups and other forms of expansive embroidery of the game and its components.

The variety of work by fans of *Final Fantasy VII* alone is hard to overestimate. Written forms come in all shapes and sizes; there are discussion groups that focus knowledgeably on specific aspects of the game such as Nobuo Umare's music, or Testuyo Nomura's artwork; fans adopt names derived from those of the characters in the game, and design visual representations of these; and they make small animated movies built around images and stories in the game.

In many ways, this is a kind of expressive and social activity typical of fans of any popular medium, and it can be researched and analysed in this way. Perhaps the most well-known recent model of this kind of analysis is Henry Jenkins's account of *textual poachers*. In his book of that name (1992) he demonstrates how fans of canonical media texts such as *Star Trek* seek to extend the pleasure they derive from them by appropriating and reworking them in various ways, through writing, song, artwork and so on. This kind of fan activity (or 'fan work') in some ways reveres the original text, seeking to remain as true to it as possible, replicating fine details of the appearance or behaviour of a character. In other ways, however, fan work can dramatically alter the original text, adapting it to express the particular interest of the fan or fan group. Perhaps the most dramatic form of adaptation is *slash fiction* (named after the slash between the sexes represented in the story, such as male/male). This form is traditionally produced by women, and focuses on homosexual relationships not explicitly present in the original text, but imagined and inserted by the fan. The classic example of this is slash fiction which elaborates a gay relationship between Spock and Kirk in the first *Star Trek* series – a relationship which, Jenkins suggests, is arguably implicit in the strong male friendships and largely male environment of the *Enterprise*, though the value systems of this kind of media text prevent any explicit development of such a theme.

The multimodal textual theory used in the last chapter raises a number of questions about this kind of fan work in relation to games, and specifically to *Final Fantasy*. First, how does the nature of the game make a difference? Fan work surrounding a TV series like *Star Trek* is largely constructed as written text and image. Although the original text is a TV series, texts and drawings are the only semiotic modes available to most fans. We might therefore consider how the transformation from moving image to written text or drawings works – what it allows the fan to say, what it prevents them from saying, and so on. Games are multimodal texts in the sense that they use visual design, animation, music, speech, writing and so on. Again, this combination of modes is unavailable to fans, so we should expect to find that they will carry out their work of remaking and appropriation as a series of transformations into the modes available to them – again, largely writing and drawing. Where this is the case, we can, again, ask how this semiotic transformation happens and how it represents the social interests of the fans.

However, games are not only made up of representational systems but of game systems based on rules, quantified challenges and economies. There is a kind of dialectic, as we have seen in the last chapter, between the *demand* structures of the game system – agitating the causal chain, pressing you over the puzzle hurdles of wrecked trains or labyrinthine laboratories, catching you in the affective tensions and anxieties of obscure routes and monstrous enemies – and the *offer* structures which lay out the context, landscape, backstory, motivation and psychology, engaging the reader-spectator in the empathetic networks and imaginative extensions of the text which also operate in conventional narratives. Although it is the combination of these which provides the kinds of pleasures Rachel describes, in the fan work that surrounds the game the combination might operate in quite different ways.

So a question this chapter will ask is: what will fans make of the game system? Will they simply ignore it, and concentrate on narrative and character? Or will they find some way to express their love of the game by reworking its game system? Or will they find ways to combine the two, as they do in the playing of the game? At the same time, we will look at what motivates fans in this kind of work – what their social interest is and what they get out of it all.

We will look at three kinds of text: a 'walkthrough' for *Final Fantasy VII* written by a fan; two pieces of creative writing about Cloud; and an amateur Japanese manga comic strip representing Cloud and Sephiroth.

The walkthrough author

The walkthrough was written by Kao Megura (2000), whose fan status has become exalted by his detailed expertise in the game to the point where he is widely regarded as something of an independent online authority. Because walkthroughs are generically not interested in the representational aspects of the game, this text omits all reference to the backstory of Cloud's former adulation of Sephiroth, his love life, his heroic appearance, the music which creates the motifs for Cloud and the other characters, and so on. The interest of the walkthrough is purely in relaying the procedural demands of the game system. Accordingly, it is structured almost entirely as a demand act itself, written in the second person, dominated by the imperative mood:

> Once you leave the train, check the body of the closest guard twice to get two Potions. Then head north. You'll be attacked by some guards. Take them out with your sword (you may win a Potion for killing them) and then move left to go outside. Now, talk to your teammates (Biggs, Wedge, and Jessie), then name yourself and Barret. Make your way to the northwestern door, and head up in the next room to enter the heart of the power plant. (Megura, 2000)

There is no oscillation here between second and third person, as in Rachel's account in chapter 6. The consistent use of the second person marks the concentrated focus on the game system, in which player and avatar are most closely linked. The 'you' in Megura's walkthrough is both player and Cloud.

For this fan, the thrill of the game seems very much bound up in his exhaustive expertise in the properties of the puzzle maze, and in the game as system. Anything incidental to this is omitted or reduced to minimal expression. The social motivation for this particular develop-ment of player preference is clearly bound up in the very public status that such a position wins in return for his hard work. His attitude to this status is quite ambivalent, however. On the one hand, there is obvious pleasure in the recognition such status brings: 'I recall that some other people were translating this FAQ into Spanish, Portugese, and other languages. If they could mail me the URLs of their translated FAQs, I'll add them here.' On the other hand, there is exasperation with online relations with people who don't measure up to his notion of minimal competence: 'I _WILL NOT_ answer any gameplay related questions about this game. It's not because I'm a prick (haha, I know), but because you wouldn't believe the types of questions I get.'

Although the walkthrough itself appears as a technical, dispassionate text, in fact the motivations that lie behind it are full of passion. Megura's online messages delineate a history of his walkthrough, which begins as a quasi-professional service, and ends in boredom and disillusionment. This appears to be partly because of magazines that have reprinted his material without acknowledgement or permission:

> I cannot express my disgust towards these people for using my FAQ simply to increase their sales. I did this because I wanted to help others, and I didn't plan this FAQ back in February just so it could be used shamelessly by people who should be responsible adults.

His disillusionment seems to proceed partly from aspirations to professional status, in which intellectual property rights become more of an issue (fan authors in general are very aware of IP and copyright issues, though this is more usually because they themselves are in danger of infringing copyright in their adaptation of original texts). Yet, it also seems to proceed from an idealistic desire to serve the fan community.

Eventually, however, Megura terminates his FAQ service. It seems that an unexpected side-effect of becoming an expert is that the naive questions of less competent players become tiresome; and, eventually, he becomes exhausted with the game itself, apparently suffering a kind of fan burnout:

> I'm not trying to be rude, but it gets a little tiring at times. I realize that there are some mistakes still in the FAQ that I never got around to correcting (the Emerald Weapon does damage equal to the materia that you wear, there is no use for the miniature soldiers, you cannot have chocobos that can fly, and any character who isn't in Disc 2 or 3 cannot be used without a GameShark code, and Bahamut Zero can be gotten from Cosmo Canyon, this is in the FAQ but no one notices . . . but I've done this thing for more than a year now and I'm tired of FF7, geez!

A contradiction in the text is that the double declaration of weariness brackets a spilling over of the kind of obsessive detail about the game which made him the walkthrough master: the ebullience of this succession of five clauses listing what can and can't be done at various points of the game system gives the lie to the profession of exhaustion.

This kind of social role is comparable to the role of 'expert' in the group of boy players whom we will meet in chapter 8. In their collaborative playing of *Soul Reaver: The Legacy of Kain*, a particular expert emerged within the group, whose social function was to tutor the others; but his fixation on getting through the game system was at the expense of other aspects of the game, or a holistic view of it, including (most importantly) its narrative. As we shall indicate, the boys' talk was characterized by Halliday's *regulatory mode* (1970), in which they sought to control each other's gameplay through imperatives – a mode which is also characteristic of the walkthrough. In other words, at the point of play, the overriding concern is to respond to the demand function of the game, which becomes realized in the grammatical structures of the boys' talk. We can see the social motivation of walkthrough authors like Megura as a kind of advanced version of the 'expert' in the *Soul Reaver* players: he wins social standing among the player community by specializing in the stripped-down, efficient sequence of commands that gets the player through the game system. He goes on to build a kind of career for himself as expert, however – a career which is characterized by the excessive, excited language of the obsessive amateur on the one hand, and by the cool, detached tones of the professional on the other.

The fiction writer

By contrast, most authors of fan fiction largely ignore the game system and concentrate on the narrative. A particular form of fan fiction is the spoiler, which effectively tells the story for those who have not yet experienced the text itself. Here is an extract from a fan spoiler from the *Final Fantasy Shrine* website, in which Cloud's story is rendered as a kind of literary narrative:

> *The Secrets of Cloud's Past*
> One of the greatest mysteries in Final Fantasy is the secret of Cloud's past. Is he a clone of Sephiroth? Is he even human? It's very hard to tell. Here, for your benefit, I will lay out the evidence and dispel all the mystery about who Cloud really is. Be advised that this is a definite spoiler, and if you want to save the mystery for yourself, leave now.
> Originaly, Cloud did leave Neiblhiem to join SOLDIER. However, he was found to be unfit, and so he became nothing more than a common grunt. During this period, he became friends with a SOLDIER member named Zack. As luck would have it, these two were assigned to accompany Sephiroth to the Neiblhiem reactor. Cloud, too ashamed of his failure to admit it to his friends and neighbors, kept his mask on when they arrive. He does, however, stop and talk with his mother a little bit. When they reach the reactor, it is Cloud who stays outside and guards Tifa. Inside, Sephiroth finds Jenova, and his mind slowly starts unraveling. He isolates himself in the mansion library, eventually burning the town to the ground in a rage. Zack and Cloud follow him to the reactor. Just as they arrive, Sephiroth slashes Tifa. Zack chases after him, while Cloud carries Tifa off to the side, fulfilling his childhood promise. Zack

and Sephiroth battle, and Sephiroth sends him flying out of the room, mortally wounded. He leaves, carrying his sword in one hand, Jenova's severed head in the other. Zack pleads with Cloud to kill Sephiroth, so Cloud takes Zack's sword, then gives chase. When Cloud reaches Sephiroth, he stabs Cloud in the chest and hefts him into the air. Thinking Cloud dead, Sephiroth lowers him back down. Suddenly, Cloud grabs the blade of the sword, lifts Sephiroth, and flings him into the liquid Mako. (This means that the Sephiroth you've been chasing around is nothing but a clone created by Hojo.) Cloud then collapses. Some scientists find them, and place them in glass tubes so they can heal them, as well as inject them with Jenova cells. Cloud has a reaction to them, while Zack does not. During this period, Cloud and Zack were linked, which is why Cloud has some of Zack's memories, and yet sees himself in Zack's role. It also explains why he has Mako eyes. They showered him with it to speed his recovery. Eventually the two escape during feeding time. They leave Neiblehiem, and begin hitchhiking to Midgar. There, they intend to become swords-for-hire, and earn a living. However, as they approach the city, they are found by a group of Shinra soldiers, who were searching for them. Zack is promptly shot to death, while Cloud, badly injured, is left to die. However, he manages to get to Midgar, where he slowly recovers. Finally, 5 years later, he finds Tifa at the train station. She at first mistakes him for Zack, because they look and act so similar. (The result of their link during their recovery.) Finally, she convinces Cloud to take the job with AVALANCHE, and you undoubtably know the story from this point on, having played it already. There are those who believe that a sephiroth clone living in a pipe in the slums is really Zack. I don't share that view, simply because I havn't seen any conclusive evidence to prove it.

There. That's the whole truth behind Cloud's past. Be this point you should know that he is a normal human being, that he never was in SOLDIER, and that he did kill Sephiroth.

(<http://www.angelfire.com/mn/midgarff7/cloudpast.html>)

Because this is no longer a game, the demand function is eliminated, unlike in the walkthrough, whose function was to deliver the wisdom of the expert in order to steer novices through the game. This account has nothing to do with game system, everything to do with narrative system: it is about filling in the gaps, developing the replete, heavy hero of popular narrative, and is a communicative act of the offer variety, entirely dominated by the declarative mood. We can also see this text as a work of reconstruction, based around moments in the game of particular importance to this player. Though he claims it is the 'whole truth' behind Cloud's past, it is in fact highly selective. It chooses moments from the complex series of cutscene flashbacks in the game in order to present a narrative with Cloud firmly at the centre – it largely omits, for instance, his relationship with Aeris.

In their social semiotic study of children's viewing of television, Hodge and Tripp (1986) note a similar phenomenon – that in their retelling of a TV cartoon, some of the children ignore the whole structure of the narrative, and make their own version by stringing together particularly powerful moments in a sequence that suits their own interests and preoccupations. Hodge and Tripp define this kind of reading as *paratactic*, a term borrowed from linguistic theory. Parataxis is a grammatical structure in which clauses are strung together in chain-like sequences, typically using connectives like 'and' and 'then'. It is opposed to *hypotaxis*, which consists of structures of subordination, such as complexes of clauses in which one clause may be the main clause of the sentence, and others are ranked in importance below it. Hodge and Tripp argue that most television and film narratives are effectively hypotactic, consisting of complex hierarchical narrative structures, but that readers may elect to read them paratactically. This kind of reading would be subversive and unpredictable, producing meanings which might be quite at odds with the apparent meaning, structure and ideology of the text.

In the case of this spoiler, we could argue that it is paratactic, in Hodge and Tripp's sense. It takes a selection of cutscene narratives in the game, and strings them together to make a story that is centrally concerned to affirm Cloud's heroic status, and to make the point that Cloud is a human protagonist, a matter of some debate within *FFVII* fan communities. However, this motivation of the player is hardly the kind of oppositional reading that Hodge and Tripp propose as a possibility of paratactic strategies – indeed, in terms of the representation of gender, it produces a conventional rendering of Cloud as warrior-hero, a feature frequently complained about by girl-fans regarding the entire *Final Fantasy* series. We might modify Hodge and Tripp's rather idealistic view of paratactic readings, then, to suggest that such readings produce interpretations of the text to fit the reader's singular preoccupations, but that these may or may not be closely aligned with the representational strategies of the text.

If we think about the game as a multimodal construct, and the game system as one of the constituent modes, this piece of writing undoes the link between game and narrative modes. However, this is not simply a function of the fan work itself – something similar happens in the game too, on which the spoiler builds. As we have seen in earlier chapters, part of the method by which games develop narratives is to insert cutscenes, short animations or FMVs (Full Motion Videos), which develop a section of the narrative. In *Final Fantasy VII*, the cutscenes are most conspicuously used to develop the backstory, a labyrinthine tale of Cloud's birth, his recruitment by an elite fighting force, his friendship with Sephiroth (later his enemy) and his love affairs. In Genette's terms, then, these cutscenes are a form of *analepsis* – an element of narrative which disrupts the chronological sequence of the story to insert previous events as flashbacks (Genette, 1980).

Two points are important to note for our purposes in this chapter. First, the cutscenes are entirely characterized by the offer mode we looked at in chapter 6 – they are simply narrative statements. They involve no interactivity, and are simply there for the player's satisfaction and pleasure. In effect, at these points, the narrative and game pull apart, to such an extent that Stephen Poole argues that cutscenes are evidence that games are not a narrative form at all, and any narrative in them is effectively decorative, structurally separate from the game (Poole, 2000). We take a different view, as we have explained in earlier chapters; but, nevertheless, in *Final Fantasy VII* it is fair to say that the backstory cutscenes do show a certain separation between the yolk of game and the white of narrative. In this respect, the fan's spoiler writing is simply taking the separation a stage further, and leaving the game system behind. It is a move for which the text provides the raw materials very clearly. Choices are available to the player – so that, where some players simply skip the cutscenes, seeing them as a distraction to the gameplay, others regard them as important and valuable (and the spoiler is a creative expression of this kind of valuation).

Second, the cutscenes, as we have observed, are effectively animated films. The spoiler writer, then, has the same set of resources and restrictions as Jenkins's *Star Trek* fans: she or he cannot develop the text in the same mode, the moving image, and is obliged to employ the mode most available, that of writing. The differences made by this are important, but we will emphasize only one. A picture paints a thousand words, as is well known; so the moving image is able to convey a brief summation of an event while retaining a wealth of descriptive detail. The cutscenes on which this spoiler builds, for instance, show us Sephiroth's flowing grey hair in close-up, the elaborate staircases of the mansion and Tifa's falling body after Sephiroth's attack. However, the scenes still construct what Genette calls *summary duration* – they rapidly summarize a series of events. In writing, this is just not possible, so this spoiler, in constructing summary duration in language, has to dispense with most of the descriptive detail. The text suggests that this is felt as a loss, and the writer struggles to provide some hints of detail about movement, especially in the verbs: *slashes, flying, flings, hefts*.

The poet

A different kind of creative writing typical of fan cultures is that of poetry. This genre is used extensively by fans of other canonical media texts such as *Harry Potter*, *Buffy the Vampire Slayer* and *The X-Files*. The poem analysed here focuses on Cloud:

The Mirror: Cloud Strife
I'm coming for you.

You stand behind the guise of a SOLDIER, a hero, and smirk down at the whole Planet.

Your unreasoned hatred
   Has tortured your soul.
Descent into evil
   Must levy its toll.

Planning your moves as if it were a chess game and not a matter of life and death . . .

   But I'm coming for you. We're coming for you.

Your crimes will not go unpunished.

You'll pay the price for
   What you choose to be.
Undaunted, unwanted
   And nothing is free.

A thief of memories, of lives, of will . . . And yet you go unrepentant, actually reveling in the chaos you cause.

   Enjoy it while you can, my former friend.

. . . for we seek to topple who has the farthest to fall: you.

Not even your precious Jenova can withstand the power of teamwork.

The shadows that haunt you
   Will spell your defeat.
The victors that taunt you
   Will take revenge sweet.

The death of our comrade will not dissuade us from our cause.

And in the end, you will fall before my blade –

– and suffer as she did before.

Beware.

Yes, a rather freakish one. I was near the end of the game when I wrote this, so I focused a bit more on Cloud's feelings towards the cute (for us girls, anyway)-but-demonic silver-haired guy we all know and love/hate as Sephiroth. =^.^= we all know and love/hate as Sephiroth. =^.^=
<http://www.geocities.com/chocofeathers/themirror/cloud.html>

The use of a lyrical (rather than narrative) poetic form here produces a very different engagement with and transformation of the game text. To begin with, lyrical poems in the Western Romantic tradition are conventionally subjective, first-person texts which concentrate on powerful emotions. This produces, most obviously, a kind of linguistic role play in which this female fan speaks as Cloud. While this is a common strategy in media fan work (there are similar poems from the point of view of Harry Potter, Buffy or Angel on fansites, for instance), the difference here is that the first-person engagement replicates, or parallels, the role play engagement with the avatar required by the game system, and expressed, as we have seen, by a move from third-person to first- or second-person accounts of play in players' discourse.

Second, however, the poem elaborates an emotional aspect of the protagonist in direct ways that the game text cannot do – it cannot, for instance, show emotion by facial expression, which would be the filmic equivalent of the feelings this fan attributes to the avatar, and in particular to the love–hate relationship between Cloud and Sephiroth. In this respect, the poem supplements the game narrative in the same way as the spoiler, which similarly refers to Cloud's shame in the direct and explicit way that language affords.

Finally, both game system (here only as the experience of role play) and narrative are generically subsumed within this emotional structure, which builds a sequence of Sephiroth's feelings rather than actions – smugness, hatred, conceit – and Cloud's counter-emotions – revenge and sorrow for the teammate who dies near the end of the game, Aeris. However, along with the role play of Cloud, this fan, like many others, finds obvious pleasure in imagining Sephiroth as a very desirable kind of enemy; and the love–hate relationship between Cloud and Sephiroth becomes a springboard for a fan admiration of both characters, enhanced by the murky moral tangles in which they are caught up.

Like all fan work, then, this can be seen as a semiotic transformation. It takes one aspect of the semiotic link between player and avatar we have explored in chapter 6 – the adoption of protagonist point-of-view by the player, constructed in the game as the character facing away from the player so that we are looking in the same direction – and transforms it into language by way of the first person. However, the offer-demand structure is quite differently dealt with. Whereas in the game, and in Rachel's talk in chapter 6, the demand mode of the game is directed outwards from the game text towards the player, demanding action in the game system, here the demand is redirected back inwards to the text, at Sephiroth, who becomes the 'you' on the receiving end of Cloud/the fan's imperatives, both grammatical and implied: *you'll pay the price; enjoy it while you can; you'll fall before my sword; beware.*

In the final section, we will see how an appropriation of elements of the text through a visual medium offers different possibilities, engages with different cultural traditions and semiotic practices, but in some ways realizes similar social motivations.

The YAOI manga artist

The visual image of Cloud is a popular subject for appropriation in the tradition of amateur (*doujinshi*) manga comics (though 'amateur' here means highly skilled independent artist). This is a tradition begun by women, both to find room for expression within male-dominated production practices, and to explore erotic images and narratives in the idealized form of manga. Though this manga subgenre develops in some ways from an earlier tradition of comics depicting love between beautiful boys (*bishoonen*), one particular subgenre, the YAOI tradition, focuses more explicitly on erotic imagery, deliberately subordinating narrative to the sexual act – YAOI is an acronym from the Japanese words for 'no climax, no point, no meaning'. McLelland (2000) also points out an obvious parallel between this provocative renunciation of narrative in American female slash fiction of the PWP (Plot, What Plot?) subgenre.

The example analysed here (Illustration 8) depicts eroticized relations between Cloud and Sephiroth in which the hero and villain of the game are represented as, respectively, submissive (*uke*) and dominant (*seme*) sexual partners.

Three important questions might be posed here. First, what does the visual medium offer that is different from the medium of writing in the spoiler and the poem; and what kinds of social interest are accommodated as a result? Second, because this kind of fantext employs the same manga aesthetic as the game, what kind of semiotic transformation is going on; and what differences does this make?

First, then, the visual mode. The adoption of the protagonist's point of view inherent in the game and easily available in language through the first-person pronoun is not available in the visual image. This then becomes an objectified view of both Cloud and Sephiroth – no vestige of the game system is possible or present. In this respect, this text is furthest from the game text than any of the four we have considered. However, the visual mode allows for elaborate specificity about the appearance of the characters: indeed, the same semiotic specificity as that of the game, which is also realized visually. However, the game realizes Cloud as several different kinds of visual design – as a finely crafted digital image in the cutscenes; and as a short, blocky polygonal doll-like creature in the gameplay sequences (a discontinuity that caused some dismay in American reviews on the game's release). The latter realization, the doll of the gameplay, is not referred to in any of the many examples of manga images of Cloud we have found. In every case, it is the more finely crafted image of the cutscene animations that is drawn upon. In this respect, too, we can say that the semiotic raw material adapted for these manga texts is appropriated from the least game-related components of the game.

Illustration 8 An example of YAOI manga depicting an erotic relationship between Cloud and Sephiroth (artist unknown).

The second question is to do with the use of manga to engage with a text which itself is designed as a kind of manga or *anime*. Clearly, there is a sense here of semiotic material – visual signs, forms, meanings, even textures – being borrowed, reworked and adapted from text to text. Furthermore, it is not simply a question of the fan manga borrowing from the original game. The game designs of Testuyo Nomura themselves grow from a tradition of images of beautiful boys whose ambiguous sexuality, combined with ferocious warrior strength, has specific roots in the *bishoonen* of earlier manga, who are arguably 'not really "men" but fantastic, androgynous creatures created by Japanese women as an expression of dissatisfaction with current gender stereotypes and the "narrow life paths" which restrict women in the real world' (McLelland, 2000).

This borrowing and adaptation of semiotic material from text to text can be theorized in different ways. It can be seen as an example of intertextuality, in which the fixed boundaries of traditionally conceived texts are seen to dissolve as signs slide between texts. It can also be seen from the point of view of Barthes's notion of connotation (Barthes, 1973), in which signs in a text carry an associative freight by virtue of their use in other contexts. In Barthes's theory, the signs developed in one context become signifier material when imported into a new context, so that they are used to make a new meaning, but bring with them a network of other meanings from a wider cultural and ideological context.

The multimodal theory we have used in this and the last chapter proposes a similar idea, but with some specific differences, in its theory of *provenance* (Kress and van Leeuwen, 2001). This theory agrees with Barthes that to make any kind of meaning, semiotic resources, or signifier material, is needed. This may come with relatively little semiotic baggage, as when a sculptor chooses a lump of rock as the basic medium for a statue (though the difference between, say, soapstone and Carrara marble is, of course, culturally significant). However, the difference between this theory and Barthes's connotation is twofold. First, Kress and van Leeuwen distinguish between mode and medium – that is, between the communicative mode at work (in the case of manga, this would be visual design), and the physical medium (paper, pencil, computer pixel). Second, they emphasize the agency of the sign-maker and their social motivation. So, in the case of manga, we could say that the visual signs of manga design which produce images of idealized and exaggerated beauty are aspects of the mode, whereas a set of craft skills built around uses of pencil, pen and ink are part of the medium, with their own signifying properties. In fact, this use of the material medium is highly prized by manga fans, who devote numerous websites to tutorial programmes in how to draw manga.

The idea of provenance, then, allows for the ways in which semiotic resources, both of mode and medium, can be successively deployed, shaped and transformed as a future resource by sign-makers. This image is arguably closer to the work of manga artists than traditional semiotics, which proposes an impersonal, fixed, abstract system, even in the case of Barthes, who is more attentive than most to the nuances of social usage.

In the case of this single image, then, we can trace a kind of history. The conventions of sculptured hair and enormous eyes are specific motifs of manga, and particularly of the *shoojo* manga aimed at young female audiences. They are among the formulaic attributes which signify the abiding figures of the beautiful boys who provide an alternative, idealized image of masculinity for the female artists and readers of closed-circulation amateur manga. We can also argue that the figure of the beautiful youth with ambiguous sexuality has a longer tradition, quite differently constituted in the history of Japanese culture than in any roughly corresponding Western history.

The development of Cloud and Sephiroth by Nomura, out of this history, then, would seem to produce a pair of characters whose visual connotations are rich and intriguing for a number of possible audiences. For boys and young men who play the game, their good looks, metal-ornamented clothes and sizeable weapons are an obvious focus of interest. Furthermore, Cloud in particular is invested with visual details suggestive of appealing modern urban style – fatigues, boots, punky spikes in his hair. At the same time, his androgynous appearance is calculated to appeal to the fans of *shoojo* manga in Japan, as well as to secondary-cult manga fan bases in America and Europe. Yet, as these images are appropriated in turn as raw material by YAOI artists, further transformations appear. In the image in Illustration 8, Cloud's raised T-shirt, his erect penis enclosed by Sephiroth's gloved hand, and his expression of sexual ecstasy are all visually explicit additions to a visual image which is impossible in the actual game, although the game contains all the elements for such a development to be plausible, both in narrative and cultural terms.

This history is also one of cultural globalization. The traditional craft of pen and ink replaces the computer graphics of the game, reaching beyond them to the concept drawings of Nomura and the manga traditions behind it. But *doujinshi* manga of this kind is enthusiastically imported into the USA, scanned on to countless websites, and offered as material for imitation and further adaptation by amateur manga and *Final Fantasy* fans in America. In spite of the cultural differences between the Japanese YAOI tradition and the American and European slash tradition, the two cultures meet up in the ceaseless global interchange and semiotic negotiation, not merging, but adopting, adapting and imagining each other.

Conclusion

On the whole, then, we have found that, in fan art and writing surrounding *Final Fantasy VII*, the representational system and game system pull apart. Fans whose interest is in the procedural intricacies of gameplay devote themselves to walkthroughs and cheats, transforming the demand structures of the game system into the characteristic imperative structures of these texts, producing themselves as experts, semi-professional guides and instructors, although precariously poised in the lawless world of online intellectual property, not always supported by their fan community, and not recognized by the industrial producers of the game.

In contrast, fans whose interest lies in the rich and complex imagery and narrative of the game build on these structures. Though it is possible, as we saw in the case of the poem, to use these to replicate the first-person identification of player and avatar, more commonly these texts produce third-person views, narrative and iconic offers which pick up the possibilities offered by the representational system of the game and select, magnify and transform these for their own pleasure. These pleasures are at least as wide-ranging as those charted by Jenkins in *Textual Poachers*; and we have indicated a particular set of cultural and sexual interests associated with Japanese women's comics here, as an example of how such fan work is both culturally local and specific and at the same time capable of global export and adaptation, just like the original game on which it builds.

CHAPTER

08

Motivation and Online Gaming

Andrew Burn and Diane Carr

A NARCHY *Online* is a science-fiction styled Massively Multiplayer Online Role Playing Game (MMORPG) set on the mysterious planet of Rubi-Ka. Players undertake missions, dodge dangerous animals and augment their character's bodies with nano-implants powered by 'notum', a rare and precious mineral. As in other RPGs, each player constructs a character according to a set of options relating to species, skills, looks and profession. These characters then level up and specialize as they accumulate experience points through completing missions and surviving combat. Because *Anarchy Online* is an online game, the world of Rubi-Ka, with its warring factions, cityscapes and deserts, is shared. Players interact with each other in real time, with varying degrees of skill, civility, hostility or ineptitude, via their colourful digital representatives and an in-game chat window. The game is accessed via a monthly subscription, but information about the game, a players' manual and the game's community forums are all accessible to non-subscribers at the developer's website.[1]

While much computer gaming is contextualized by shared cultural activities of some description, an online multiplayer game like *Anarchy Online* is unavoidably public: the persistent, graphic world is shared by thousands of players. And, like other computer games, *Anarchy Online* is *multimodal*: that is, it combines a variety of audio and visual information as well as text. Players dress, arm and manipulate their character, and type/chat live to other players, while in the background thunderstorms or a moody score lends atmosphere. In analysing how players engage with the game, therefore, we need to pay attention to how these modes combine – for instance, how the text-based chat through which the players communicate relates to the animated images of their avatars.

In this chapter, we focus on three kinds of motivation that characterize players' interaction with the game. The word *motivation* needs some explanation. Within social semiotic theory, it is used in a technical sense, and derives from a classic debate about the nature of the sign. The debate begins with the original idea of the Swiss linguist,

Ferdinand de Saussure (1916/1983), that the sign was *arbitrary* – that the use of the signifier *tree* to denote the idea of that plant was simply a matter of convention, as becomes clear if we look at another language which chooses the word *arbre* or *ki* (in French or Japanese) instead. Social semiotic theory disputes this idea (Hodge and Kress, 1988; Kress and van Leeuwen, 2001). It argues that signs are always motivated by the *interest* of the sign-maker. Whoever chooses signifier material is doing so for a social purpose: social actors and communicators reach for the sign-making modes that are most suited (socially shaped) to their purpose, and combine them in ways that are partly determined by generic conventions. However, these modes are always transformed in use, according to the motivations of the sign-maker.

From a social semiotic perspective, then, we need to be asking two related questions. The first is to do with the specific sign: what is there in the combination of signified and signifier that reveals a social motivation? The second is more general, but perhaps more pressing: if each act of sign-making is socially motivated, what is the motivation of the sign-maker, and how does it relate to their social context? On the whole, this chapter focuses more on the second question. In this respect, our use of the word motivation is quite close to its everyday sense: why is this person making this statement? However, the former, more specific semiotic sense will be borne in mind as well.

In order to investigate these questions, our first task was to learn how to play *Anarchy Online* ourselves. We dedicated many hours to this end, and regularly found ourselves lost and confused on Rubi-Ka. The game is not easy to learn because of its scale, and because players choose to participate in a wide variety of ways; partaking in player-versus-player combat, joining temporary teams or forming guilds, or embarking on full 'in character' role play. Because of this diversity, motivations will vary from player to player (and even from session to session). Nonetheless, we propose the following three broad, inter-relating and overlapping categories with which to explore the variety of motivations behind the sign-making and sign-reading in *Anarchy Online*.

First, we suggest that some of the motivations involve *representation*. This category involves visual imagery, characterization, performance and narrative factors. Second, we suggest that there are *ludic* motivations. These relate directly to gameplay, to the skills necessarily acquired, the rules, competition, statistics and objectives. Finally, we propose that there are motivations relating to *communal* aspects of the game. This classification refers to the social, shared nature of *Anarchy Online*, as well as to the fact that the game itself is located within different generic communities, including other forms of science fiction, other role-playing games, and other online computer games.

Representational motivations: 'Welcome to Rubi-Ka'

Anarchy Online situates gameplay within a science-fiction setting. Episodes of 'The Story' of Rubi-Ka are available at the game's website in various forms. Prose updates such as 'A Return from Oblivion' fill readers in on recent political developments. There is also the *Anarchy Online Animated Series* that can be downloaded from the website. These weekly updates are designed to 'run concurrently with the game, elaborating on the story and providing a context for the events, missions, characters, dungeons, monsters, items, and other story-related content that players will encounter in the game'.[2]

As we have previously noted, RPGs typically begin by offering the player the opportunity to construct their own characterized protagonist via a set of templates relating to profession, species, talents and physicality. *Anarchy Online* dramatizes this process: when we played during 2002 and 2003, the player 'arrived' at an orbiting space station, and was welcomed by an intercom-style announcement to the territorial space of Rubi-Ka. An animated sequence swooped them along the corridors of the space station to a lab where he or she was invited to begin DNA sequencing a body for a new life on the planet below. Because *Anarchy Online* is science fiction, familiar classifications (elf, gnome, human) are exchanged for more alien suggestions (solitus, opifex, nano, etc.), but the idea that a character's strengths are offset or balanced by a corresponding vulnerability is maintained.

Players choose from a limited set of options in order to construct the 'syntagmatic bundle' that becomes their character (in semiotics a 'syntagm' is a meaningful combination of signs), but in actuality these few options combine to produce considerable variety. To begin with, the player selects from four very different species, each with different strengths. The player then selects a gender (interestingly, in *Anarchy Online* the most macho-looking species is classified as androgynous). This choice of species and gender then determines the player's subsequent options, when selecting a face, then a height and body weight. Variation is multiplied again when the player decides on one of twelve professions (which will determine the character's initial wardrobe, among other things). Then the player is required to use the keyboard to give the character a name, which the game will reject unless it is unique. Finally, the player decides on the political alignment (neutral, clan or corporate) of the new character. These options relate directly to the game's backstory, and the choice made here will have geopolitical consequences for the new resident of Rubi-Ka.

This apparently limited sequence of options, or semiotic possibilities, multiplies to produce many different possible characters. Variety and distinctiveness are further developed during play. Players can win

Illustration 9   Representational motivations in *Anarchy Online*: Aisea dancing in a blue dress. Reproduced with the permission of Funcom, Inc.

or buy clothes (party dresses, protective hoods, boots, etc.), wear tattoos and find new armour during missions. We created and played with various characters during the months that we subscribed to *Anarchy Online*. The characters we used initially were neutral martial artists called Aisea and Nirvano. While we went on to experiment with different sexes, professions, allegiances, body types and species, these were the characters in which we invested the most time.

As beginners, our character-construction choices felt like a whimsical or playful dressing up, yet once we began playing and interacting with other players, our characters did *feel* like partial representations of our offline selves. For one thing, their composition reflected our preferences and decisions. For another, the mistakes that Aisea and Nirvano made as they stumbled and died all over the training ground felt public and occasionally embarrassing – in other words, they were *our* mistakes. When Aisea and Nirvano joined other characters in the cities of Rubi-Ka, it became clear that the seemingly incidental choices we had made in the privacy of the character-generation chamber had repercussions. Andrew, for example, opted to create an 'honest' rather than a wishful persona, and so his character Nirvano is portly rather than muscle-bound. As a consequence, he found himself in the surreal position of taking another character's derogatory comments about Nirvano's weight personally (as discussed later in this chapter).

Over time it became clear that the private frameworks through which we assembled our avatars, using the resources supplied by the game, were more revealing and autobiographic than we initially appreciated. Our choices related to how we feel (however vaguely or unconsciously) about managing social relationships and identity in real life. Relationships between on-screen avatars and their players are complex (Taylor, 2003: 27, 39), and in our case there was a degree of blurring, a mingling that revealed our lack of experience with online invented personas. Yet we expect that, for all players, their offline identity will infuse their on-screen activities to some degree, whether they decide to create a fictional identity or not.

Perusing the players' forum does make it clear that some players do make very specific 'Role Play' choices right from the start. They have intentions to play a type of character, with a particular background and allegiances. This might involve choosing a weapons specialization, or a particular trait of strategic value, but it might also involve the creation of an invented personality.

Once players enter the world of Rubi-Ka, there are different ways to play the game. A percentage of participants are committed to full Role Playing. These self-described Role Players (or RP'ers) invent characters with biographies and histories, in order to participate in shared events and improvised scenarios while acting and speaking in character. There is an active Role Player forum on the *Anarchy Online* website where players debate the state of the game. A few frequent topics of discussion include: the relationship between Role Players and the general player population, the best way to begin Role Playing as opposed to just playing the game, how to spot a fellow Role Player, or the right way to play a 'baddie'.

This split between players and Role Players is not new, and is not confined to computer RPGs. Gary Fine studied North American table-top RPG culture in the late 1970s and found a similar schism within the community: 'The gamer plays the game as himself, while the player who wishes to lose himself to the fantasy is the true role-player – he plays the character' (Fine 1983: 207). While we are not using the same distinguishing terms as Fine, the pattern is familiar enough.

When advising new Role Players, a contributor to the player forum named Vixentrox (31 December 2002) suggests that when creating a character 'a brief background outline is a good place to start' and 'If you have multiple characters . . . make sure they RP as different people. My main character has a "step sister". They trade insults and don't like each other very much. The one is more fun loving . . . the other is more serious and stern.' It is obvious that Vixentrox is referring to traits that have little to do with the options offered by the game. Another contributor, Lillemjau (5 January 2003) replies to a beginner's request for Role Playing advice with the following: 'I want to address your character development . . . in between the background history and personality traits, add some good and bad habits, strengths and weaknesses, things your character loves and hates. Those little things makes the depth of him/her more interesting.'

As Lillemjau's and Vixentrox's posts to the player forums indicate, for committed Role Players the character generation templates offered by the game are only a set of starting positions. The ways that a player might interpret and perform the identity of his or her character exceed any statistical attribute. In this sense, the character-building resources offered by the game are what Kress and van Leeuwen (2001), following Halliday (1985), have described as systems of *meaning potential*. In a game, resources and rule systems are offered – but, as for language, there are not necessarily limits on what can be 'said' using these resources.

Role Players make choices about the personality and the personal history of their character, but even if the player does not want to play 'in role', he or she will still, at the very least, make choices about the look of their character. These choices reflect expressive, narrative, aesthetic or dramatic concerns, rather than strategic or game-related choices. There are, however, motivations that directly concern game-play. We have termed these 'ludic motivations'.

Ludic motivations: game, goals, strategies

The representational motivations discussed above might hinge on information that is not necessarily on-screen, or essential to the game, such as a character's invented biography or extensive wardrobe. When we turn to ludic motivations, however, we are looking directly at those parts of *Anarchy Online* that make it a game: strategy, goals, real time events, chance, rules, skills acquisition, exploration and levelling up. Yet the borders between these ludic and representational motivations are not firm or distinct. As we have noted, there is some discussion on the player forums as to what, for example, distinguishes Role Play (play with a pronounced narrative or dramatic agenda) from general play, where players go on missions or explore the game world using the avatar more as a game tool, and less as a character per se. Some players argue that, as all characters involve specialization (e.g. as a martial artist, a doctor or an engineer), then all play in *Anarchy Online* involves playing a role to some degree. In fact, the ludic and representational qualities often blur. For instance, we did not participate in full Role

Play, but we did spend more time and game currency on our characters' outfits than was warranted by the game rules (and Aisea discarded helmets altogether, purely on aesthetic grounds).

While these various motivations overlap, it is still possible to distinguish between them. Ludic motivations include those that emphasize the function of the avatar as a game component, a symbolic unit of strategic value (like a chess piece), rather than as a character. Accordingly, this category of motivation revolves around considerations of how to play. Ludic activities in *Anarchy Online* include going on missions, selecting one style of profession over another based on a preferred style of strategizing (sniper over martial artist, for example), or directing time and energy towards the accumulation of experience points (through goal attainment) that will enable an avatar to level up.

Expert players traverse the game world with ease, but beginners struggle to move their avatars at all. At first it is difficult to see what you need to see, and tricky communicating properly with others. Our characters Nirvano and Aisea staggered around, made false starts, rotated wildly or froze. When we wanted to quit the game, we realized we didn't know how. We selected 'quit' from the menu, and were instructed that we must sit down before we could quit – but we could not find out how to sit down. Fortunately, the training ground is full of other players of varying degrees of expertise. Once you have mastered the ability to type/enter basic conversation (which is not as simple as it might sound), it is possible to ask for advice from your fellow-players. There is also an open chat channel just for 'newbies', which is full of questions and requests for aid.

Just as the character templates supplied by the game initially appear limited, the various movements of the new avatar are stiff and mechanistic, and they remain stilted and disjointed until the player has gained a certain level of familiarity with the controls. At first the player has to make a considerable, concentrated effort just to drive their avatar through simple actions, such as turning a corner or following a path. However, the commands that are constantly used soon move to a stage of less deliberate manipulation. The avatar moves in the game world thanks to a combination of a set of technological potentials, and the player develops a skill or a fluency in deploying them, much as you might move through the world in a car, making both a functional journey and a social performance, by exploiting those potentials through learned manipulative skills.

The actions of the avatar depend on the player – and these actions involve the manipulation of technologically mediated signifiers. These signifiers recall what Halliday (1989) has called the *restricted language of games*. His example is contract bridge, where very limited sets of

Illustration 10 Ludic motivations in *Anarchy Online*: the character Japhis' statistics screen. Reproduced with the permission of Funcom, Inc.

signifiers (such as the four suits in a deck of cards) can multiply with other sets (such as the numbers of such suits which can be bid) within the rule structure of the game. In spite of the restrictions, the range of possible combinations, the ways in which they relate to the rules of the game, and the way all this in turn is determined by strategic collaboration between players, all combine to make for a complex and creative activity requiring considerable skill. In computational linguistics, too, restricted languages have found a new significance as bounded systems which computers can handle easily, as opposed to the unpredictable, unbounded nature of natural language.

The player responds to the game's rules, which are expressed in semiotic terms as missions, weapons, rewards and first-aid kits. The player has available a restricted language of avatar movement – run and walk, jump, take a particular direction – but each movement, however simple, is immediately a more complex act, because the movements are not made against an empty white background: the game world contains both a landscape and other characters and creatures. Any move of our avatar makes a syntagm – a combination of signs. A step forward combines our avatar's motion with the landscape, and with the actions of other avatars. If we, for instance, decided to take our avatars for a walk outside the city gates of Borealis, we might 'walk forward' and immediately other signs in the 3-D multimodal world would collect around this simple action – we would 'see' a new landscape of hills and lakes outside the city, the music would change, and the sound of our feet on the ground would change to the crunch of a sandy path.

Simply wandering around in the game world involves the combination of a restricted language (the avatar's actions) with the much bigger language of the game world and its contents. The latter is, in principle, an unrestricted language, as anything can be designed into it, whereas the avatar's movements depend on the game's rules and mechanics, and the player's fingers. The 'design' of our avatar's journey is a joint activity, with three principal co-designers at work. The player designs a walk through the woods; the game's programming designs elements around us; and our fellow-players may affect our experience to a greater or lesser degree. And the presence of other players means that, in addition to the representational and ludic motivations we have discussed, there are social and communal factors shaping the player's experience of the game world.

Communal motivations: Sharing Rubi-Ka

Our final category of motivation involves a mix of what we might call 'communal' factors. This category includes the game's relationship to other games and the expectations that players bring to the game from elsewhere, as well as the shared nature of the game world itself.

We explored the question of players' expectations by enlisting three volunteers and arranging subscriptions for each of them. We interviewed our three (male, teenage) player consultants about their expectations of the game before they began to play, and were struck by how adamant they were about certain aspects of the game, despite never having played it. All three boys had played other online games before, and from this prior experience they confidently predicted how best to enjoy themselves, survive and prosper on Rubi-Ka. They had well-articulated expectations about play, including the kinds of combat they wanted to engage in, the best ways to level up and the best kind of character to construct. After one of the interviewees, Tim, began to play *Anarchy Online*, he sent us an email describing how he built and named his character:

> Name: Belithralith – Soulish (my nickname) translated into elvish on an Internet translator.
> Breed: nanomage – just look kind of mysterious

>Gender: male – 'cos that what i am i 'spose
>Profession: Agent – all i can say is: sniper rifles :)

As Tim's email indicates, he arrived at *Anarchy Online* armed with a variety of discourses inherited from associated texts and other games. The boys were interested in the exploration and combat potentials of *Anarchy Online*, but very dismissive of the game's RPG associations. All three expressed distaste for the 'dressing up' potentials of the game. This makes it all the more interesting that Tim gave his character an 'Elvish' name that harks back to the game's *Dungeons & Dragons'* fantasy roots, rather than its science-fiction setting (Elvish is a made-up language deriving from Tolkien's work). All our interviewees, including Tim, explained their predilection for sniper rifles in terms of their past experiences in online games, more specifically, combative online First Person Shooter games. And, just as we had initially wondered how closely to construct our characters to our offline selves in terms of physicality or gender, Tim framed certain decisions about representation in terms of a connection between his online persona and himself – ''cos that what i am i 'spose'.

Tim's account of constructing his character involves several different types of motivation. His choice of avatar name provides one indication of the specifically semiotic dimension to this process. On the face of it, the name appears to be a good example of Saussure's arbitrary sign – it seems to be a nonsense word associated arbitrarily with its meaning only by an obscure set of conventions. However, it can be said to be motivated in two ways. First, it is a translation of Tim's real-life nickname Soulish, itself a motivated sign representing, presumably, both musical and personal tastes. Second, as an example of 'Elvish' it has generic and historical origins: it has to 'sound' like Tolkien's Elvish; and Tolkien's Elvish was in turn based on his own scholarly knowledge of real runic languages. In this respect, the word *Belithralith* is not simply an arbitrary collection of phonemes, but a socially motivated sign.

Our interviewees' expectations about the social aspects of the game were interesting, especially as regards gender. When asked what kind of avatar they would choose, they all said they would be male, human and as like themselves as possible. Yet, at the same time, the boys were certain that it would be necessary to 'read past' the appearance of other avatars because, they explained, behind all female avatars are 'fat American (male) teenagers'. They quickly revised this to 'fat middle-aged American men'. The boys were half joking yet they were very insistent on this point. Their distrust of alluring female avatars was expressive of a discourse of 'Internet suspicion', born of an alarmist and wary attitude towards online predatory sexual duplicity. The expectations expressed in the boys' dubious comments also rest on the 'common-sense' notion that 'women don't play', an assumption fed by past experiences of other online games, and buttressed by commercial gaming culture at large. So 'obvious' is this to our interviewees that it potentially overrides alternative interpretations of female characters in the game world, even when they are talking about the game to a female interviewer/player.

In an online game like *Anarchy Online*, other players and their characters also populate the game world. It is possible to go solo when playing, and to refuse to engage with these other players. However, it is not possible to ignore their existence: they will run past you, hold you up in queues at mission terminals, stand next to you in shops, have conversations you can 'hear', and approach you with questions or requests to join them. Additionally, because levelling up tends to involve specialization, there are strategic incentives for playing on teams. As we explored these possibilities, it became apparent that the interaction with other players is channelled primarily through two (occasionally disarticulated) modes: the visual, animated aspect of the avatar (how they act, how they look); and the in-game live chat that is typed and entered by players in real time, sometimes 'in character', but more often 'out of character'.

The first, visual mode of this interplayer communication is generated by the visual design, actions and animating of the individualized avatars. Our avatars enable us to occupy the game world, to assume a form (perhaps macho and militant, or small and innocuous, bizarrely alien, or blandly handsome) and to approach others. This particular system of *meaning potential* also involves the avatar's repertoire of 'emotes' – animated movements expressive of emotion or certain kinds of social communication. These include waving, nodding, laughing, pointing, dancing and various other rude, humorous and expressive gestures. For instance, when Aisea first appeared next to Nirvano at the appointed time and place, she waved her arms and danced about in vigorous greeting. Within minutes, Nirvano had been introduced to the emote menu, and he too was waving wildly, performing ballet and turning back flips. This visual aspect of the avatar employs various potentials – costume, body, face and movement – but it is not infinitely flexible. The player's presence in the game depends on and manifests through the avatar, and the motions, proportions, actions and 'look' of the avatar are subject to the rules of the game.[3]

Semiotically, these movements can be seen as paradigmatic choices (from a class called 'emote'). The *paradigm* is the 'selection' axis of semiotics: choices can be made from classes of items, so, in a sentence, you must choose from a class called 'nouns', a class called 'verbs' and so on. In this case, the class is a group of actions expressing emotion. These choices are then organized in a *syntagm* (the combination axis). In language this might be a sentence, but, in the game, it is a sequence of animated action constructed by the two players. The language is restricted to the choices made available by the game's resources; although the meaning intended by the player will always exceed the generic meaning assigned by the game. For instance, Andrew's waving of Nirvano's arms signified for him a mixture of embarrassment ('why have I only just learnt how to do this?'), as well as a greeting to someone he knows in real life, and so on. Furthermore, the syntagm is multimodal: the animation combined with the text-based chat to allow Andrew/Nirvano to greet Diane/Aisea in type, 'Hi', and salute her virtuosity visually, with a hearty wave.

Players type live to one another during the game. This text-based chat can be 'in character', but often it is clearly the player who is talking. This so-called speech has no actual vocal or audio component, it is typed and read, and it is entirely at the player's disposal (although the game does have rules about unacceptable behaviour and language). Thus, with the chat mode it is possible to play out different shades of commitment to the avatar's identity, to slip in and out of role – to maintain the role at a low level, to speak in character, or to speak as the player, from 'behind the mask'.

In-game chat might swing from 'in character' dialogue, to the stripped pragmatics of team formation, to completely unrelated sociable chat ('Hi, where R U from?'). This chat mode, unlike the relatively specific and restricted visual language of the character, is an unrestricted or natural language. Like our characters' nicknames, this chat is a form of semiotic work that is player-produced. Yet the majority of in-game conversations that we witnessed were as abrupt as the example we include here. In this sequence, Nirvano is trying to join a clan that is in the process of being formed by Storm, Rigret, Artspider, Thel, Demon and Helement:

STORM:	make name
STORM:	first
NIRVANO:	yeah
THEL:	fighters of the lost rhelm [sic]
STORM:	I got to go now
RIGRET:	athen whompa? [a 'whompa' is a portal to another city]
STORM:	hurry up
ARTSPIDER:	make me leader
THEL:	ok
STORM:	u can make name
THEL:	ok me
STORM:	fith hurry up
RIGRET:	thx anyway ☺

Storm, although she expresses no ambition to be leader, or to decide on the name of the group, is assertive in assigning tasks to others, using brisk, imperative forms ('make name', 'hurry up'). A dominant theme of the conversation is the choosing of a name for the group. Team formation is appropriate to RPGs, yet the name itself appears to have strayed in from an alternate subgenre, that of fantasy: the group agree to call themselves 'Fighters of the Lost Realm'. Nirvano's eventual, sole contribution to this discussion is to correct another player's spelling of 'realm', because he can't bear the thought of wandering around belonging to a misspelled guild – and this is another marker of Nirvano's symbiotic relationship to Andrew's offline identity.

In this conversation, the players appear motivated by communal rather than narrative concerns: they are negotiating with real people, they choose between being demanding or persuasive, polite or abrupt, and between agreeing or arguing. Of course there are also ludic motivations evident in that they are organizing a team with strategic, rather than dramatic, ends in mind. The avatars are not talking in a manner dramatically consonant with the visual style of their character. Rather, the players are communicating in the compressed dialogue of synchronous chat, with typical orthographic (spelling) and stylistic features. This style of written communication implies certain cultural and perhaps age-related attributes, including a familiarity with online environments and an ability to talk and read 'txt'. Werry (1996) has outlined the linguistic features of Internet Relay Chat, such as abbreviation, paralinguistic cues, and actions and gestures, each of which is an adaptive strategy to allow it to behave as much like speech as possible. The 'talking' in *Anarchy Online* displays many of the same features. The game identifies who is speaking on behalf of the group. Abbreviations are used, both grammatical ('make guild') and orthographic ('u can make name'), while facial expression is simulated as with Rigret's smiley. These features indicate a desire to replicate the 'feel' of speech within a typed and read mode, and it is also completely possible that the urge to save time (or 'hurry up') is motivating the players.

So in this particular example of synchronous chat, the players display a high communal (and ludic) motivation, and a low commitment to Role Play or characterization. Nobody is interested in the character, history or personality of his or her fictitious characters – only in getting the job done. The dynamic properties of the exchange are not the dramatized elements of invented roles, but the real impatience, assertiveness and indecision of the human players. In semiotic terms, the effect of this is a kind of pulling apart of the two modes through which the avatar acts: the animated image and the written chat. In this instance, the two modes are only loosely joined, because at this moment the visual aspects of the characters and the strategic, decision-making chat of the players are themselves only loosely connected. The communal motivation is more strongly vested in the language; the visual signs, here, are more weakly motivated, because the players are not, for this moment, assigning them meanings.

We have no space here to develop an account of how the modes of image and speech might be combined when players are committed to full, in-character Role Play, but we can give a brief illustration of what such an analysis might entail. Role Players infuse their exchanges with invented personas, and in such cases abbreviation is not a priority, as seems clear in this comment witnessed by Andrew in passing: 'I bow to your superior wit and wisdom, and withdraw from combat.' This fragment could represent a dialogue between two characters speaking in role. On the other hand, it could be a snippet of dialogue between two friends who find florid formality amusing. It could even be the snide and sarcastic 'last word' in an out-of-character confrontation. To satisfactorily account for this enigmatic quotation, we would need to see it in context and know the broader frameworks of meaning that the players themselves were invoking.

Conclusion

The three categories of motivation we have been exploring in *Anarchy Online* do not occur in isolation from each other. On the contrary, as we have shown, they combine during play. We conclude this chapter by recounting an episode where the three categories are thoroughly entangled. To recap, we described these styles of motivation as *representational* (dramatic, performative, figurative, graphic, narrative); *ludic* (game orientated: scoring, levelling up, the avatar as tool); and *communal* (generic and other expectations, wider online culture, the shared nature of the game world).

In the middle of a play session we – Nirvano and Grayse, another of Diane's female characters – were trying to decide whether to head straight out on a mission, or go shopping, when we were interrupted. A 'voice' intruded on our conversation (in the form of a line of text) to ask if Nirvano 'was pregnant'. Andrew immediately felt affronted, as he understood this comment to mean that the new arrival was making an offensive remark about his avatar's girth (and Andrew had consciously designed Nirvano's physicality as an 'honest' personification). Diane was immediately riled because she assumed that the player was mocking Nirvano for associating with females. As far as we can make out, we were both wrong, and if anything the interloper was actually flirting with the unsuspecting Nirvano. It subsequently emerged that the 'voice' belonged to Rafayel, an avatar with a 'male model' physique, wearing high heels, thong style underpants and sunglasses.[4]

For Andrew, Rafayel's comment was confronting because Nirvano wears aspects of Andrew's real body image. Diane's (Grayse's) response was also triggered by her offline identity. Rafayel made more jokes about Nirvano's appearance ('i can hear the baby kick') and then compounded the provocation with mildly confrontational actions, walking close enough to Nirvano to make contact, and then apparently bouncing off his tummy. In his dialogue and in his stance, Rafayel completely ignored Grayse and directed all comments and actions at Nirvano. Grayse resorted to conciliatory compliments about Rafayel's shoes, but to no avail. Inspired by the tattoo that Rafayel sports across his chest, Grayse asked about where or how to get one. Rafayel ignored Grayse. Nirvano repeated the question, and Rafayel immediately replied: 'on missions mostly' (the tattoos are a mission reward).

We responded warily to the representation in front of us. His manner 'felt' confrontational. Rafayel initially offended both of us, for completely different reasons. And we both assumed throughout the encounter, and afterwards, that Rafayel represents a male player. There is, of course, no reason to believe that is the case – 'Rafayel' might be an adolescent girl or a grandmother, but while in this particular embodiment, he was male to us. Rafayel presented as male, or perhaps it is truer to say that Nirvano and Grayse (Andrew and Diane) experienced him as a male presence, because of the way he looked, the way he acted and the things that he typed. The pronouns here reveal how knotted together various modes become during play. 'He' is a designed fictional character, a barely dressed male humanoid. 'He' acts according to the directions of an off-screen agent, the 'he' that types comments about Nirvano's physique. Rafayel's comments could have been the expression of a player's acting 'in character' as a confrontational or flirtatious person, or the comments could have been a player's genuine attempts to make friends. As it happens, Nirvano and Rafayel met by accident later that same afternoon, and enjoyed a more amiable conversation. Rafayel offered Nirvano an object for his in-game apartment (a lava lamp, actually) and typed that he was 'from Sweden'.

As these encounters demonstrate, while it is possible, in part, to distinguish between the various motivations shaping the reading and making of signs in a massive, shared, graphically rendered world like that of *Anarchy Online*, in practice, these motivations are simultaneous and intermingling. Just as a deceptively simple set of templates combine to create a huge range of possible avatars, the motivations (representational, ludic, communal) that we have examined mesh together during play, proliferating, compounding and informing one another. In practice these motivations become ambiguous and multiple. The invented persona of the avatar remains curiously shot through with aspects of the everyday. The online persona and offline identities of participants interrelate, while gameplay is infused by the expectations that different players carry with them into the game world. The game's exotic inhabitants and elaborate science-fiction locale play against the abbreviated pragmatics of chat, levelling and team formation, and the flexible bond between the visual and the speech-like semiotic modes allows for these ambiguities.

CHAPTER 09

Social Play and Learning

Gareth Schott and Maria Kambouri

IN the early chapters of this book, we analysed the structure of particular games from our own perspective, both as players and as critics. However, we also drew attention to some of the limitations of the 'player-as-analyst'. Over the previous few chapters, we have gradually widened the scope of our inquiry, in order to examine different aspects of the relationships between players and games including role play and fandom. In this chapter, we take another step back from the screen in order to consider how players use and enjoy games, the role that the games console might perform in their social lives and the implications of social play in terms of informal learning.

As we have shown, players may engage with a game in a variety of ways, both during the course of play and in the activities that take place around the play itself. These forms of engagement are most evident (and, for researchers, most easily accessible) in the context of fan activities of various kinds (chapter 7) and in the context of online games (chapter 8). It is much more difficult to explore what players actually do when they play console or PC games, particularly if they do so alone. Somewhat more easily accessible, however, is the experience of collaborative play, and the social pleasures that it affords; and it is this that forms the focus of our analysis in this chapter.

This line of inquiry means that we need to engage with research traditions drawn from the social sciences. Without denying the importance of textual analysis, it is these traditions that seem to provide a more developed account of the experiences of players, and of the social settings and networks in which gameplaying is situated. We agree with Henry Jenkins's claim that game research should be:

> more attentive to the experience of playing games rather than simply interpreting their surface features. We need to situate them more precisely within their social and educational contexts, to understand them more fully within their place in children's [and adults'] lives. (1993: 69)

In fact, there is a growing body of work on computer gaming within the disciplines of psychology and, to a lesser extent, sociology. It is here that we might expect to find plausible interpretations and accounts of the pleasures and experiences of gameplaying. Unfortunately, however, much of this research is quite problematic. Most of it is preoccupied with what we would regard as a very narrow set of concerns about the negative psychological, moral and behavioural effects of computer games. Thus, numerous research studies have attempted to assess the impact of playing computer games on aggressive behaviour; on psychological variables such as self-esteem; on educational achievement; and on the development of stereotyped attitudes. Researchers have typically used survey methods, although there have been some more experimental studies of short-term effects. As reviews of this research have suggested (e.g. Durkin, 1995; Gunter, 1998), the findings of such studies have been uneven and inconsistent.

In many respects, the limitations of this research reflect those of parallel research on the effects of television, for example, in relation to violence. These would include, first, a crude approach to categorizing games themselves, which rarely goes further than superficial distinctions based on content. Second, such studies often rest on untested and inadequately defined notions of the mechanisms by which effects are assumed to be caused. As in the television violence research, key terms such as 'addiction', 'arousal', 'identification' and 'modelling' are often loosely defined and measured. Third, and perhaps paradoxically, such research often tends to neglect the social context of gameplaying, and the social interaction that surrounds it: it is often solely concerned with the interaction between mind and screen (for further discussion, see Buckingham, 2002).

Nevertheless, there is an emerging body of work within social psychology and sociology that is adopting a more considered approach (for instances, see Jessen, 1999; Schott and Horrell, 2000; Tobin, 1998; Walkerdine, 2004). Such research typically moves beyond simplistic assumptions about effects, to take fuller account of how players actively construct and define their own social identities, both in the course of gameplay and in the interactions that surround it. Such research also tends to leave behind surveys and experimental methods in favour of in-depth ethnographic observation. It was these approaches, in combination with some aspects of learning theory, that we employed in the research we describe in this chapter.

Exploring social play

One of the popular concerns that is frequently voiced about computer gaming relates to its allegedly 'antisocial' characteristics. Gaming is frequently seen as an isolated activity that undermines 'natural' human interaction and ultimately leads to the atrophy of players' social skills. In the case of children, it is also seen to displace more traditional forms of social play, which are frequently considered to be vital for the development of 'healthy' peer group relationships. In some instances, this is regarded as part of a wider historical development: for example, Brian Sutton-Smith (1986) argues that play has steadily moved away from social, collective and public forms to private, personal and solitary ones. Likewise, we frequently read of the 'holding power' of computer games and the 'new kind of intimacy with machines that is characteristic of the nascent computer culture' (Turkle, 1984: 66) – and indeed of the emergence of a new 'Nintendo generation' (Green and Bigum, 1993), whose most meaningful relationships appear to be with – or at least conducted via – machines rather than through face-to-face encounters with real people.

With this, it is argued, comes evidence of disruption to parent–child communication as a result of video gameplay (Bonnafont, 1992). Yet careful examination of these research results reveals that it is not the children who are retreating, but parents, as a result of their own insufficient understanding of, and unwillingness to partake in, game cultures which appear to captivate this new generation (Casas, 2001).

In evaluating these kinds of concerns, it is also necessary to identify the particular kinds of engagement and game experiences to which they refer, as it is difficult to apply them to all aspects of gaming. For example, they must exclude the necessary sociability of online games (as discussed in chapter 8) or that of pervasive games, that require an interplay between real-world location-based action and digital communication (see McGonical, 2003). We can only assume that such concerns are typically aimed at one-player games played on stand-alone, independent game systems, such as games consoles. Although such systems do incorporate player-to-player game experiences, in which two players can take action in real time without fixed turns (for example, in fighting games such as *Tekken*) and (in some cases) networking capabilities, they do for the most part engage the player in player-to-game interactivity in which predefined virtual worlds are navigated.

Nevertheless, early psychological research into the social effects of PC gameplay showed little effect on peer play (Fein et al., 1987), while other studies suggested that the presence of computers actually increases social contact amongst peers (Borgh and Dickson, 1986; Wright and Samaras, 1986; Ziajka, 1983). More recent research strongly refutes the popular idea that gameplaying is an antisocial activity (Buckingham, 1993; Jessen, 1999; Livingstone and Bovill, 1999). While the actual playing of games is sometimes an individual, isolated pursuit, it is also often collaborative, and the focus of a great deal of talk and interaction. Furthermore, the culture surrounding the games is an important means of establishing and sustaining interpersonal relationships – from the swapping of games, advice and 'cheats', through to participation in the more public culture of games shops, arcades, magazines and TV shows. The culture of gameplaying involves the ongoing social construction of an 'interpretive community' (cf. Radway, 1984) – and in this respect, as Jessen (1999) argues, it may be better suited to the pattern of children's play than older media such as books, which one is alone in consuming.

At the same time, this social process is mediated by the operations of the market. Much of the discussion is about what you can buy, what you have bought or what you are going to buy – and this is a discussion in which players are not all equal. Furthermore, it would be at least optimistic to assume that such 'interpretive communities' are necessarily always warm and cosy. Game culture can serve as an arena for the creation of hierarchies and for bullying of weaker members of a group; and it can also be a vehicle for the 'border-work' that marks the boundaries between boys and girls, and thereby prevents girls from gaining access to technology or to the knowledge that is required to use it (Orr Vered, 1998).

Observing players

As we have noted, previous research on gameplay has tended to neglect the specific nature of particular games: 'gameplaying' is too often seen as a unitary activity, with little attention being paid to the distinctive features of games, game genres and the different experiences they offer players. In contrast, what we present in this chapter is a single case study of one group of players, and their experiences with an action adventure game, played on an individually owned CD-based console system at home.

Our initial focus of examination was the nature, frequency and length of adolescent gaming experiences with console gaming systems. The research design was longitudinal: that is, it aimed to observe and chronicle playing habits over time in order to gain a representative account of the degree and nature of gameplaying in everyday life. Rather than attempting to explore how the individual player is cognitively experiencing gameplay, we sought to provide an account of the 'actuality' of social play, and to consider the 'social envelope' (Giacquinta et al., 1993) in which computer gameplay becomes embedded.

We sought to achieve this through video recording a group of pre-adolescents' use of console systems within the context of their own homes. Video cameras (plus tripods) were left in participant gamers' homes with various instructions on how to record their gameplay over

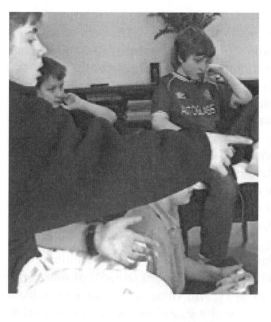

Illustration 11   Boys engaging in collaborative play. Photo: Schott and Kambouri

a one-week period. During the research, several methods of video recording and scheduling were experimented with. All participant gamers were given instructions on the positioning of the camera and the length of recording required. In the example we describe below, the participant was instructed on how to achieve a sideways/over-the-shoulder shot that would enable the player and their screen action to be viewed (see Illustration 11). By securing the assistance of participants and in some cases their guardians, it was the intention to capture user activity at the times when the participants *chose* to play games. In addition to the video material collected, participants also recorded details of all their gameplay during the course of a week, including gameplay outside the video schedule or home context. Participants submitted an account of the length of time spent playing, the title(s) of the game(s) played in a given session, the level at which games were played and an account of the progress achieved.

During our piloting, an interesting occurrence took place which altered the focus of the research. The video footage revealed an interesting contradiction between the intentions of the game designers and the ways in which players behaved. Games intended to engage a single player were shown to be able to incorporate cooperation with, and the contribution of, others. Furthermore, gameplay in groups appeared to constitute quite a natural and consistent component in the life cycle of an individual's progression through such games. We found that participants successfully transformed one-player games into an effective and highly structured social performance, in which roles and identities within the group were constantly being negotiated and redefined. Indeed, it became clear that a significant part of the pleasure of gaming involved this interaction with other gamers during the actual experience of play. Just as games located in social spaces (such as arcades) foster and/or incorporate social interaction, so gameplay in the home also appears to promote particular forms of collective and collaborative engagement.

The game

To illustrate some of what we observed, we will focus on a single case study of collaborative play among a group of four pre-adolescent boys with the console version of the game *Soul Reaver: Legacy of Kain* (Eidos). In the game, the player(s) adopt the character of 'Raziel', a mysterious entity cast down to the material world in order to seek vengeance for his betrayal by his master 'Kain'. Like other action adventure games, *Soul Reaver* incorporates the need to traverse puzzles, overcome traps and defy enemies in an endeavour to reach a final showdown with Kain, although it has elements of the Role Playing Game in that the player has the chance to augment the avatar's abilities during the course of play.

In the opening cutscene we learn that, having served Kain for a millennium, Raziel has followed his master's evolution by gaining his own gift, that of flight. We see Kain tear Raziel's wings for his transgression, and order his brothers to throw him into the 'Lake of the Dead' where he will experience eternal damnation. Inside, the disfigured and enraged Raziel is spared from 'total dissolution' by an Elder God who declares Raziel 'worthy' and offers him the opportunity to avenge himself and become an 'Angel of Death', leaving behind the desire for blood, and replacing it with a need to devour souls. The demands of the game require the player to sustain Raziel's strength as he pursues Kain and revenge. Raziel is able to move between the spectral and material planes of the world – giving him the ability to manifest in the physical world and return to the ethereal environment of the 'Underworld' should his physicality become weakened. The movement between these two states of existence is crucial to the gameplay, as areas of the game that are forbidden to Raziel become accessible when planes are transcended.

During the course of the game, the player travels as Raziel through Kain's Empire, Nosgoth. The game environment is littered with cataclysms caused by the earth's attempt to 'shrug off the pestilence of Kain's parasitic empire'. The decay set about by Kain has Nosgoth on the brink of collapse. Raziel begins at his tomb and the womb of his rebirth, the Lake of the Dead, before entering and navigating through various clan territories of his brothers Melchiah, Zephon, Rahab and Dumah. During his journey he moves through cathedrals, tombs, a drowned abbey, the city of Dumahim and an oracle's cave, encountering wraiths, clan vampires, tomb guardians, sorcerers, his siblings, and ultimately Kain himself.

Playing the game

In addition to the video material captured by the console owner of his solitary play, he also captured gameplay in a group. During the sequence we will discuss, the roles occupied by the four boys are fairly clearly defined: in addition to the 'Owner', there is an 'Expert', an older boy who also owned the game but had progressed much further than the 'Owner'; a 'Novice', a boy the same age as the 'Owner', who possessed the same console system but not this particular game; and a 'PC Gamer', a boy who neither owned the game nor the same console system, but was computer savvy and played PC games.

At the beginning of the group footage captured by the Owner he is observed sat on his own in front of his television, playing *Soul Reaver* while picking at food from a plate positioned in front of him. Shortly afterwards, he is joined by the three friends who have called round. They enter the room and position themselves in a semi-circle behind him in front of the television. Beyond turning his head to acknowledge his friends, the Owner does not adjust his position or really disrupt his play. After spending some time exchanging pleasantries and discussing other matters with the Owner, the friends quickly start to fix their gaze upon the on-screen action.

Console gaming has not been an obvious focus for psychological research interested in how social discourse and interpersonal dynamics are developed within play. Yet, contrary to the concerns identified above, the video footage initially appeared to have captured circumstances comparable to the behaviour of 'casual' visitors to video arcades (Fisher, 1995). Video arcade studies have shown how a proportion of those who attend arcades give equal value to both 'hanging out' and playing (McMeeking and Purkayastha, 1995). In our case study, a significant period of time passed in which the Owner progressed with his gameplay while simultaneously engaging in non-game-related conversation with his visitors. However, as play advanced, group 'chat' abated and the group began to organize itself effectively within a form of collaborative play. Footage showed that observations and advice from members of the group began to have a significant impact upon on-screen events. Indeed, analysis unearthed examples of the way that the relationship between player and console was orchestrated and structured under the guidance and advice of peers, creating an effective form of 'mediational interaction' (Feuerstein, 1979).

Although many paragraphs have been devoted to discussion of the drama that occurs within the agreed boundaries of play (Adelman, 1992), little attention has been given to the social dimension of console gameplay. Issues such as how the utilization of objects is negotiated and agreed within the 'politics of play' (Sutton-Smith, 1979) therefore remain unexplored. In order to direct on-screen events it is necessary to possess control of the joystick. Within the context of this encounter, the handling of the joystick largely remained with the Owner, although it was occasionally passed to the Expert. While this may have been indicative of the power of ownership or territoriality, observation of the effectiveness of the multiple roles assumed by members of the group led us to question the importance of the role of joystick controller within collaborative play. Although one person was nominally in charge of manipulating the joystick, the contribution of all four participants became fused within gameplay. Pointing out, reminding, suggesting and praising all served to assist and structure the on-screen activity. As Schott and Horrell (2000) have stated: 'The problems that require solving within adventure games often transcend the physical dexterity required by the joystick controller. Decisions concerning direction, orientation, utilization of discovered objects are often more pressing and benefit from the input of others' (p. 40).

Over the course of the session, each member of the group appeared consumed by the game and their role within it. A 'truly collaborative style' (Orr Vered, 1998) ensued in which group contributions were communicated either verbally or via pointing or touching the screen (see Illustration 11), rather than contesting who should control the joystick. Within learning theory, the term 'scaffolding' (Wood et al., 1976) has been widely used to describe the nature of support offered between tutor and student. Yet, in this context, group play was serving this scaffolding function, for example by demonstrating how to achieve goals and highlighting critical features of the task that a novice may have overlooked (Wood and Wood, 1996).

Only the Expert, who showed occasional signs of frustration with the way that the group was conducting gameplay, contested control of the joystick. To this effect he was observed extending his arms out as a sign that he wished to receive the joystick and take over control of Raziel. This occurred when he was agitated by the way that his directions were either being ignored or not executed accurately or effectively. The collective strategy put into practice by the group appeared to accelerate the progress of the Owner beyond what he might have achieved in a solitary play session. However, it also appeared to conflict with the strategy employed successfully by the Expert in his own unassisted play. Consistent with the way that progress was showing itself to be contingent upon the multiple roles operated by group members, the Expert made little reference to the relevant aspects of the task beyond the manual dexterity and speed necessary for the movement of Raziel. However, Raziel's narrative from the game expresses the need for specificity and strategy, for example, when engaging in battles:

> A vampire's immortal flesh begins to close as soon as it is cleaved. Vampires need only fear those wounds that impale or inflame. Water scorches like acid, and fledglings are devastated by sunlight's touch. I would have to modify my tactics to suit my foes.

The Expert failed to narrate the story in these terms and showed little variety or rationale for the methods he wished to see the Owner employ. In contrast, the other members of the group, who did not have direct responsibility for on-screen action, demonstrated a greater ability to detect and locate a wide range of environmental features that were relevant to the character's progression or life force. Indeed, when control of the joystick was relinquished to the Expert, he revealed that he was making the same mistakes that he did within his solitary play.

Traditional models of learning recognize that new tasks cause the learner to engage more fully in monitoring and making sense of immediate events. Coupled with dexterity, aim, response time and steadiness, comprehension of computer games also requires the ability to decode a complex system of representational devices. In addition to mastery of procedures and moves, the presence of others within collaborative play permitted the group of players to discern what was happening in the wider narrative and representational context of the game. For example, as an active observer, the Novice became particularly adept at recognizing how objects within the game environment should be incorporated into gameplay. In one of the game's many block puzzles, where the objective is to stack the blocks in a specific way in order to permit Raziel to reach higher ledges, the Novice's field-independent observations were indispensable. The Owner was thereby permitted to concentrate on developing 'local expertise' as he grappled with the movement and precise placement of the blocks, while the Novice concentrated on the visual-spatial demands of the task.

Observation methods of this kind are not comprehensive enough to establish whether collaborative play generates higher order thinking in the individual player. The degree to which the group, in the first instance, supplied the Owner with 'psychological tools' that provided 'general and optimal methods of dealing with certain classes of problems' (Lidz, 1995: 143) is difficult to ascertain. What the observation did establish was the capacity of the group to direct the Owner towards the essential characteristics of the problems (Karpov, 1994). Such actions are consistent with interactionist models of learning (Vygotsky, 1978), which argue that the development of theoretical learning occurs through 'socially meaningful mediated activity' (Kouzlin, 1990). As distinct from traditional activity-centred theories of learning which focus on the gradual unfolding of internal, individual capacities within adult–child dyads, the present study established the potential that exists for 'groupings of people engaged in tool-making learning' (Holzman, 1995: 201). Gameplay within a group situation appeared to provide a bridge between the learner's existing knowledge and experience with the game, and the skills and the demands of new levels and puzzles.

Regardless of the roles taken up by different members of the group, further confirmation of the collective nature of the group play was apparent from the synchronized ways in which the boys responded to the frustrations of play. In their reactions to the events of the game, the group would often respond with almost identical facial expressions and body movements (Illustration 11). As we have noted, the boys sat in a semi-circle round the television, with the Owner assuming the central position directly in front of the set. When faced with a mistake, failure or general frustration, the group's collective response was rarely aimed directly at the Owner as joystick controller. In conveying their exasperation, the group rarely averted their gaze from the events occurring on-screen.

One aspect of games that is often neglected is the type of sound effects that accompany events occurring on-screen. In addition to atmospheric or 'ambient' music and sound, many games feature occasional non-diegetic sound motifs – short files activated by player movement that signify events such as killing or being killed or the successful collection of items. Such sound effects rarely seek realism in sound reproduction, but instead their artificiality serves to emphasize and confirm the failure or success of the player's intended action. Like other action adventure games such as the *Tomb Raider* (Eidos Interactive) series, *Soul Reaver* also contains ambient background music that functions effectively to build suspense and indicate either that a significant event is drawing nearer, or that time to complete a task is running out. As the mood of the instrumentation changed and became more intense, so the Owner's discomfort and tension became more evident as he attempted to maintain his concentration, precision and accuracy. The stress of the situation and the increased salience of success meant that mistakes produced angry responses from the Owner, such as self-criticism and raising and dropping his arms in despair. More interesting, however, was the manner in which the group members mirrored each other's postures as they observed the action unfold. As the suspense and tension rose, it was common for group members to lean closer and closer to the screen until failure or frustration sent them falling back into their chairs.

Narrative and play

How does this account relate back to our earlier analysis of the relationships between the 'game system' and the representational dimension of games? In particular, what does it tell us about the significance – or lack of it – of narrative? Like most games of its type, *Soul Reaver: Legacy of Kain* possesses a sophisticated quest structure. It has a clearly delineated backstory that is present in the game packaging, official solution guides, web 'walkthroughs' and pre-animated sequences within the game itself. Yet these elements seemed relatively insignificant in the observational material that we gathered on our videotapes.

For example, the way in which *Soul Reaver* deals with the consequences of screen death, so integral to Action Adventure Games, is highly original. In this game, on-screen death does not lead to a 'start again' return to a previous screen, but movement into a 'spectral realm'. This permits play to continue in the same environment but with a 'twisted, Boschian air' (Poole, 2000: 234) which contains previously non-existent pathways. Yet, despite such inventive and atmospheric gameplay, members of the group showed no disposition towards describing the game and its objectives in narrative terms. Instead, the talk was dominated by directive-based instructions such as 'go there', 'jump on to one of those', 'run away from the other one fast', 'land on that' and 'push that'. Auditory analysis alone would not have imparted any information on Raziel or his position on his journey through clan territories, or his movement between the material and spectral plane. The urgency of gameplay appeared to demand a more direct and instructional mode of communication rather than any more discursive speculation as to the motives of the character or the potential plot twists ahead.

The boys' talk was thus heavily reliant upon what Halliday (1970) terms a 'regulatory' use of language, via imperatives intended to control the joystick controller's actions. Thus, the Expert commonly advised the Owner to press X, Y, A or B on the joystick, rather than 'Push', 'Jump', 'Shoot', 'Run' and so on. In this instance, the physical elements of the technology were referred to, rather than their narrative function within the *Soul Reaver* game. Although the progress of the group illustrated how they were mastering the narrative concept of the game, they showed no evidence of expressing this mastery in talk – at least in the talk that took place during the act of play itself.

This 'regulatory' form of language is characteristic of the kinds of questions and commands that are exchanged between the game and the player, and between players themselves. As we have seen (chapter 6), within social semiotic theory, this is referred to as a 'demand' function. In this sense, the Expert in this group of boys is operating rather like the walkthrough author described in chapter 7. He focuses entirely on the game system, and on instruction, from which his social standing in respect of the game derives.

To some degree, this is inevitable. The visual and auditory fascination of computer games clearly reduces the need for extended face-to-face discussion during play: if the story is unfolding before your eyes, it is perhaps redundant to describe it or even refer to it in any detail. However, consistent with previous research on children's play with toys (Pelligrini and Perlmutter, 1989), the video footage clearly demonstrated how group members' motivation to participate in gameplay led them to focus primarily on developing competence in their interactions with the game system. In attempting to explore the pleasures of the representational dimension of the game, we would need to supplement this kind of observational account, for example, with interview material gathered at a later stage. As Juul (2001: 3) points out, 'games may spawn narratives that a player can use to tell others what went on in a game session'. As we have shown in the case of *Final Fantasy*, these post-play narratives can reveal much more about the narrative fascinations of games and the ways in which narrative considerations undoubtedly do play a part in the immediate act of gameplay.

Conclusions

Research on the development of play has shown that, by adolescence, the majority of recreational activities revolve around a strong need for self-awareness, socialization and communication (Hultsman, 1992; Zarabatny et al., 1990). Socialization, in this instance, has been defined less as *doing* something with others and more as simply *being* together (Hughes, 1999). Like the arcade, the personal console system has revealed itself to be an object around which a group can congregate and interact. However, the evolution of gameplay from coin-operated to home console systems has altered the emphasis from speed of thought and quick reactions to a more strategic style of play – at least in the case of the kinds of games we have been considering here. Thus, in this instance, group play was not only found to be an effective means of advancing through the game, but also a natural constituent in the life cycle of learning to play.

In comparison with solitary play (also recorded and documented by the Owner), the context of group play meant that the individual player was better equipped to identify the relations between the task demands and his existing skills and knowledge derived from practice with the game. In conjunction with psychological models of 'scaffolding', the occurrence of instruction, advice and support within the group enabled the boys to retain sight of the overall goal of the activity. As a form of guided activity, collaborative play also appeared to be more effective than explicit attempts to instruct. Within the study, attempts to instruct the Owner and advance the group's progress were limited to the Expert's attempts to assume control of the joystick. Unlike instruction within activity, demonstration of this kind is often found to be less effective, as it requires the player to break down what is shown into component operations or actions (Wood, 1994).

By attempting to account for the 'social envelope' within which computer gameplay is embedded, our observations have revealed how a one-player game can be transformed into a social activity characterized by effective instruction and communication. Video footage captured an example of 'informal learning' that was embedded within the everyday lived experiences of participants, as distinct from learning that occurs in more formal institutional settings. The study also shows that the players engaged with the agenda set down by game developers in their own fashion, negotiating and developing a shared way of pursuing their interest.

In these respects, the study reinforces the value of theories of 'situated learning' (e.g. Lave and Wenger, 1991). This approach sees knowledge not as an abstract possession, but as a form of competence within a socially valued activity; and it defines knowing as a matter of participating in a 'community of practice' that collectively pursues the activity. Both in the context of online games (chapter 8) and in the everyday social settings described in this chapter, gaming offers a good example of a form of learning that fosters community and identity. The competence that players acquire is configured socially, not only by the industry and the game designers, but also within social practices at all levels of gaming culture. Participation in this culture is negotiable, shaped by differing forms of ownership, expertise and motivation. Our study suggests that collaborative play increases the opportunities for individuals to participate in the practice of this community, by making constructive use of the skills and repertoires of the group members.

Informal, cooperative play of the kind we have outlined is so pervasive within game culture that it surprising to find that it is often ignored by game research. Our study here was fairly exploratory; and it points to the need to develop more systematic ways of conveying the nature and function of social play. Nevertheless, it suggests that we need to take a broader view of interactivity – one that looks beyond the relationship between the player and the screen to take account of the social contexts and relationships that are inherent in so much gameplay.

Agency in and around Play

Gareth Schott

THE notion of 'interactivity' is often used to explain the appeal of computer games. During the experience of play, players often come to feel that their actions are not just orchestrated by the game system, but that they have a considerable degree of power to determine what takes place. For some theorists, this is effectively a political issue: games are seen to offer the player a form of freedom and control that is apparently denied to them by traditional 'mass' media (Aarseth, 2001). Yet to what extent is this merely an illusion? Players may be engaging in a great deal of *activity* as they play, but to what extent do they really possess *agency* – that is, the power to control and determine the meanings and pleasures that they experience?

In this chapter, we will be exploring questions of agency and inter-activity through a case study of players' engagements with a console action adventure game. On the face of it, such games present a more structured mode of play and storytelling than the online games and RPGs we have considered in earlier chapters – and hence, perhaps, fewer opportunities for active engagement. Yet it is important to distinguish between the different kinds of 'activity' and 'agency' that may be at stake in different types of gameplay. Rafaeli (1998), for example, makes a useful distinction between *declarative* communication, where a source sets the agenda and receives no (or only indirect) feedback, and *reactive* and *interactive* modes of communication. Reactive communication involves bilateral interaction, while interactive communication is an iterative, ongoing process that leads to jointly produced meaning.

If we apply this to action adventure games, it would seem that they are more appropriately seen as 'reactive' rather than 'interactive': play is a bilateral process by which one side (either player or game) responds to the other. Meaning is not jointly produced, since the choices available to the player – for example, in respect of character development, goals or outcomes – are, to a greater or lesser extent, already circumscribed. For example, in console action adventure games it is frequently the case that character development occurs within the context of animated cutscenes. Often used as rewards for the completion of a level, cutscenes may not reflect the manner in which the end point has been achieved. More broadly, the essential dynamic of the game is one in which the player follows directions, and the game system provides a limited set of opportunities for the production of events. Although the structure of the game allows for different ways of fulfilling its potential, progress and movement is very much guided, pre-structured and moulded by the game's developers.

Nevertheless, it remains to be seen whether this account really captures the nature of the player's experience. In particular, it may fail to account for the way that the human mind of the player is not just 'reactive' but generative, creative, proactive and reflective. As Janet Murray (2000) argues, it is the subjective experience of 'agency' that players seem to desire from their engagement with gameplay: they need to feel that they have exerted power or control over events. To this extent, we might conceive of gameplay as arising from the interplay between a sense of agency and the requirements of the game system – an interplay that operates in different ways at different points in the game.

Focusing on agency, then, implies that the player does more than simply respond to stimulation, but also explores and manipulates the environment and seeks to influence it. In this respect, gameplay may be no different from many other areas of human activity. It is a regulated activity, governed by the boundaries of social and physical environments, but equally in real life we live in environments that place constraints on our behaviours. Many human transactions involve 'inducements' to behave in particular ways, but, as in games, these do not always succeed in determining what happens. Likewise, gameplayers may seek to accommodate themselves to the game's rules and objectives, but they may also seek to exercise control and behave otherwise.

Albert Bandura (2001) employs a model of agency that extends conventional understandings of direct *personal* agency to also account for *proxy* agency and *collective* agency. Proxy agency is a socially mediated form of agency, in which the individual makes use of the mediating effects of others with the necessary resources or expertise in order to secure a desired outcome: one of the most obvious manifestations of this in relation to games would be the use of walkthroughs. Meanwhile, *collective* agency reflects the fact that certain outcomes are only achievable through socially interdependent efforts – as, for example, in the creation of a shared 'fan culture' that may extend well beyond the game itself (see chapter 7). Applying this model to console gaming allows us to account, not just for the complex, multidimensional nature of some players' personal engagement with games, but also for players' collective participation in the wider fan community, and their use of games as a basis for creative practices of many kinds.

Entering the Oddworld

Released by the developers Oddworld Inhabitants in 1997, *Abe's Oddysee* was the first game in what became the 'Oddworld Quintology'. The main character/avatar is Abe (see Illustration 12), a Mudokon (Moo-DOCK-un) who begins the game as an ignorant and happy floor-waxer working in the meat-packing plant 'RuptureFarms'. However, Abe's introductory narrative tells us that his bosses, the Glukkons, have exhausted all the meat reserves in the local ecosystem for their meat products ('Meech Mynchies', 'Paramite Pies' and 'Scrab Cakes'). To his horror, Abe has come to learn that the solution to the Glukkons' dilemma is to use their Mudokon workforce as the main ingredient in their new range of meat products ('New and Tasty'). The game's intro-duction ends with Abe fleeing for his life, issuing a plea to higher forces to 'get me outta here!' Before he can free himself, it is Abe's destiny and the aim of the game to sabotage 'RuptureFarms' and secure the release of as many of his ninety-nine co-workers as possible.

The popularity and success of *Abe's Oddysee* subsequently led to the release of a bonus game (rather than sequel), *Abe's Exoddus*, the follow-ing year. The bonus game allowed its developers to extend many aspects of gameplay found in the first game and also address some of its shortcomings (introducing a 'quick save' feature, and decreasing the need to use screen death as a problem-solving strategy). Following the saviour of the Mudokon workers in *Abe's Oddysee*, the spirits of dead Mudokons now need Abe's help. The spirits reveal that, although altru-istic and heroic, his actions in the first game have had severe reper-cussions. It is revealed that the Glukkons were also using Mudokon bones as a key ingredient in their ultra-addictive beverage SoulStorm brew. However, since the destruction of their sister company RuptureFarms, the Glukkons' supply of bones to the SoulStorm brew-ery has subsequently dried up. Now the Glukkons are digging up the bones of the Mudokon dead, disturbing their spirits. The inevitable subversive acts follow and Abe's reputation as the former 'employee of the month' is further soiled.

Oddworld Inhabitants have always possessed a clear vision for the evolution of their franchise. This was evident from the way they mapped out their quintology from the outset. Likewise, *Abe's Oddysee* and *Abe's Exoddus* were released as '2.5D' games when most others were working in 3-D. The level of technology at that point (PSX, 120MHZ PC) was not considered sufficient to handle the vision that Oddworld Inhabitants possessed for their game universe in 3-D. Lorne Lanning, co-founder of Oddworld Inhabitants, stated that: 'We won't do real time 3-D and compromise art, animation, or charm.' Lanning (2002) has also expressed an intention that each Oddysee game will be accompanied by

Illustration 12   Abe (right) interacts with a fellow Mudokon. Image courtesy of
Oddworld Inhabitants, Inc.

a major technological leap in gaming hardware: thus, the second game
in the quintology, *Munch's Oddysee*, shifted from the Playstation to the
superior processing power of the Xbox.

   Unusual for a character/avatar in a console action adventure game,
Abe's strength lies in his agility, versatility, humour and ability to interact with other characters, either directly through 'gamespeak®' or
through his ability to possess and embody other characters. Likewise,
the Mudokons pass through a range of collective and individual
predicaments (enslaved, dependent or incapacitated) and emotions
(angry, wired or depressed). The game series also delineates the depth
of Oddworld with its ever-expanding cast of characters (Sligs, Scrabs,
Paramites, Fleeches, Slurgs, Slogs, Greeters and Glukkons) and detailed
landscape environments (factories, temples, forests, vaults and mines).
The game has a distinct cinematic feel, not only in its rich landscapes
but also in its mood-sensitive soundtrack and seamless cutscenes.
Indeed, *Abe's Exoddus* received the honour of being the first video game
to gain an Oscar Nomination for 'Best Short Animation'.

   In terms of the generic attributes outlined in chapter 2, the games
reflect a range of influences. In the case of the character of Abe, for
instance, the green colour of his skin can be traced back to the traditions of comic-book and sci-fi iconography. In combination with the
bulbous eyes, gleaming bald skull and skinny body, Abe's skin colour

references a particular vision of the alien. These features originally signified menace and strangeness, as in the figure of the Mekon in the Dan Dare cartoons of the British *Eagle* in the fifties and sixties. However, with growing familiarity, the image of the 'little green man' has arguably become an affectionate stereotype with almost comic properties. The evocation of this figure in contemporary popular media thus produces a mixture of strange, magical qualities and a familiar, almost pet-like appeal, as in Dobby the House-Elf in *Harry Potter and the Chamber of Secrets* or Gollum in the *Lord of the Rings* trilogy of films. In both cases, the figure of the hairless, bug-eyed creature is also seen as enslaved, Dobby to the wicked Lucius Malfoy, Gollum to the power of the Ring. Both are in need of emancipation, at the hands of Harry Potter and Frodo Baggins respectively. These meanings are also imported, with the image, into the Abe narrative. Abe also begins life as a slave, along with the Mudokons in general, and his quest is for emancipation, albeit through his own agency in this case.

However, Abe consists of more than just an image – he is an animated and interactive character, with sounds as well as visual properties. His most celebrated sound is a powerful fart. The meaning of this element may have its origins not in the popular comic strip but in cult fanzines such as the US publication *Mad* magazine or the UK's *Viz*, which includes in its pantheon of scatological anti-heroes the character Johnny Fartpants.

Although there are potentially many other references in the iconography of Abe's world, these two make the point that quite different cultural worlds are being invoked. The cultural world of Dan Dare, Harry Potter and Frodo Baggins all have quite sober heroic aspirations, and can be located in traditions of popular narrative reaching back to the quest-based sagas of medieval Romance literature and folk tale. By contrast, the popular culture of *Mad* and *Viz* is essentially anti-heroic. Its social function is directly oppositional and subversive. Like the Rabelaisian practices of Bakhtin's (1968) carnival, it operates to upset the pomposity and arrogance of official culture, to displace it and substitute its own defiantly grotesque version of authority, if only for a day. What we get with Abe, then, is a curious mixture of the two. We have something of the seriousness and heroism of the quest-sage, as Abe struggles for the liberation of the Mudokon slaves, but also something of the subversive irreverence and grotesque humour of the carnival anti-hero.

In addition to these artistic dimensions, Oddworld Inhabitants have also emphasized the strong ethical and moral issues that underline the game's narrative and drive its characters. Indeed, Lanning (2002: 2) has commented that Oddworld's 'characters are driven in a way that is fired by larger issues'. The basic situation and objectives of the game clearly reflect concerns about the environment (food safety, pollution, unregulated industrial growth) and, more broadly, about a rapacious and exploitative form of modern capitalism. Lanning, Oddworld's creator and designer, has explicitly expressed his desire to 'inject' ecological dilemmas into a package that players can interact with, and ultimately overcome. Thus, despite its fantastical setting, the game mobilizes broader political motivations that have a strong contemporary relevance.

Researching player agency

The data presented in this chapter focus on the contributions that fans of the games make to the discussion lists, Oddworld Forums (<www.oddworldforums.net>). The forums facilitate a variety of discussion topics that are divided between Zulag 1, 2 and 3 (drawing on the factory zones found within RuptureFarms). The whole site currently (early 2004) has 2,437 members who have amongst them contributed 9,864 threads and 164,933 posts – numbers that grow every day. Within Zulag 1 there are three discussion forums, the 'General Oddworld Discussion' devoted to speculation about upcoming games, queries, theory building and general enhancement of Oddworld knowledge and trivia (51,222 posts). *Proxy* agency is achieved by players of the Oddworld games through the 'Spoiler Forum' (2,625 posts) that addresses the narrative direction of future games, and 'Oddworld Help' (2,468 posts) in which technical support and advice is offered to fans continuing to play the games. Within Zulag 2, members can also offer feedback on the running of the forum within 'Forum Suggestion and Help' (5,671 posts). Additionally, members may engage in 'Off-topic Discussion', which constitutes the most popular communication forum (79,733 posts): in this space, friendships are formed and cemented. *Collective* agency is particularly apparent in the remaining forums. 'Oddworld RPG' (6,025 posts) represents an ongoing text-based RPG game that expands upon Oddworld Inhabitants' original concept and allows fans to transport themselves into the environments of Oddworld. Finally, there is the 'Fan Corner' forum in which those who enjoy writing fan fiction and making fan art converge (15,089 posts).

The collective nature of this overall endeavour is also clearly shown by the fact that contributors to the forum environment take responsibility for its governance. Fans are elevated to supervisory positions, maintaining the etiquette of online communication. They steer discussions and contributions into acceptable realms, sanctioning those who attempt to violate the ethical or political 'values' of the game; and they encourage participants to contribute in ways that are mutually supportive rather than destructive.

Analysing some of these thousands of contributions – particularly to the general discussion board and the fan corner – provides us with some concrete instances of the three forms of agency identified in Bandura's model, outlined above. In the discussion that follows, we refer to the online nicknames of the contributors in italics. The postings we discuss were all made between April 2001 and October 2003, and are reproduced *verbatim*.

Personal agency

As we have noted, the concept of agency conventionally refers to the ways in which people make things happen, or influence events, through exercising some element of personal control. Agency, then, involves *intentionality*: it is not just a matter of expecting or predicting future events, but also of intervening proactively in order to bring them about. Computer games invite the player to act in and on the material world, traversing gateways to unseen territories that set in motion a chain of uncertain events. Such actions are performed with the intention that they will lead to desired outcomes, but they can also produce outcomes that are neither intended nor wanted.

By not featuring the 'quick save' option, that allows the player to return to an 'opted for' point in the game that guarantees their efforts up to that point are retained in the event of screen death, the first Oddworld game, *Abe's Oddysee*, would often lead to unintentional outcomes. The first game contains alternate endings, depending upon whether the player follows one of the key objectives of the game: the rescue of ninety-nine Mudokons from the RuptureFarms meat-packing factory. When leading Mudokons to safety it is necessary to prioritize and order how obstacles are cleared, whether you clear them first ('stay here') or take the Mudokon with you ('follow me'). This decision can sometimes lead to the loss of the Mudokon to automated chainsaws, falling objects, bombs or beatings from overzealous Sligs. Although screen death enables the player (as Abe) to replay the same events over and over, it does not bring back perished Mudokons. Despite their best intentions, the player has ostensibly sent the very individuals they are supposed to be liberating to their deaths.

Yet, as we have noted, games also offer degrees of freedom that give the player the power to make desired game events materialize and unfold. In the case of *Abe's Oddysee*, the player has the power to originate actions in order to 'ensure that all the lost brothers in the corporate grinder are liberated' (as *Sad Mudokon* puts it). However, agency is also adaptable (Bratman, 1999): as initial intentions are partially met through action, so they are adjusted, revised or even reconsidered in the face of new information – including materials embedded within the game text itself. As *Silversnow* comments: 'It's not just a regular game . . . It's a world, with possibilities for you and itself.'

The Oddworld fan forums provide many indications of the ways in which players monitor their behaviour during gameplay and seek to exercise personal agency. Thus, there are discussions of dormant actions and capabilities at the disposal of players, in which a different set of performances can be unearthed that sit alongside the expected standards of competencies set by the game designers. An example of this can be found in such acts as 'Meep flipping':

> you can make a Meep flip over on its back he he . . . They sort of squirm around before they get up. Its kind of weird. You have to throw or move one to the wall . . . in order to make them flip upside down. (*Paramiteabe*)

Pinkgoth is another fan who has used the forums to express this kind of pleasure in playing with the minor characters that Abe can possess and control. Many of these creatures are more primitive than Abe and wild in nature. The ability to possess such creatures allows Abe to reposition them and avoid attack as he passes through different landscapes. These characters offer little contribution to the environmental activism driving the game's aims. However, *Pinkgoth* provides this rationale: 'My favorite creature is the most savage: the scrab. For me, the scrab is a symbol of nature's power, which mirrors itself in my life philosophy, one of the instinct and the carnal.' Taking into account the expanse covered by the leading character's odyssey, the game offers *Pinkgoth* very little opportunity to engage with Oddworld as a scrab, yet this is still identified as a key pleasure in engaging with the game world. Similarly, *Fazerina* argues that the 'non-important stuff like farting (well, it is VERY important) and your buddies' [Mudokons'] reactions to it are just plain fun.☺'

Fans also show a deep appreciation for the space of Oddworld and the design and movement of its characters. As *Xavier* states, 'the games are incredibly rich. Thousand of details in each screen. Stop and look at the picture, it's really beatifull [*sic*].' Likewise, *TyA* uses the desire to explore Mudos (the continent in which *Abe's Oddysee* and *Munch's Oddysee* are set) as an explanation, arguing that 'every screen has a personal beauty to it'. *Lampion*, a Brazilian fan, argues that, 'the levels of the game are so detailed and complex in appearance, thus creating an increasing sense of expectancy and curiosity about what comes next'. And the importance of the communicative function of 'space' is reinforced by *Dequibenzo*, who states:

> Oddworld reminds us of what it takes to make a classic story, no matter what the medium. You have to create your world, truly make it real for

yourself, then, when you let visitors in, engage them . . . A true story-teller creates the universe and uses the story to explore it, and that is exactly what OWI [Oddworld Inhabitants] have done.

Fans' interest and engagement in the game is also sparked by the storyline, which is essentially a critique of the profiteering of capitalist industrialists. The potential of games as an opening for debating wider political issues can be found in *Scrubs'* question to the fan forum: 'I was just interested to know how many people on this board started recy-cling, and supporting charities such as WWF [World Wildlife Fund] to try and save animals and their habitats that have been around much longer than we have?' Here, perhaps, we see an extension of the notion of agency beyond the game itself and the goals defined by its develop-ers, reflecting the potential role of the game as an incentive for actions in the real world. Other contributions to this discussion thread high-light this political impact of the game upon players:

> Yes, we're all Khanzumerz really, our lives depend on the products and services of companies and corporations . . . I'm definitely against mate-rialism and commercialisation . . . it really sickens me the way holidays are converted into, and even created as, selling points . . . I'm positive that growing up with Oddworld over the last few impressionable years has helped make me aware . . . and for that I'm really grateful. (*Max the Mug*)

> Oddworld totally changed me! I suddenly realized the hell we put the African Americans through and the Indians through way back before the Civil War. I had made the connection between Mudokon slaves and Tainos or African American slaves. (*Slig Hunter 72*)

Other players' comments on the forums reflect this sense of the rele-vance of the Oddworld universe to the contemporary world: as *Sad Mudokon* states, Oddworld is a 'universe, akin to our very own, appeal-ing to a sense of understanding, our grasp of the excessive, merciless theologies behind the corporate system. The industrialists represent to us what is real.'

As these contributions suggest – and as we have maintained at several points in earlier chapters – players' engagement with a game can take many forms. Despite the strong narrative objective – the salvation of Abe's fellow-workers – *Abe's Oddysee* can be read on several levels, visually, emotionally and thematically. The world can be explored at will, and seemingly incidental details or characters are made the subject of play 'for its own sake'. Although these choices and potentials are all encoded within the game system and the visual design of the game, it clearly permits forms of personal agency during the activity of play that are not confined to the achievement of a singu-lar objective.

Proxy agency

As we have noted, games resemble the real world in that individuals do not always have direct control over the conditions and practices that affect their actions. Just as in real life, few people possess the time, energy and resources necessary to master every realm of their activities. Under such conditions, Bandura (2001) argues that individuals can employ a socially mediated form of agency, which he calls *proxy* agency: they try, by one means or another, to enlist those who have access to resources or expertise to act at their behest in order to help them secure the outcomes they desire. We saw some clear examples of this in the previous chapter, where players collaborated on gameplay; and this kind of function is also apparent in a more mediated way through online message boards.

An obvious example of proxy agency can be found in players' production and use of walkthroughs. As we saw in chapter 7, walkthroughs retrace the successful strategies employed by someone who has successfully completed a game. Although gaming magazines produce hints and cheats for players, more instant and comprehensive walkthroughs are produced by gameplayers online. However, the Oddworld fan forums also reveal other less chronicled examples of proxy agency.

One of the most contested debates amongst gameplayers is the role of non-interactive animated cutscenes. Within console games like *Abe's Oddysee*, cutscenes are typically used at the end of a level to introduce turning points in the narrative. Some players feel cutscenes detract from the gameplay experience, enforcing particular versions of the game (from the developer's perspective) that may contradict the way the player has conducted him or herself and engaged with the character up to that point. Yet, for fans of Oddworld, this does not appear to be the case, as *Sad Mudokon* argues:

> I played for the cutscenes, for the elaboration on the world, and for insights into the personality of the characters. They were and are a key element of the Oddworld phenomenon.

Likewise, *Lampion* also articulates the importance of cutscenes:

> the cutscenes of the games are as important as the actual game, because they create the storyline, and portray the characters in such a deep and detailed way that it otherwise couldn't be achieved through gameplay.

Here we see the perception of cutscenes not only as a reward for successful play, but also a means of accessing the official narrative, as players shift between parallel storylines.

Within the context of the game, developers avoid accounting for all objects and artefacts contained within its environment. In creating a complex and extensive world, Oddworld Inhabitants have included

detailed ecosystems and landscapes distinguishable by their relationship with nature and the technologies that are utilized. As a
Mudokon, Abe is a member of an ecologically admirable race that lives
in respectful balance with the land. Players enter the story after the
point of breakdown in the natural order. The game thus seeks a route
back to a communion with nature and the acceptance of a philosophy
of a new environmental order free from industrial oppressors. In the
process, players witness and experience species that have been taken out
of their natural habitat by the Glukkons and either put to work, experimented upon or used as ingredients in their food and drink products. As
Abe escapes the confines of the factory grounds, he moves through
lands that offer a glimpse of the past. He passes through vaults, mines
and temples that contain wall paintings, carvings and discarded tools
and technologies that offer players hints of a pre-history. In this way, the
developers present players with historical and cultural 'gaps' that they
are able to fill in. As *TyA* states, 'the mystery of Oddworld remains, and
it's the mystery that means most to me.' One of the functions of the fan
forums, then, is to provide theoretical explanations and accounts of the
various species' biological evolution, lifestyle and traditions.

The discussion thread entitled 'Vykkers Feet' is typical of the theoretical discussions in which fans engage. Here we see *The Khanzumer*
beginning the thread with a query about the anatomical accuracy of
the Vykkers, given their backstory:

> Vykkers were originally tree dwelling creature right? Well, to me at
> least, it doesn't seem like they have very good means of doing this
> (climbing trees) . . . I think the stitches on their legs are the result of
> them amputating their other arms. I think that their three 'legs' used
> to be their primary limbs for climbing. But they were terrible for walk-
> ing on the ground . . . What do you guys think?

This thread generated fifty-eight posts by twenty-two fans over a period
of seven days. During the course of the discussion, it is suggested that
the stitches resemble a self-inflicted modification to deal with a change
of environment or that the creatures possess a masochistic nature.
Ultimately, it is established that Vykkers reproduce themselves, 'similar to stickbugs from Australia that do the same thing' (according to
Mac the Janitor). What we see here is a consensual process of establishing
a backstory, a history prior to the current storyline. This practice
involves proxy agency, as players subsequently refer to the outcomes of
such discussions as established knowledge; but it also entails collective
agency, as players collectively construct meanings that go beyond those
contained in the game itself. As *TyA* demonstrates:

> I've . . . read very interesting theories about the moons of Oddworld,
> as well as a theory that Oddworld might be a moon itself. Theories

regarding the time before Glukkons [the industrialists] . . . theories regarding how the gender of Mudokons could not be perhaps 100% male but female instead.

Collective agency: fan production

The practice of fan production – fan art and writing – is perhaps the most obvious example of collective agency, although it also reflects elements of proxy agency as well. Artwork produced by fans might be regarded by those with a negative view of the cultural value of games as derivative, mechanistic, superficial and facile – particularly when compared with the traditional view of art as original, individual and based in hard-won craft skills. Behind the smooth surface of the digital aesthetic, however, all games contain a design phase rooted in traditional craft skills. Japanese games are well known for having designs based on the elaborate paintings of their concept artists; and Oddworld is no different. The official website is at pains to emphasize the hundreds of iterations of pencil sketches of Abe, and presents some of them on the site. Here we see how the old, individual craft technologies of the hand and pencil sit alongside the digital modelling of animated characters and interactive worlds. Fans who produce artwork and submit it to the forums for comment and reaction engage with these same practices and values in their own tributes.

Exhibitors of fan art on the forum explore the aesthetic concepts of Oddworld through the manipulation of different materials and processes (e.g. pencil sketches, inked illustrations, puppets, plasticine models, computer-edited montages and original art). In doing so, fans publicly refine and control their use of art tools and techniques, and evaluate their own and others' work, alongside the lessons they learn from Oddworld Inhabitants' artists and designers. Indeed, the artistic practice engaged in by contributors to the Oddworld Forums could be compared with the apprenticeship practices of Renaissance studios, in their admiration of the master-practitioners of cartoon, manga and digital art, and in their diligent attention to graphic techniques that are often surprisingly traditional. Consider, for example, this advice from *Paramiteabe* about how to do pencil drawings based on a kind of brassrubbing technique:

> It's not that hard after you know what the type of method is used it's quite easy. Anyone can do it and it involved outlining the photograph. All you do is get a photograph of anything black and white. Take a pencil and just scribble on the back of the photograph. Turn it over and outline the image on the photograph onto the paper don't press hard.

You will altimatically get a line because you scribbled on the back of the photograph you will get a line of the image transfered altimaticallly to the paper. In other words your traceing it. Then altimatically you have the shape. The only thing you do now is fill in the tones of darks and lights by only using small line strokes. That's it its that simple . . . and believe it or not Concept artist are aloud to trace when its the right time. So trace and that will be great.

Examination of forum members' responses to submitted work also reveals the common use of 'industry standard' (as indicative of career potential in the game industry) as the highest form of compliment offered to exhibitors of artwork. For example, in response to the artwork of *Tybie_odd* and *Red Muse*, *Splat* declares: 'Wow those pics are really great! You should all become desighners for computer characters! You'd make millions a year!' Similarly, comparisons to Oddworld artists and other artists (for non-Oddworld art and literature) also characterize a well-received and highly acclaimed submission to the forum. Again, the approving *Splat*, this time in a different thread, is the thirteenth person to respond to the work of *Canned Gabbiar*, exclaiming:

> WOW! Those were brilliant! I laughed, I cried, I stared in awe at your pure artistic genius! No exaduration! I'm being solely truthful when I say that you should take up a job as a character designer for Oddworld! You'd get the job, no competition. Honestly, I just applied your fuzzles [game characters] as my wallpaper! Brilliant!

Here exhibitors are receiving direct and immediate reinforcement from an audience that is deeply entrenched in the visual design of the game. Members' duty to support and encourage both new and experienced artists and writers submitting work to the forum is illustrated by forum moderator *Al the Vykker*, who interrupted a long and exclusive thread communication with a request that members 'try to be fair and go and read other peoples' work and artwork also, instead of just going to one in here. I suggest that most people around FC [fan corner] try and be a bit more attentive and give some other artists . . . feedback.'

When praise turns to advice, thread posts are tender in their approach to dispensing constructive criticism. In no threads were posts unearthed in which any member excessively denigrated the contribution of another member's art. For example, when *Dipstikk* submitted work under the title 'Abe art' (see Illustration 13), *Sligslinger* commented: 'Nice drawings . . . keep up the good work, ps: may I suggest u make Abe look less elfish.' *Dipstikk* acknowledges this critique, conceding 'Yeah, the ears were a problem. I forgot that they were immobile, plastered to the side of the head.' Meanwhile, after praising *Dipstikk*,

Illustration 13   'Abe Art' by Dipstikk that stimulated discussion of appropriate materials for presentation of work and the anatomical accuracy of his depiction of Abe. Image courtesy of Oddworld Forums.

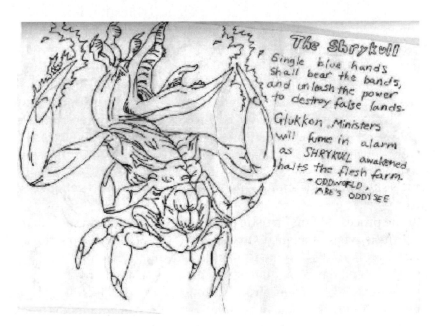

Illustration 14   Depiction of a Shrykull, a powerful force that transforms Abe and permits him to defeat those who have exploited his people. Image courtesy of Oddworld Forums.

Alector focuses on standards of presentation and materials for exhibiting art in the thread:

> But notice: Drawings look <u>much</u> better when you draw them on white non-lined paper. The lines disturb the pencil drawings a lot. The . . . picture with the yellow background looks good [Illustration 13]. It shows the power of the Shrykull. The havoc and the danger of it. The poem gives the drawing a mysterious touch.

In line with the emphasis here on collective agency, an influential thread on the forum entitled 'Share Your Artwork Tips' begins with a statement by *One, Two, Middlesboogie* which reads: 'Among true artists, there are no secrets. Pooling our knowledge can only make us better, so share the secrets of your success.' The thread provides comprehensive tips on pencil drawing, pastels, inking and computer-colouring techniques, a guide to buying art supplies as well as links to other web-based art tutorials (e.g. by computer artist Kristen Perry) and texts (e.g. Andy Smith's 2002 text, *Drawing Dynamic Comics*).

It is also not uncommon for sketches to be redrawn or altered in line with feedback. Here the text is regarded as a process, as unfinished business, rather than a static object, which can be collectively transformed, adapted and reworked. Likewise, it is not uncommon for fans to employ/commission other fans to illustrate their fan fiction: input and feedback is expected from the author(s) and the readers of the fan fiction as to the appropriateness of the graphical illustrations. *Tybie_odd* provides a good example of this in his work, which he posted in the form of four character pictures titled 'Work at Rupture Farms', based on characters created by other fans in the text-based Role Play forum. In the case of one character, a Glukkon named 'Arnie', *Dripik*, the creator of that character, comments that despite appreciating the work, there was 'maybe one thing: I imagined smaller shoulder pads for Arnie'. In response, *Tybie_odd* is happy to oblige and accurately realize the creator's mental image of Arnie: 'YAY! They like them! Now I am encouraged to do Otto [another fan-created character] Coming right up, dripik! I changed Arnie's shoulder pads smaller, I post the new pic when I get done with Otto.'

In the process of fans' artistic production, then, we can see elements of all these types of agency. On one level, the postings show the anxiety, stress and risks attached to acts of personal agency and the cultivation of personal competencies. Fans make use of proxy agency by supporting and learning from each other's feedback, advice and expertise. And this is clearly a collective process, in which fans feed off each other's work (sometimes across different media), and work together to set standards for their own production practices. To some degree, of course, all this activity remains within the terms laid down by the original creators of the Oddworld; yet it also extends and goes beyond it in several ways.

Conclusion

Henry Jenkins's work on fan communities provides several illustrations of the tensions and power struggles that may emerge between media producers and their audiences over the 'ownership' of a particular text or symbolic world (Jenkins, 1992). For example, fans strongly resisted attempts by Lucasfilm Ltd to maintain the PG-rated world of *Star Wars* and censor fan-fiction that engaged its characters in 'pornography'. By contrast, Oddworld fans appear to honour their role as representatives of the game brand; they are rarely critical of – in fact, they often celebrate – the stock Oddworld universe. Although we do not have evidence to this effect, it is also very likely that the forums function as a means of market research for the developers, providing them with insights into the appeal of the games and possibly even suggesting likely future lines of development.

Of course, it would be a mistake to romanticize this, or to see it as evidence of a radical democratization of cultural production. By and large, the producers still define the terms and parameters within which players' agency is exercised. Nevertheless, as we have shown, gameplay to some extent *depends upon* and *requires* a positive experience of agency on the part of the player; and the forms this agency takes may be different in several respects when compared with older media such as television. At the very least, we can say that a focus on the agency of the player should lead us to re-evaluate popular assumptions about what a game is, who produces it and by what means.

Film, Adaptation and Computer Games

Diane Carr with Diarmid Campbell and Katie Ellwood

IN John Carpenter's 1982 film *The Thing*, an isolated Antarctic research community is infiltrated and gradually annihilated by a voracious shape-shifting alien. The film was based on 'Who Goes There?' – a short story by John W. Campbell published in 1938,[1] and filmed as *The Thing from Another World* in 1951. The scientists discover an apparently dead alien frozen in ice. Once defrosted, the alien goes on the rampage. The creature has the ability to mimic other life forms. This enables it to infiltrate the research team. Unable to tell which of their companions are still human, the team begins to disintegrate.

In 2002 a computer game sequel to Carpenter's film, also titled *The Thing*, was released by the London-based Computer Artworks.[2] Computer games have rules and chance, and they are played – the player plots events and interacts with objects in the game world. This means that even if a game shares a title, a setting, a villain and generic features with a movie, there will be marked differences in the experience offered by each. As this implies, considering the adaptation of *The Thing* from film to game involves revisiting questions of genre (horror, in this case), and looking again at the relationship between the ludic and the representational within a particular game. In this chapter this relationship is examined from the perspective of game development and design, rather than the player. This was made possible through the involvement of Diarmid Campbell, *The Thing's* lead game programmer, and Katie Ellwood, a games producer and writer with a professional interest in cinematic and story-driven computer games.[3]

Computer games based on feature films (and filmed versions of computer games) have become common over the past two decades. Some games, such as *Star Wars* (1983) make no attempt to add to the narrative of their source. Instead, the game is 'a three-dimensional space shoot-'em-up which abstracted elements from certain battle scenes in the film and turned them into simple game objectives' (Poole, 2000: 88). Other games, such as *Enter the Matrix* (2003) arguably prioritize the source material (the *Matrix* film franchise, in this case) at the expense of playability, with uneven results (Carr, 2006). As this implies, movie and game tie-ins are diverse in approach. They also vary a great deal in quality. In this chapter the discussion will be limited to one particular adaptation, rather than the phenomenon in general.

Horror – from film to game

As Patrick Crogan (2000) has pointed out, Carpenter's film is a generic hybrid (science fiction and horror), and it stars a monster that is the ultimate hybrid – an endlessly adaptive and apparently indiscriminate consumer. The game is also a generic amalgam – it is an adaptation of a film (that itself incorporates material from a previous film and an earlier short story). Additionally, *The Thing* borrows characteristics from a range of different computer game genres. It incorporates elements of First Person Shooters and RPGs, and fuses these varied parts into an action adventure 'horror-survival' whole.

Prior to discussing the production of *The Thing*, it would be pertinent to investigate the relationship between horror movies and computer games in general. As Tanya Krzywinska writes in 'Hands-On Horror', the 'horror genre has made the transition to video games for a number of reasons. Horror offers death as spectacle and actively promises transgression; it has the power to promote physical sensation, and the genre appeals to the youth market that is central to the games industry' (2002: 207). For Krzywinska, the interactive nature of gameplay amplifies the dynamics of generic horror, including patterns of passivity, peril, attack and flight. By switching between gameplay and cutscene, games are able to 'intensify an awareness of the dynamic between *being in control* and *out of control*' (2002: 215, emphasis in original).

Both the game and the film of *The Thing* are horror, and both feature monstrous 'things' that blur the divide between human flesh and alien otherness. Transgressive, all-consuming monsters are common in horror. The power of these fearsome hybrids has been analysed using the notion of 'abjection', a concept developed by psychoanalytic philosopher Julia Kristeva. According to Kristeva, abjection involves disturbing phenomena that cross or threaten the borders that are necessary to our sense of self. The abject evades categorization, thwarts clarity, undermines order and undoes differentiation.[4] A corpse, for instance, is 'the utmost of abjection. It is death infecting life. Abject. It is something rejected from which . . . one cannot protect oneself as from an object' (1982: 4).

Film theorists have used the notion of the abject to probe horror and science-fiction cinema. Barbara Creed (1990), for instance, applied it to the 'Monstrous-Feminine' in the 1979 film, *Alien*. Films including *The Thing*, or *Shivers* (1976) offer viewers repellent monsters that skip and lurch over the border from one form to another, from one sex or species to another; aliens that are sticky, who leak profusely, who reduce human beings to snacks, or egg incubators. These horrific creations are compelling and repulsive by turn, thanks to their power to disregard the divisions between the internal and the external, between the self and others, or between life and death.

Carol Clover has written about the ways in which horror movies and their rowdy audiences hark back to pre-cinematic forms of entertainment. Generic horror relies on its viewers' 'knowing consumption'. These films make a virtue out of a formula. As such, horror movies have strong ties to folkloric practices. Generic horror bears 'all the hallmarks of oral narrative: the free exchange of themes and motifs, the archetypal characters and situations, the accumulation of sequels, remakes and imitations. This is a field where there is in some sense no original, no real or right text, but only variants' (Clover, 1992: 11). What this reiteration suggests, argues Clover, is that the rendition or performance of the formula (who gets killed where, in what order, and by what means, for instance) is more important than innovation for its own sake. This emphasis on performance, constraint and repetition is reminiscent of gaming, and avatars, as we argued in chapter 6, in some ways resemble the heroes of oral narrative.

For *The Thing*'s developers, showing humans turning into thing-monsters involved using computer animation techniques. As Diarmid Campbell explained, 'our people were built up out of skinned components (arms, legs, heads, etc.). So we used a combination of changing the underlying bone hierarchy, and scaling different bones, particle effects and swapping components in and out to create the transformation.' In the fifties' film version, 'the alien is finally revealed to be nothing more than (an actor) dressed up in a monster suit and rampaging through the camp as only a man in a monster suit can do' (Billson, 1997: 16). The monster-thing in Carpenter's movie is made up of 'clay, foam latex, metal machinery, cabling, heated Bubble Yum gum, strawberry jelly, mayonnaise, cream corn, melted crayons and food thickener' (Crogan, 2000: 3). The horror of Carpenter's film is loud, visceral and gooey. Despite the comparative cleanliness of the digital processes that underlie monstrous transformation in the game, it is still possible to find parallels between horror films and gaming that involve the body.

The ability of Carpenter's movie to produce sensations of shock, revulsion or fear in the viewer has been analysed by film theorists, including Linda Williams (1999). Williams, in fact, singled out three film genres with a propensity for evoking physical sensations. Porn, horror and 'weepies' are associated with low cultural status, youth, women, marginality or deviance. Sensory rather than cerebral, these films promise their audiences quite specific embodied experiences, and they will be judged successful according to whether they deliver, respectively, sexual arousal, fear or tears.

These 'body genres' involve excesses that are gratuitous, that go beyond any narrative function. Yet, as Williams argues, to describe these excesses as gratuitous is actually to miss the point, because overflow and sensation are the stated purpose of these films.[5] The reactive and physical nature of gameplay (and the lowly cultural status of computer games themselves) suggests affinities between film horror as a body genre, and certain computer games. Computer gaming is physical, on a number of levels. Scary games provoke sensations of fear. The player must trigger the avatar's gestures and movements, and guide it through space, which implies a particular, embodied symbiosis – plus there is the player's tactile manipulation of the game controls.

Williams argues that 'fantasies are not, as is sometimes thought, wish-fulfilling linear narratives of mastery and control leading to closure and the attainment of desire. They are marked, rather, by the prolongation of desire, and by the lack of fixed positions with respect to the objects and events fantasised' (1999: 711). The continuing salience of these fantasies explains their enduring popularity – they are 'a cultural form of problem solving' (1999: 710). Williams attributes various temporalities to the three forms of fantasy associated with body genres. While pornography is described as 'on time', and melodrama is cast as 'too late', the temporality of horror is 'too early!' This anxiety is characteristic of (but not limited to) adolescence, and corresponds to fantasies of being caught out, exposed or ambushed.

The idea that horror fantasies involve the compulsive reworking of a 'problem' recalls computer games' capacity for repetition. Repetition in *The Thing* occurs at the level of task and mission (opening doors, locating keys and codes, accessing rooms), as well as in confrontations with the various monster-things. The things in the game are an array of variations on a theme. Toothy, tentacled, bi-pedal or quadruped, the monsters spawn in dark corners and wait behind doors; they burst out of live teammates, or bubble out of corpses. They are a host, to be repeatedly dispatched, rather than a singular enemy locked into a relationship with the hero protagonist. If anxiety around readiness is pivotal to horror, it has found its perfect match in computer games. Ambush is frequent in games, as is the need to identify and load the appropriate weapon without hesitation. Failing to expect the former, or carry out the latter, will result in injury or death. Walkthroughs are marked by this anxiety – they are distinctly cautionary:[6]

The (alien) will thrash the room a bit and if it breaks the wall next to you, it will reveal a scuttler pod. If you edge out, you can burn it from around the corner of the box (Use your first person view). Take care of it and you won't have scuttlers pestering you. However, if it doesn't destroy that wall early, expect some scuttlers to have spawned and (they) will begin attacking. (Morgan, 2002)

Adaptation and *The Thing*

The developers of the computer game were faithful to the 1980s film, but it is a game and, of course, games are played. This means that even when content is borrowed from a film and faithfully reproduced within a game, its meaning will change. As Patrick Crogan argues with reference to *The Thing* (film) and *The Thing* (game):

> the modelling of a situation to explore its parameters and methods for controlling it interactively describes a computer game's response to cultural themes or content in contrast to a filmic one that is based on a narrative procedure of retrospective configuration of event-elements, a procedure that serves an interpretive function. (Crogan, 2004: 16).

In other words, when playing a game, the player is exploring the limits, choices and the strategies inherent to a situation. The protagonist, the environment and the monster(s) entail variables that are manipulated or experimented on. In this case, the situation involves a military unit, in the Antarctic, who must survive an infestation of homicidal aliens. To function as a game, *The Thing* must confront the player with challenges, but it must also be winnable. This distinguishes the game from the film. In the game 'the threat of an unpredictable and sometimes unidentifiable enemy and the paranoia it engenders are replayed as precisely playable challenges able to be overcome at the end of a training process' (Crogan, 2004: 16). The thing(s) that lurk in the game are killed by the player, once he or she has acquired sufficient skills, and generally only after the protagonist has been injured or killed a number of times. The viewer of the film cannot kill or outwit the monster, and the film's hero will not die repeatedly because of the viewer's lack of dexterity. The game does represent material from the film, yet in the move from film to game, its function and meaning are altered.

As noted in chapter 3, the player has influence over the arrangement, frequency or duration of events in a game. This is one of the major differences between temporality in gameplay, and time in conventional narratives. There are also significant and associated spatial differences. The term 'space' here refers to the setting, to distance and proximity, and to the potential for exploration and navigation.[7] The design of space and the arrangement or manipulation of existents within it, are central to gaming. It does not follow, however, that the spaces in the game should be seen as irrevocably divorced from those of the film. As this online, player-authored walkthrough of *The Thing* shows, for some the appeal of these rooms is due to their prior appearance in the film: 'Access the CCTV camera station. This will switch you to a view of the room behind the door . . . Fans of the movie will instantly recognize this room.' The author adds that once the room has been accessed, 'I'm sure movie fans will want to nose around' (Morgan, 2002).

Playing *The Thing* means crossing dangerous terrain, accessing particular zones, disarming barriers and unlocking doors. Death by exposure is possible because the game characters are susceptible to the extreme weather. They are only safe outside for a short amount of time, after which their health will begin to degrade. Inside spaces might be warmer, but this is also where the monsters tend to be waiting in ambush (according to the film's famous tag line 'Man is the warmest place to hide'). Doors, insides, and exteriors form arrangements to be negotiated by the player.

> Close the doors behind to each room once you are done with a wave. This keeps the next wave from pouring into the room while you are fighting the previous one. You can also open the door, pitch in a grenade and kill several since they are so bunched up [. . .] You have just enough time to get into the recreation room, however, you can also use the door to corral your enemies to avoid being surrounded [. . .] If you're lazy and don't want to figure the doors to open out for yourself, open 9, 8, 6, 3 and then 2. There be monsters behind the other doors . . . may as well make this easy, right? (Morgan, 2002)

It is hardly surprising, then, that the arrangement of space, and things in space, is fundamental to the design process. The developers selected a few core themes (such as infection, isolation and trust) from the film, to develop into dynamics within their game. The next step was to begin the design of the game itself. Designing a game level entails making decisions about balance. It is important to align the degree of difficulty with the amount of resources on offer: the number and variety of weapons, the frequency of confrontations or the strength and resilience of the enemy. After arriving at a few 'ballpark figures', the level was planned out on paper. As Diarmid said:

> Someone might propose, 'right, so the player is going to come here. We're going to plant a key here, then we're going to have these monsters here, or here . . . and these weapons hidden here.' This rough design is reviewed by the designers and they play the level through in their heads, thinking 'OK, I'm going to walk this way, and now I'm going to go over here.' They have to try and imagine what it's like to play it, which is quite difficult to do. It is one thing to design an additional level

for an existing game, but trying to imagine playing a level of a game that does not yet exist, is much more difficult.

As well as mapping out the level on paper, the development team found it useful to physically perform the various happenings. When developing the whole idea of distrust, for example, and the idea that a character can turn and become the enemy, it was useful to act it out. Using these methods they arrived at a rough design of a game level. At that point, the process moved on to a computer. The developers planted weapons and monsters in a terrain mesh-style environment, and began to actually play it, testing out the timing, getting a feel for the space, and moving things around to the point where it began to 'feel right'. Diarmid explained that:

> Various controls are on the screen, and the user would select from these variables, changing or adding the objects to the game, or moving the camera. So, you could decide, 'right, I'm going to add this kind of monster here but, let's see, he's just going to stay there until . . .' and then you could place something called a 'position trigger' somewhere on the level. Once the player's character trips the trigger, the monster will begin to approach them. The level editor could set this up in a few minutes, and then they will just play through it and see how it feels.

This stage of the process should be seen as editing rather than composing, and it should not replace the earlier, paper-based stage of design. There is a danger, for one thing, that when the designer plays out the new level, he or she may experience it as satisfying due to an intimate prior knowledge of the terrain. In order that the level works just as well for other gamers, it is important to ensure that the level's logic is sound, prior to playing it through. There is another reason to work on paper. It is possible that the assets and tools needed to realize a new game level are not initially available to the designer. They might be working with new technology or with new software developed specifically for the game. This means that tools and applications must be defined prior to or concurrent with the construction of the level. If there is no 'blueprint', it is possible that the technology developed will work against, rather than for, the designer.

Characterization and cutscenes

The developers viewed the Carpenter film, and identified features that could be adapted meaningfully into a game. This does not mean merely replicating imagery. It means selecting features from the film, such as infection, the setting and the extreme weather, or the attributes of the alien, and converting these elements into game mechanics. A game mechanic is 'simply any part of the rule system of a game that covers one, and only one, possible kind of interaction . . . A game may consist of several mechanics, and a mechanic may be part of many games. The mechanic trading, for example, simply states that during the game, players have the possibility to trade' (Lundgren and Bjork, 2003).

In the film the team disintegrates as they realize that any of their number may be infected, and might no longer be human. The game developers elaborated on this dynamic. Each team member has a 'trust meter' that shows the level of confidence that he has in the protagonist. A high level of trust will mean that he will obey without question. A very low level of trust might mean that he turns on the protagonist in self-defence. Certain actions will result in a loss of trust, while other acts will result in its increase. Similarly, when members of the team are afraid, their performance deteriorates. According to the game manual 'Your Squad-Mates are entirely aware of the circumstances they're in. You'll have to manage their fear in order to keep them stable' (p. 11) and to prevent them from becoming a liability. Infection, trust and fear in the game are interconnected, as Diarmid explained:

> Adapting the standard action game rules to reflect this change (infection) was a logical step in creating the game of *The Thing*. Having a trust system as a mechanics might not seem such an obvious step. However, while in standard action games, the baddies are the baddies and the goodies are the goodies and everyone knows who is who, as soon as you introduce the idea of infection this distinction becomes much more complex and dynamic. An NPC does not know which side another character is on. While the introduction of trust as a mechanic was something we wanted to do anyway, I think that even if we hadn't wanted to, we would have had to do it in some form to allow the A.I. [Artificial Intelligence] to cope with the infection mechanic.

As game designers Salen and Zimmerman have explained, compelling play relies on the player being offered meaningful choices, with discernible outcomes (2004: 61–6). In *The Thing* narrative elements (including characterization) function to contextualize goals, missions and obstacles. In this way suspense is heightened, and in-game events are made meaningful – granted validity and coherence. As Diarmid reported:

> Characterisation in the game was important. We wanted the player to get attached to their characters and so be more disturbed when they got infected and not want to shoot them. Each character had a set of generic speech that could be triggered in certain types of situation (e.g. seeing someone burst out, getting scared, finding a friend). All generic speech was said in a manner appropriate to that character. The idea was that you could put any of the characters in any of the situations in the game and they would say things appropriate to the situation. They then also had a set of character-specific speech that would be

triggered at specific points in the game to tell you something about their background and lead the story along. Then some characters would appear in cutscenes. We also tweaked some of the A.I. parameters to make some characters more likely to get scared or go mad.

The characters in *The Thing* are less athletically mobile than the avatars in other action adventure games – they do not jump, roll or climb, for example. There were various reasons for this. For one, the developers saw the gritty realism of Carpenter's film as one of its strengths. This informed the realistically human (or limited) abilities of the characters in the game. Second, as Diarmid explained, 'People get scared when you take away their freedom. Stopping the character being able to look up and down and stopping him jumping confines the player in his environment much more and intensifies the suspense' (see Krzywinska, 2002, for a discussion of control in horror games). A third reason involved ease of use. As Diarmid pointed out, 'the more movements you can do, the more buttons you need to do it. We already had loads of buttons taken up with squad communication and weapons operation. We didn't want to make movement any more complicated than it needed to be.'

As noted, the 1980s version of *The Thing* was a remake of a 1951 film titled *The Thing From Another World*. This black-and-white feature differed from the original short story and the later film in several ways. For one thing, its cast included a number of women. Carpenter and *The Thing*'s scriptwriter, Bill Lancaster, toyed with the idea of admitting women, but decided against it on the grounds that this was, in Carpenter's words, 'more realistic' (Billson, 1997: 35). For Lancaster, including women would have been 'gratuitous' (quoted in Billson, 1997: 35), and would have necessitated adding 'obligatory love scenes' (ibid.). Notions of realism are, of course, relative. The film does, after all, revolve around the antics of a hideous monster from outer space.[8] As Diarmid reports, women were left out of *The Thing* (game) for less odd and more prosaic reasons:

> As far as I am aware, it was simply a question of economics. All the male characters shared a skeleton and an animation set. The animation set consisted of approx 120 different animations ('run', 'walk', 'side-step', 'throw grenade'). To introduce one woman would have meant a new skeleton and redoing most of the animations. Given our limited number of animators and the limited memory on the PS2, we decided not to.

Like many other 3-D console games, *The Thing* contains cutscenes. In one sense these real time animated sequences show the debt owed by computer games to cinema. For some designers and game writers, cutscenes are functional (rather than merely decorative), because they re-establish continuity, plot and characterization – features that tend to become lost during the played levels. Associating cutscenes with narrative, and levels with gameplay is an oversimplification. However, it is true that traditionally in action adventure games the levels are associated with play and interactivity, while cutscenes are equated with non-interactive storytelling.

Actually there are various degrees of interactivity in a game like *The Thing*. There are, for instance, points where the player's avatar might be approached or spoken to by a Non-Player Character. This would involve a minor animation, and the player might not necessarily lose control entirely. At other times, there may be a need to relay more complex information in a particular sequence, or there could be details that need to be related to the player without interruption. At these points control is taken away from the player, and animations are used.

For game developers the creation and insertion of animated segments into a game raises several problems. During a cutscene the player has no control over on-screen events, so it is necessary to ensure, first of all, that nothing else in the game will move during it. As Diarmid pointed out, 'you don't want the player going into a cutscene while a monster is mauling them, especially if the attack continues while it's going on!' For the developers of *The Thing*, finding ways to effectively and efficiently integrate cutscenes into the game was a process in itself, not least because it was crucial to avoid situations where glaring inconsistencies emerged between a played level and a subsequent cutscene. The more complicated or elaborate the cutscene is, the more likely it is that there will be obvious discrepancies between it and the game level. The environment is the same during both, so it is noticeable if blood splatter or dead bodies, for instance, disappear and reappear. Diarmid said that these ramifications only became fully apparent during the development process:

> It was only after we had completed quite a lot of the cutscenes that we realised we might have problems. Eventually we developed a system whereby we would look at each individual cutscene and decide which characters are essential to it, and which are not. The essential people (a character who says or does something important, for example) must still be alive at the point that the cutscene starts. On quite a few occasions we ended up having to make squad members 'mission critical' – they needed to survive, because they turned up in the cutscene a bit later!

Cutscenes fall into two categories: pre-rendered, and real time. The definition of a pre-rendered cutscene is an animation that is rendered into a piece of pre-edited, pre-recorded, predefined movie file that is stored on the game disc and played when it is triggered by a level completion. The characters, set and props may all be derived from the game, and perhaps even rendered through the game engine, but the animation has been created, captured and saved before the game left the development studio: it is inherently unchangeable. As Diarmid's comments suggest, games with pre-rendered cutscenes must be elaborately planned, in order to avoid undermining the continued 'reality' of the game world.

Levels are unpredictable, with variable sections of real time gameplay, manic button pressing, repetition, exploration and experimentation. The game is a designed experience involving certain constraints, but a player's moves cannot be predicted. Careful planning will help to eradicate a percentage of errors in continuity during the move from played level to cutscene, but it is almost impossible to predict all of the possible outcomes, especially as, due to tight production schedules, the cut-sequences are often compiled at the same time as the levels. It might be argued that clever design should render inconsistencies impossible, but this involves a level of overdetermination that is detrimental to gameplay.

Unlike pre-rendered scenes, real time cutscenes are loaded through the game itself. There is little difference between these scenes and the level – they are the same characters moving and speaking within the same locale. These events will have the exact 'look' of the rest of the game, because everything, from the characters, to the lighting, is rendered as it happens. For some game designers, real time cutscenes will only be used to maximum potential when they become seamlessly integrated into the levels. This, suggests Diarmid, might entail focusing on scenario creation rather than action:

> By specifying the story in terms of the emotional situations we want the player to find themselves in, we give more freedom to the game to determine the exact nature of the event (who is involved, where it happens, how it happens, etc.). To do this, though, we will need to have our characters able to respond to different events in realistic ways and algorithms for writing realistic dialog. These are challenges we are some way from addressing.

This is a technical issue, and it is expected that integrated scenes (and, by extension, storytelling within games) will become less scripted and far more code/A.I. driven. As a result, cutscenes may become less rigid, to the point where they become as flexible as the levels themselves. This is where, some predict, we would see representational factors (such as narrative, for instance) and gameplay collide. In such a case, the challenge would be to maintain the freedom, agency and unpredictability of gameplay. The danger would be that the capacity for narrative to create mood, or generate emotion, would be lost.

Adaptation – game to game

There are other elements of adaptation and genre that might be less apparent to users than those discussed above. Underneath the on-screen action, which may differ significantly from one game to another even within a single genre, there are different layers of programming. Some of this programming will be specific to a particular game, but much of it will be more general. This is because there is a great deal of functionality in similarly structured games that is actually shared. Many games will, for example, take user input, play recorded sound samples and vary their pitch, and position objects in 3-D space. Games have moving entities in their worlds with collision volumes. These elements are common across many games; they are just differently adapted, in different instances.

The game engine will allow for all the fundamentals: the physics simulations, the entities in the world, control systems, user control. On top of the game engine will sit the various, specific games. For instance, in *The Thing* there are mechanics of infection, trust and fear – and the relevant code is situated at this more specific level. The real challenge for developers is that of calculating what might be considered generic across all of their games, and what must be regarded as 'game specific'. Diarmid estimates that 20 or 30 per cent of *The Thing* is actually specific, and the other 70 or 80 per cent is reusable. Given the cost of creating a game from scratch, it is not difficult to see the value in creating general and transferable computer code.

One of the challenges faced by Computer Artworks when developing *The Thing*, was that the team were developing a game engine, and a game title at the same time.

> We had the game engine in part from when we developed a previous game, *Evolva*, but there was definitely a big jump when we went from this game, to doing *The Thing*. Now, however, we find that we can do much higher quality games for much lower cost, because we have several different products that are all contributing to the game engine – and they all benefit from each other's technology.

The goal, then, is to make the game engine generic enough to allow the developer to build a series of games with it. Of course, there are limits – the engine for *The Thing* is very much tuned to doing 3-D graphically rendered games, rather than text-based RPGs, for example. Apart from that, however, it is very open-ended. As Diarmid explained, 'The trick is to make your game engine as flexible as possible, so that there's very little the games designer could come up with that the game engine couldn't do – and if it can't do it, we would alter it so that it could.'

Conclusion

The Thing combines original game-mechanics with borrowed monsters. As Crogan has suggested, the alien thing-monster itself

> is arguably the most profound attempt ever conceived to represent visually the paradox of genre: like 'genre' the thing has no identity in itself but must always rely upon exemplifying its attributes from specific incidences. Each new form it manages to assimilate becomes another attribute or set of attributes it adopts as proper to it, so that it has no independent or stable identity but mutates each time a new example of it appears. (2000: 4)

Examining links between horror movies and horror gaming allows for the identification of continuities. Both, for instance, are associated with formula, performance and repetition. Both are popularly associated with youth. Horror films recall oral or folkloric narratives and embodied sensations, as do computer games. *The Thing* (film) and *The Thing* (game) share a monster and themes of transformation – the alien's own parasitic mutations, as well as the shifting between trust and fear within the team.

The depiction of distrust and infection within the film re-emerges in the game at a narrative level (within non-interactive, plotted cutscenes) and as a game mechanic (as a variable that impacts on play, that the player must respond to or otherwise manage). Similarly, the creation of tension and suspense within the game relies on both representational and ludic factors: the isolated setting, for example, is atmospheric, eerie. It also has gameplay ramifications, in that the characters' health will degrade if they remain exposed to the extreme cold for any length of time. The characters are granted personality traits, in the hope that this will amplify the player's investment in their well-being. These character traits also involve ludic variables, in that different characters are more or less susceptible to fear, and possess different necessary skills.

For some within the games industry, developments in console capacity and A.I. will lead to the existing distinctions between storytelling and gameplay being further eroded. However, as production of *The Thing* demonstrates, during development (as well as during play), it is already the case that ludic and representational features operate in tandem. They are mutually informing. Each plays a part in establishing the constraints and allowances that will eventually structure the experience of playing *The Thing*.

CHAPTER 12

Games and Gender

Diane Carr

ONE of the more interesting paradoxes within the existing computer games literature is that, while the majority of players are reputed to be male, most of the critical attention directed at questions of gaming and gender has focused on girls and women. For some researchers these issues are important because the marginalization of girls and women within gaming culture is sexist and thus reflects troubling inequalities in society more generally. Other analysts, particular those focusing on equity and education, have proposed that the use of leisure software including computer games could help to interest girls and young women in technology, science and maths related subjects (see Gorriz and Medina, 2000; Gansmo, Nordli and Sørensen, 2003). There is concern that girls avoid these subjects at school, with the consequence that women are not entering related high-status professions. Some games producers and designers, meanwhile, have studied girls and gaming because they have an interest in expanding and diversifying their audience (Laurel, 1999; Graner-Ray, 2003).

As this suggests, issues of girls, gender and games have been tackled by an array of theorists with different interests, motivations, methods and professional backgrounds. In order to introduce these debates in this chapter we will touch on questions of representation, players and player culture, as well as aspects of the games industry. When it comes to questions of gender and computer games, it would be possible, and valid, to limit our discussion to the analysis of representations of the gendered body on-screen. Yet, if meaning (as in 'the meaning of an image') is associated with interpretation and reception, we also need to be looking at the player. Players (and analysts, of course) are informed by and situated within social and cultural contexts. In addition to this, computer games are developed, published, publicized and distributed by an industry that has typically addressed a male audience. In this chapter, therefore, issues of text, gender and representation will be introduced, and followed by a consideration of contexts: contexts of reception, and contexts of production.

Games as representations

A report titled *Chicks and Joysticks* (Krotoski, 2004) recently published by the Entertainment and Leisure Software Publishers Association (ELSPA) contains statistical data on female players. The figures show that more males play than females, but only in certain countries, and not in all genres, and that the 'average age of British female gamers is 30–35 years old. They represent 27.2% of UK gamers [and on] average they spend 7.2 hours per week playing games' (p. 11). Patterns of gender and gaming vary significantly from country to country, and this suggests that gender alone is not a consistent predictor of gaming habits: 'Internationally, British women play less than games-dedicated countries like the US, Japan and Korea where 39%, 36% and an astounding 65.9% play respectively' (p. 10). As these figures make apparent, women and girls do play games, and it would be a mistake to associate computer gaming solely with children or teenagers. Despite this, in the public imagination games remain 'the preserve of adolescent boys' (Krotoski, 2004: 6). Other research has found that women gamers do not necessarily regard computer gaming as a male hobby, 'but they did feel that many non-players viewed it as a boy's pastime' (Kerr, 2003: 283).

Some theorists have argued that representational factors – the 'look' of female avatars – are partially responsible for alienating women and girls from computer games (see Bryce and Rutter, 2002, for a review of 'content analysis' literature). It is arguable that until fairly recently females were planted in games either as rewards (titillating decor) or as goals (princesses to be rescued). Over the past few years, however, the range and availability of female avatars has expanded to the point that this is no longer a straightforward, viable claim (see <www. womengamers.com> for a discussion of 'digital women'). In many, although not all, RPGs the player is given the option to select the gender of the protagonist. In some MMORPGs (as we noted while discussing *Anarchy Online*) the player's choices might extend to details of the avatar's physique – from body weight and height, to hairstyle. Other online multiplayer RPGs might not offer the same degree of flexibility. T. L. Taylor's (2003) research into women, pleasure and gaming shows that the ability to shape an avatar's body (or the necessity of accepting the body types provided) is indeed an issue for women players of online multiplayer games. Taylor studied the game *Everquest* (an MMORPG with a fantasy setting), and found that 'women in *EQ* often struggle with the conflicting messages around their avatars, feeling they have to "bracket" or ignore how they look' (Taylor, 2003: 36). Both male and female avatars in the game have exaggerated physiques, but exaggeration in the case of the female avatars is specifically sexual, and while 'chests and biceps on male characters act as symbolic sexual characteristics, they are simultaneously able to represent power . . . large breasts *only* act as sexual markers' (Taylor, 2003: 39).

There are many game worlds where the highly 'marked' or marginal, or altogether absent, gender is female. As we noted in chapter 11, all the characters in *The Thing* are male. In the game *Abe's Oddysee* (the action adventure game discussed in chapter 10), it might be argued that the protagonist Abe and his alien brethren are androgynous or neuter but – as the name 'Abe' makes plain – the game is actually quite clear that the protagonist is male (although fans might 'read' against this). The masculinity modelled by Abe is of a different style from the masculinity of the game's broad-shouldered, bullying master race, the Glukkons, but the point is that maleness seems to permeate the game's population as a more-or-less universal characteristic – as a neutral, default category. This implies that femaleness is somehow 'difficult'. It has been argued that the attainment of a 'neutral identity' within a culture – whether it is maleness, or indeed whiteness (Dyer, 1997; hooks, 1992) – is linked with the power to define, and it is always and only ever possible from a position of power relative to the 'marked' and the marginal. Judith Butler argues that 'only the feminine gender is marked, that the universal person and the masculine gender are conflated, thereby defining women in terms of their sex and extolling men as the bearers of a body-transcendent universal personhood' (Butler, 1990: 9, referring to de Beauvoir).

Representational factors in games cannot be ignored, yet such considerations need to be reconciled with the fact that computer games are actualized through play: the user is a *player*, as well as a viewer, a reader, a consumer and a spectator. At first glance, theories of representation and identification developed within Film Studies would seem to offer viable models for the analysis of avatar gender, or the impact of avatar gender on player 'identification' or 'projection' – but this is not necessarily the case. Playing an RPG or action adventure game might well involve gazing at a gendered body as it leaps across a screen, but at the level of the apparatus (a projector and camera vs. a computer, keyboard or joystick), and in terms of the conditions of participation (gazing or viewing vs. playing and manipulating), film viewing and computer gaming are very different activities. As mentioned in chapter 5, degrees of recognition between off-screen user and on-screen body may arise during gaming, as when we lean over in vicarious response to gravity in a game world, for example, but as yet these resonances are undertheorized. It would be difficult to establish, at this point, if the object on-screen evoking recognition in this way even has to be humanoid – let alone representative of a particular gender.

As this indicates, satisfactory conceptualizations of the player-as-gendered-subject manipulating the game-as-text are not yet available. For this reason, assertions that commercial games necessarily entail 'homogenising effects on the viewer/user' (Spielmann and Mey, 2005) are premature. As we have discussed throughout this book, games deliver information, content, narrative, spectacle, invitations and demands in multiple modes. The diversity of this address suggests that a variety of simultaneous 'reading positions' are open (or closed) to different players. As yet these offers and the manner in which they might mesh with different aspects of player subjectivity (in particular contexts) remain under-investigated.

While the 'look' of a body represented on-screen can be analysed in terms of its face, physicality or wardrobe, the realization of an avatar through play will involve a combining of its menu of movements with the player's operational skills and playing style. The input of players and their ability to determine the actions of an avatar (to some degree or other) means that, while avatars are characterized, there are important differences between avatars and characters in films or novels. A trait expressed by the game, through dialogue, via gestures or actions, or by an avatar's body, might become either emphasized or irrelevant – depending on the player's actions and priorities. While a partial account of an avatar's meaning is possible, the actualization of the avatar and its traits will vary from player to player, and even session to session. A player might 'read' the avatar as an attractive, annoying or amusing character one moment, only to become absorbed manipulating it as a tool the next.

The ludic and the representational

Games involve rules. Players consent to work within these parameters, whereupon they are offered a set of variables, economies and components that are manipulated and reconfigured. We have used the term 'ludic' to cover these aspects of a game. The genres that we have been concerned with feature an emphasis on graphics and storytelling – they have locations and characters that are represented in compelling detail. We've referred to this material as the representational aspect of a game. Together, the ludic and the representational facets present a player with a set of offers, demands and invitations. These are selectively actualized through play. Each player is a culturally and socially situated subject who is manipulating a keyboard or a console control, interpreting menus and on-screen action, and participating in an experience within a particular context (say, a lounge room, as discussed in chapter 9, or within an online, shared world, as is the case with

Anarchy Online, discussed in chapter 8). The game may overtly reference non-game texts (as with *The Thing*), or other, non-computer games (as with table-top RPGs). Images or figures from within the game may reappear in other contexts – whether it is in fan fiction, or on billboard advertisements. For these reasons, part of the meaning of a game resides in its relationship to wider cultural contexts.

Many avatars are simulations of people – and simulations are simplified models. Simplification involves leaving things out. The inclusions and exclusions built into a simulation might reflect cultural and social values (or biases, or assumptions), as well as game design decisions. Avatars in *Baldur's Gate*, for instance, stagger if they are forced to carry too much; they need regular rest, or their performance will be impaired – but they do not need to eat, go to the toilet or shower. The rules of a computer game might express design choices that relate to gender and sexuality. The scores attributed to character strength in *Baldur's Gate*, for example, are affected by species (elves are comparatively puny), but not by gender. Females are not programmed to be physically weaker than males. So it is possible for the player to assemble an all-male or all-female team, if they desire, without it impacting on gameplay. In other games, avatars might feature different variables. In *The Sims*, for example, the characters' affections are quantifiable. Sims can be gay or straight. They can live together as friends, as family, as lovers or as spouses. Sims are liable to be unfaithful if plied with gifts – but they are also programmed to become jealous, so romantic relationships involving more than two at a time are difficult to maintain.

As we noted in chapter 1, a game can be defined as 'a structured framework for spontaneous play' (Pearce, 2002: 113), and different games will allow for different degrees of scope in relation to these structures. As we described in chapter 4, the player-generated *Baldur's Gate* character of Bad Joan had wicked intentions, but her worst impulses were disallowed by the game's rules. Thus the player might ignore traits attributed by the game to an avatar, while traits attributed by the player to the avatar might be over-ruled by the game. In comparison with the player-generated protagonist in *Baldur's Gate*, the identities of Cloud and the other characters in *Final Fantasy VII* (as discussed in chapters 6 and 7) are more deeply embedded in an extensive narrative. As a result, characterization and gender roles in the game are relatively determined. This, however, has not stopped fans from 'reworking' the characters' gender, sexuality and relationships in their creative outpourings.

So, the meaning of gender in a game needs to be examined in terms of its rules, and in terms of representation. Yet meanings are also created through processes of use, interpretation and reception – which implies that the meaning of a particular representation could also be investigated as it emerges during play, at the hands of a socially and culturally situated user. Play involves repetition, ephemeral actions and improvised experimentation – and this variability will impact on any attempt to formulate a 'once-and-for-all' definitive account of the meaning of a gendered body on-screen.

The meaning attributed to an avatar by a player is likely to be provisional and shifting rather than static. Experienced gamers routinely distinguish between gameplay and the representational 'dressing' or the trans-textual associations of a game. Newer or more casual users, in their turn, might accord a higher degree of importance to these factors. Neither position is 'more correct' – the point is that the meaning ascribed by a player to an aspect of the game is likely to change over time in response to the player's own shifts in familiarity and competence. Furthermore, an avatar's actions might alter to reflect the player's increased skills, and its traits might vary from player to player according to their preferred gaming style (to become more aggressive, or more cautious, for example). For these reasons it is arguable that, in the end, the manner in which gender is inscribed in the game at a representational level might simply be over-ruled by the player. Consider again our experiences on Rubi-Ka, the world of *Anarchy Online*.

When we played this game we had the choice to play as male or female characters. From what we could ascertain, a cheerful mix of inhabitants populated the game world (male and female, big and small, humanoid and more alien). It appeared to be (and we felt it to be) a diversely inhabited place. From our perspective the other avatars reflected the participation of both female and male players. A player, however, might 'read' all the female avatars as actually representing male players, in which case the visible diversity would be overturned by a homogenizing interpretation. The male teenagers we interviewed were insistent that all the female avatars in this online game represented older, duplicitous male players (see chapter 8). In actuality it is difficult to establish with any certainty the percentage of subscribers who are playing against their real-world gender. The game's developers, Funcom, 'does not have any statistics about the gender distribution of their players. They claim they have many female characters signed up, but they cannot know whether these female characters are representing male or female players' (Gansmo, Nordli and Sorensen, 2003: 15).

During a game the operational, ludic aspects of an avatar will intersect with issues relating to representation – and this is also true of the process of avatar design. For example, when describing the creation of an avatar named Jen for the action adventure game *Primal* (released in 2003), the lead designer, Katie Lea, outlined a complex process that incorporated casting and working with actors (for motion capture, and for vocal recordings), as well as animation, 3-D modelling and texturing, programming, wardrobe and costume design, dialogue writing and backstory invention.[1] Jen is a quirky, urban girl on a mission and her adventuring across dimensions is made possible by her ability to shift between demon forms. These demonic forms are based on elements – earth, air, fire and water, and each allows for a particular set of skills. As this indicates, her 'look', dialogue, demonic forms, gestures and gait, combat skills, controls and weapons are all integral to her character design. After the game's European release, its characters were adapted for different international markets. The Japanese producers, for instance, were concerned that Jen's demonic forms were unattractive, and that her hazel eyes, strong features and dark hair made her too ambiguous for the Japanese market. After discussing whether Jen should become either Japanese, or more emphatically Anglo-European, the Jen for Japan acquired:

> very blue eyes (and) a nose job – quite subtle changes really. Changes to the demon forms are more noticeable; they're really toned down, quite pretty demons. Bizarrely she now has matching eye-shadow, depending on the demon form – so in [her earth demon] form she's wearing a glamorous green . . . (email, Katie Lea)

In contrast to Jen and other commercially produced avatars, there are the avatars generated by players within the open source movement. 'Open source' refers to game engines, programmes or coding accessible via the Internet and open to reworking by computer literate users. There are, for instance, modding (from 'modification') communities who work with the Infinity Engine (*Baldur's Gate*'s game engine) to create new quests, additional Non-Player Characters, extra banter and dialogue and new relationships between teammates (see <www.gibberlings3.net>, or <www.blackwyrmlair.net>, for example). The open source movement is interesting in terms of games, gaming culture and gender, especially as it relates to online First Person Shooter (FPS) games like *Quake*. The avatars in these games were originally all male. This situation was remedied thanks to the direct intervention by players, who created and distributed female avatars through resources such as the Quake Women's Forum at <www.planetquake.com> (for 'women with attitude, and plenty of ammo'). Hacking, patching, modding and skinning practices resulted in 'female heroines like the "Female Cyborg Patch" and the "Tina-bob" patch for Marathon [that] were among the first patches to offer active female avatars (in place of trophy princesses) for gameplay in shooters, prefiguring the official release of *Tomb Raider*' (Schleiner, 1999: 4).

These practices indicate that the imposition of stereotypical attributes on to either players or game genres is problematic. Online FPS games are susceptible to gendered categorization because they involve macho, muscle-bound, militaristic avatars with guns, engaging in intense competition and fast paced action. Yet this is less than half the story. As Schleiner (1999) has documented (see <www.opensorcery.net>), these games exist within a matrix of active, online communities, where creative innovation, mentoring and resource distribution are practised primarily – but not only – by male players.[2] As such, these FPS games and the communities in which they are situated manage to embody the traits most typically associated with 'masculine' gaming (guns, shooting, competition, pace), as well as those often attributed to the feminine (collaboration, creativity, sociability). The point is not that particular genres or preferences are the proper domain of one gender rather than the other. The point is that attributing a certain playing style or gaming preference to one gender is simplistic. As FPS games and their collaborative communities indicate, questions of games and gender need to be considered in context. This involves looking at gaming culture, production and the industry.

Gender, games and contexts

No single factor can be held accountable for the apparent alienation of women and girls from computer gaming. Nor is there a simple answer as to how this imbalance might best be addressed. As it currently stands the majority of computer games are produced by a primarily male industry that tends to assume a male audience. Computer games are publicized and reviewed in magazines that address a male (usually adolescent) reader, and they are often sold in retail outlets where men outnumber women on both sides of the counter. These factors in combination result in women and girls having less exposure to games, and less first-hand experience of gaming. Girls and women who are unacquainted with games will have to answer researchers' questions about their gaming preferences based on their impressions of games, rather than on actual experience. Girls and women who have not been introduced to the pleasures of gaming will not be motivated to buy or play games. This disengagement will 'prove' or perpetuate the notion that males are more inclined towards gaming. So fewer girls will be encouraged to take up gaming, and fewer girls than boys will grow up wanting to create or produce games – and the games industry will remain primarily male.

Different, cumulative historical and economic factors have contributed to the construction of maleness as the default gender for computer games and gamers. The gender bias has become ingrained in games production and reception. Over time it has become self-perpetuating and self-fulfilling, with the result that developers who attempted to remedy this imbalance by deliberately targeting female consumers were often less than successful. As Laurel (1998) has pointed out, 'whenever a "girl" title was attempted, it was launched all alone onto the shelf without adequate marketing or retail support, and the inevitable failure easily became a proof that girls would not play computer games'.

It is quite common within game production to follow a design approach known as the 'I methodology' – a process in which 'designers see themselves as typical users and use their own tastes and preferences as the basis of making design decisions' (Gansmo, Nordli and Sørensen, 2003: 5). Consultants International Hobo conducted research into *Demographic Game Design*, and found that the industry tends to produce games that will appeal to the tastes of 'the vast majority of game programmers' (iHobo, 2003: 12). At the games company Funcom (the Norwegian developers of the online game *Anarchy Online*, discussed in chapter 8), the employees are '90% men. The women work mainly within the administration' (Gansmo, Nordli and Sørensen, 2003: 16). Employment figures within the UK industry are not dissimilar. Approximately 16 per cent of employees within the UK games industry are female, and 'anecdotal evidence suggests that women are concentrated in marketing, PR and administration' (Haines, 2004: 3).[3] Women are employed to promote games – industry trade shows, for instance, hire female 'booth babes' who are, according to one games correspondent, 'lovely, captive women that pretty much have to let you ogle them and take pictures' (Dove, 2004).

Theorists, educators and designers who have investigated the alienation of women and girls from player culture have often focused on questions of gaming preference. The implication is that if games were produced in accordance with 'female' preferences, the number of women or girls active in gaming culture would increase. The problem with this approach is that it runs the risk of abstracting the problem ('girls are not playing games') from its contexts – the cycle of production, marketing, consumption and reception outlined above. Asking 'what games do girls like?' also implies that preferences are determined by gender, but is it the case that gender is that aspect of player identity most responsible for shaping tastes? What of age, class, peer groups, cultural affiliations or sexuality? The fact is that our stated preferences will inevitably reflect the experiences, the pleasures and the actual computer games to which we have had access. Mapping patterns in preference is possible, but preferences are an assemblage, made up of past positive experiences, and subject to situation and context. The constituents of preference (such as access) are shaped by gender and, as a result, gaming preferences may manifest along gendered lines. It is not difficult to generate data that will indicate that gendered tastes exist, but it is short-sighted to divorce such preferences from the various practices that form them.

For these reasons theorists addressing questions of gender and preference have had to tread carefully, researching and acknowledging the power of socialized patterns of play on the one hand, while resisting essentialist notions of gender on the other (Cassell and Jenkins, 2000). Gender is a demographic category, with measurable social, cultural, economic and political repercussions for individuals – yet contemporary theory argues that gender is fractious and multiple; that gender is continually negotiated and performed, that it is provisional, rather than a fixed, attained condition (Butler, 1990; de Castell and Bryson, 2000: 235). Gender 'involves possibilities that are always in flux and that are determined by many things' (Cassell, 2000: 300). While theories of gender emphasize negotiation and mutability, the way in which masculinity and femininity will manifest in day-to-day life continues to impact on income, access and opportunity.

The literature on gender and games often underestimates the variety of computer games available. Investigations into gaming preferences tend to establish separate camps for male and female players, who are then depicted as possessing diametrically opposite tastes. Males, for instance, are expected to 'gravitate to games that incorporate scoring and fighting' (Gorriz and Medina, 2000: 44). Boys want fast-paced, skills-based games 'that involve substantial amounts of fighting and killing' (Gorriz and Medina, 2000: 45) Games, as well as players, are classified: 'boy-based games consist of repetitive shooting, violent graphics, and loud noises . . . Girls tend to prefer games that encourage collaboration with other players and involve storylines and character development' (Gurer and Camp, 2002: 122). Researchers repeat that girls don't want 'to outdo someone else' (Gorriz and Medina, 2000: 47). Girls reputedly possess 'an avowed dislike for aggression and [a] preference for cooperation over competition' (Subrahmanyam and Greenfield, 2000: 55). These statements could be used to argue that RPGs are a female-friendly genre, but such accounts of gendered preference could also be used to argue that RPGs do not appeal to male players at all – which is obviously not the case.

Furthermore it has been noted that, in interviews, children (or adults, for that matter) may answer questions with 'what they are supposed to say' (Cassell and Jenkins, 2000: 19), and the result is that they supply researchers with 'gender appropriate' responses. Research shows that girls interviewed about computer games may be less than forthcoming about their level of experience. Pelletier (2005) for example, encountered twelve- and thirteen-year-old girls who, when interviewed in mixed company, would only admit to having played *The Sims*. Yet these same girls would later inadvertently demonstrate detailed knowledge of racing or fighting games.

These issues complicate the collection of data on gaming, gender and tastes. Game developers relying on 'empirical research as a justification for design and development decisions run the risk of reinforcing (and naturalizing) this gender-polarized play culture rather than offering an escape from its limitations on their choices' (Cassell and Jenkins, 2000: 20). Yet perhaps the need to have girls engaging with computers and technology is so pressing that appealing to gendered tastes is justified? Games for girls, or 'pink' games remain a controversial issue, but games tailored towards stereotypically masculine tastes are not subject to the same forms of interrogation, for several reasons. To begin with, computer games are very diverse, and the assumed male audience is not imagined to be a homogeneous group and nor is this male audience generally referred to as a specialist market. Additionally, the under-representation of men in media, science or technology careers (on the basis of their gender) is not widespread. Finally, boys and men who are participating in online games culture, buying computer games or reading games magazines are not generally treated as interlopers, intruders or eccentrics.

The call for pink games has often been countered by reference to so-called 'grrl gamers' – girls and women who enthusiastically participate in apparently macho genres like online First Person Shooters (FPS). The grrl gamers interviewed in *From Barbie to Mortal Kombat* express dismay at the idea of pink games, arguing that such games perpetuate female meekness and marginalization. Grrl Gamer Nikki Douglas, for example, has suggested that research indicating that girls shrink from competition or combat due to a preference for 'quiet contemplative games with well rounded characters and storylines' (Jenkins, 2000: 335) merely demonstrates how effectively girls are conditioned to be passive. Douglas argues that the problem is not that boys are openly competitive; the problem is that girls are not, and maybe, she adds, 'that's why we are still underpaid, still struggling, still fighting for our rights' (p. 334). Of course, to argue that all females should be satisfied with access to either 'girly' games *or* online FPS games would be to miss the point.

Research by AOL published in 2004 made apparent that women (at least in North America) are playing a great deal, but they are playing online puzzle and card games, rather than high-profile console games. According to this research, 'female gameplayers over 40 spend the most hours per week playing online games [and these] women were also more likely to play online games every day than men or teens of either gender' (AOL, 2004). This could be a sign that these games offer something to these users that is more appealing than console titles. Others have argued that women generally have less free time and less income than men – and this is going to inform leisure pursuits, including gaming habits. As Cardwell (2004) has pointed out, online puzzle games are easy to learn, yet impossible to master, and thus they appeal to people without the time to invest in learning a complicated set of commands or travelling through a vast game world. This is also the kind of game that is easily accessed and enjoyed while at work, although it would be difficult to establish just how many women (or men) are sitting at the keyboard during office hours playing puzzle or card games. It is also possible that part of the appeal of these games for women is that they do not entail venturing into territory that has been assertively designated male.

Sectors of the games industry have woken up to the fact that alienating half the population is commercially unwise, yet there is continued caution and conditionality about female participation. Retailers in general continue to make gender distinctions when selling games and games hardware, presumably in part because it compels parents to buy twice as much. The UK department store John Lewis, for instance, distributed a catalogue for Christmas 2003 titled 'Top 5 Gifts For . . .', in which they listed a Playstation 2 as a suitable gift for a boy. On the facing page a pink karaoke machine was touted as the equivalent present for a girl (and this kind of separatism must be difficult for the boy who covets the pink karaoke machine, as well as for the girl who yearns for equal access to the console). When it comes to computer games, a great deal of money is spent making games for, and selling games to, a male audience, and in all likelihood that is the main reason why there are more male players. Even when releasing an action adventure game version of a 'girl friendly' title like *Buffy the Vampire Slayer*, the developers focused on those aspects of the television programme that they believed were more likely to appeal to a male audience. The game 'draws more on the action-adventure aspects of the show than the more 'soap' style interactions . . . For some potential players the generic alignment with fight-based action adventure, designed as it conventionally is to attract a male rather than female audience, may prove a step too far' (Krzywinksa, 2003: 3).

A particular audience has been consistently sought and served by the games industry, and thus has expanded – while other sectors of the potential market have remained relatively untapped. In other words the association of masculinity with computer games is a construct, the result of a series of inventions, trends, practices and commercial decisions that have settled into a particular pattern. Fantasies and fears relating to new technologies are expressed most repetitively in the practices (such as games marketing) that proliferate between new technological devices and the contexts of their reception. Female marginalization appears to be merely a side-effect of an anxious drive to situate the male player as the 'natural' user of technology. There may be other explanations, but this is the simplest way to explain the level of nervous aggression aroused by the notion of women's participation. Countless accounts of harassment and gender policing are available on the Internet. Here, as a representative example, is LegendaryMonkey's account of an online FPS gaming experience:

> For those of you who don't know, *Halo 2* online is supported by the Xbox live voice chat – so you can not only shoot and stab others, but talk shit over their corpses as well. Fun! When I started, I asked the husband how many girls he'd ever heard. I expected him to give it a moment's thought, y'know, to count. Not so; the answer was immediate: 'None. Not one.' Huh, thought I. No girls ever? I soon found out why. My third or fourth game in, I was greeted with, 'Oh, look, there's a whore playing with us. Shut the hell up, whore, get back to your place' (memory may betray the exact wording, but it was close). What girl wants to face shit like that? None that I know. It's sad that the Internet's anonymity fosters this sort of acting out, and while it affects everyone (the constant screams of 'faggot' aren't great, either), it really works to create a hostile environment for girls. (LegendaryMonkey at Sudden Nothing: <http://www.suddennothing.net/archives/2005/04/girls_and_games.php>)

Laurel makes the point that in reaching out to female players, game developers or associated publications risk losing their existing male audience: 'Even as late as 1994, major game companies steered clear of the potential girls market because they feared that being seen as doing things for girls would alienate their male audiences. By the way, our research showed that – initially at least – their fears were indeed well-founded' (Laurel, 1998). This caution appears to be expressed in a special issue of *Edge*, a respected UK games magazine, titled 'The Girl Issue' (issue 121, March 2003). The magazine had good intentions, and yet mixed feelings about how to locate itself in relation to the question of sexism in games. On the one hand, to quote from the editorial: 'As this themed issue should show, our concern is with the bigger picture: that the gaming community is and will continue to be worse off by ostracising girl gamers' (Diniz-Sanches, 2003: 3). On the other hand, the magazine used a close-up of a digital girl's bikini-clad lap as its cover shot. According to the letters page of the following issue, both male and female readers found the image embarrassing or ill-judged. *Edge* responded that they were being ironic – a statement complicated by the erect nipples and bare thighs (female, in each instance) that graced the full-page advertisements paid for by games industry recruitment agencies in the same issue (pages 116, 117). While *Edge*'s gesture towards inclusion was cautious (it was a single, 'special' issue, after all), it was still too much for some, as this (presumably male) reader's letter indicates:

> The fact is ladies, that you didn't pay your dues. You can't turn your nose up at a pastime, label it 'sad', then bitch about it twenty years later because it's evolved into something you don't like. You only get out what you put in, and with some very honourable exceptions, women have given us jack, bar some rather delightful inspiration . . . (Letter R. Casewell, *Edge* 122: 127)

The publishers of *Edge* at the time, Future Publishing, hedged their bets by releasing a special issue dedicated to sex and subtitled 'Games, Girls, Guns, Gyrating, G-strings' two months later on another of their titles, *Playstation 2*. The issue included an article on women avatars titled 'Who's The Sexiest' – with a follow-up feature where various female characters were rated as either 'Swingers or Mingers' ('minger' is UK slang for ugly). Throughout the magazine the reader is addressed as male and heterosexual, and the assumption is that only female avatars can be sexually attractive. Yet anecdotal evidence, audience research (Carr, 2005) and common sense would suggest that male and female players have noticed the relative attractiveness of various male avatars. In material produced within Japanese fan cultures (as discussed in chapter 7), the sexual appeal of male avatars is openly celebrated.[4]

Research we have recently undertaken at a South London girls' school found signs that (for some, at least) the links between computer games and masculinity is becoming less pronounced than prior research has documented (Carr, 2005). For these twelve- and thirteen-year-old girls, computer games were a regular feature of their social and family lives. They were all casual rather than hard-core gamers[5] in that none of them played for hours on a daily basis, and they tended to borrow, share or rent games rather than make regular purchases, which also means that they would not be visible as consumers (Kerr, 2003: 282, 284; Bryce and Rutter, 2002). Their gaming did not set them apart from their peers. On the contrary, most talked to their friends about games. In interviews and conversations, the girls would refer to playing with their older cousins, sisters or especially their dad as a regular and enjoyable yet otherwise unremarkable part of their younger childhood.

So there may be signs that things are changing. Fantasies of natural female disinterest and associated practices of female disenfranchisement might become increasingly obsolete, yet it is only to be expected that social and cultural factors will continue to impact on users according to their gender (as well as their age, income, class, ethnicity, etc.). When new leisure technologies arrive in homes the terms of their use are negotiated through existing patterns of gender and power, as Gray's study of women and VCRs demonstrated (Gray, 1992), and this applies to computer games too (Schott and Horrell, 2000). Girls and boys might well be socialized to engage in different forms of play (Laurel, 1999), and there is a long, well-documented tradition of male gaming and game-related socializing that alienates women, and which certainly pre-dates computer games (for an exploration of this see Fine's study of Role Playing Gamers in the Mid Western US in the late 1970s, *Shared Fantasy* (Fine, 1983), as well as Bryce and Rutter's (2002, 2003) work on LAN parties and the competitive games scene in the UK).

Conclusion

It might be the case that more girls and women are playing, and that games production and marketing forces are gradually broadening their focus to include female consumers, yet any such progress may not be the result of timely intervention by academics, educators or progressive developers. It could be that it is becoming less necessary to fantasize that women and girls are inherently disinclined towards gaming, because computer gaming itself has grown in the popular imagination to the point where it can accommodate differently zoned, and differently defined, spaces – and this expansion creates room for diversification.

Over recent years computer games have shifted out of the cultish margins and into the mainstream of popular culture. This could be the result of many different factors, but the phenomena that might be most responsible is the success of cross-media licences and faddish collectables – from *Pokémon* and *Tamagotchi*, to the games based on highly popular, pervasive franchises, including *The Matrix* films and game, the *Harry Potter* series (books, games and films) or the recent *Lord of the Rings* related products (books, films, computer games and board game).

In the wake of computer games' movement into mainstream popular culture, older distinctions between people who play (male) and people who don't (female) might become outmoded or discarded – or perhaps they will merely be reworked. At the time of writing another distinction appears to be emerging to take its place: the categories of the hard-core gamer, and casual gamer. Hard-core or 'committed gamers' are those who play for hours a day 'and who buy games on a weekly/fortnightly basis' (Kerr, 2003: 278), and they are generally identified as male (or renegade female), while the casual or social player is less definitely gendered. A parallel division is made between 'real games' and various, playful alternatives (culprits would include *SingStar*, *Dance Dance Revolution* and *Samba de Amigo*). It is not clear which market is regarded as the more lucrative by the industry. Kerr (2003: 278) found that Sony, for example, 'admitted that they were only really interested in hard-core gamers'. On the other hand, Gansmo, Nordli and Sørensen (2003: 5) found that the industry professionals they interviewed identified two kinds of male gamer: 'the hard-core gamers who play a lot, but who were not considered very interesting as a market because they tend to buy few games [and a second more interesting group] described as the casual gamers . . . boys and men who play now and then'.

From the perspective of game studies and game culture analysis, it might become increasingly important to distinguish between serious gamers and casual players, as these groups are likely to look to games for different pleasures, express different preferences, and engage in gaming in distinct ways. It does not follow that either group's engagement with computer games would be more meaningful, significant or credible – or that one group would be the more legitimate to study than the other.

Emerging distinctions between hard-core and casual gamers might shift the focus from gender at an explicit level, but if fewer women have the time or income to devote to gaming on anything more than a casual basis, the division is likely to reflect a gender divide. As this implies, the disenfranchisement of women and girl players from computer games and gaming cultures cannot be addressed by a single solution or a straightforward equation. The notion that more female avatars or more 'female' games will lead to more female players, and that more female players will result in more women entering the games industry, might not prove correct – not least because other factors including race, age and class will continue to intersect with gender, determining access to education and technologies, which, in turn, impacts on the numbers of women entering into technology-based careers or the games industry.

The increased variety and availability of female avatars is certainly welcomed, but establishing the meaning of a gendered and played body on-screen is a complex task. The manner in which an avatar (of whatever gender) is constituted within a game (by its rules and its representational aspects) can be analysed – with the proviso that these factors might not manifest in a particular or predictable manner during actual play. The meaning of a game, or the portrayal of gender within a game, can be investigated as they emerge during play within a particular context, at the hands of a particular user – with the proviso that this interpretation is not assumed to be universal. Finally, a game's relationship to wider culture is also part of what 'it means'

– and this too can be analysed. The game may foreground its links to a particular film or book, or a popular sport, or it might incorporate certain gender or racial clichés, and as such a game might be collaborating in the perpetration of particular norms or values within wider culture. Whether any such values or patterns survive the unpredictable, variable and ephemeral nature of play would be another question.

CHAPTER 13

Doing Game Analysis

David Buckingham

Oᴜʀ primary aim in this book has been to offer a range of concepts and strategies that can be applied in the empirical analysis of computer games. We have not sought to develop a holistic, all-encompassing theory – not least because we believe that any such theory would be premature. Rather than seeking to address games in general, or the whole range of game genres, we have provided a series of case studies of specific games that illustrate broader issues in game analysis. Our theoretical approach has been eclectic, drawing principally on literary theory, film and media studies, semiotics and social psychology, as well as on recent work within the emerging field of 'game studies'. We hope to have provided a set of analytical frameworks – a conceptual toolkit – that might be applied to specific aspects of computer gaming, for example, in the context of student projects. In this brief conclusion, we draw together some of the key concepts and approaches we have used, and provide a kind of *aide memoire* for further research.

Defining games

In chapter 1, we reviewed a range of approaches to defining 'gameness' – that is, what makes a game a game. Celia Pearce's (2002) definition of the key elements of games – in terms of goals, obstacles, resources, rewards and penalties – provides a useful starting point here. She also draws attention to the different kinds of information that are available – to all players, to individual players and to the game itself – and to the ways in which information may be progressively revealed.

We also looked at a range of other theoretical approaches that allow us to explore some of the diversity of these different elements. For example, we can analyse the system of rewards and penalties (the 'economy' of the game), or the balance between elements that can be controlled by the player and those that cannot (which will include elements of chance). Likewise, we can explore the different kinds of obstacles within a game, as static or dynamic, controlled or random, transient or intransient, and so on. And we can analyse the different types of rules, as they define the properties of various components in the game, the procedures that must be followed, the characteristics of the game 'world' and so on. These approaches provide a useful first step in game analysis, particularly when it comes to comparing games. They help to define what is specific or distinctive about any given game, and they alert us to significant exceptions or deviations from the norm.

However, all these definitions focus on what we have called the *ludic* aspect of games, or the *game system*. They define what makes a game playable, and the limits within which play can occur. What they do not address is the *representational* dimension of games: that is, elements such as visual design, narrative, character and the game 'world'. These elements are less specific to games, and in many instances find their origins in other media. Yet, as we have argued, the analysis of computer games needs to address *both* the ludic and the representational dimensions, together with the relationships between them.

Game genres

Nevertheless, we argue that the most important distinctions between different genres of games derive from the game system. In chapter 2, we identified some key distinctions between the two main genres we explore in the book, Role Playing Games and action adventure games. We argued that genre conventions are not an abstract set of 'rules', but evolve through a dynamic relationship between text, producer and audience. In this sense, genre is a social practice, which needs to be understood in its social and economic context. However, it is possible to identify the various formulae that computer game genres employ: genres such as RPGs or action adventure games will offer different styles of gameplay, as a result of their distinctive configurations of elements like goals and obstacles, economies and rules.

Thus, in a typical action adventure game we play via an avatar who is provided by the game, and who generally follows a predetermined path through the game world, overcoming obstacles in a given order. The goals of the game are generally unambiguous, and its economies relate to quantifiable properties such as health or ammunition. The key emphasis in gameplay is on speed and accuracy. The player acquires skills as s/he proceeds through the game, but the avatar tends not to change or develop.

In contrast, with RPGs, the protagonist may be constructed by the player from a series of choices, and is often accompanied by a team of helpers with specific specialisms. The player has more freedom to explore the game world and to follow multiple quests, and may have the option to overcome obstacles without conforming to a set order. While the ultimate goal may be clear, there are often numerous subsidiary goals that may be irrelevant to this. Economies – in the form of experience points and inventories – are important, but they are more open to negotiation. The key emphasis in gameplay is on strategy rather than speed, and play is often a more reflective experience.

The differences between these two genres are far from absolute, and several of the games we discuss incorporate elements of both. Even so, we would argue that the key differences between these genres are to do with the game system, and not with the representational dimension: they apply whether the game takes place in a futuristic science-fiction world, in a medieval setting or in a contemporary urban wasteland.

The three case studies in chapter 2 indicate some of the diversity of the RPG genre in terms of representation. While the primary origins of the genre lie in the 'sword-and-sorcery' of table-top *Dungeons & Dragons* games – and, beyond that, in the work of Tolkien – this has been reconfigured in different ways through globalized encounters with other media forms such as science fiction and Japanese manga. As the genre shifts and mutates, so do its characteristic imagery and thematic concerns. Furthermore, different instances of the genre may have implications in terms of gameplay: the online game *Anarchy Online*, for example, is significantly less linear, and offers much more opportunity for player input, than the console- or PC-based *Final Fantasy* series.

Narrative and play

Our case study of *Baldur's Gate* provides a more developed account of the relationship between the representational and ludic dimensions of computer games. In chapter 3, we applied approaches from narrative theory developed primarily in relation to literary texts. Following the work of Genette (1980) and others, we distinguished here between story (the events of a narrative), discourse (the plotting or arrangement of those events) and narration (how the story is told). We considered the game in relation to this theory and, in the process, identified some of the key differences between games and narratives. These relate particularly to the management of time, and to plot.

Like many RPGs, *Baldur's Gate* insists on telling a story, regardless of how the player chooses to play the game. Underneath and around the variations of real time play, there is a conventionally structured narrative whose sequence cannot be altered; and this is conveyed via cutscenes, on-screen text boxes and scrolls, and the testimony of Non-Player Characters, which narrate the backstory and determine further developments in relatively straightforward ways. Meanwhile, players themselves also generate events through their play, which are 'told back' to them via the actions of animated figures and text boxes that function as a form of simultaneous narration akin to a sports commentary. The fact that the player is involved with plotting these events, however, means that they do not fit within classic models of narrative.

Our analysis also shows that readers (or, in this case, players) occupy different positions as regards the narrative: at times, the player acts in the first person, generating events; at times in the second, being addressed as 'you' and being told of events by other characters or by an invisible narrator; and at times, the player's character is swept up in events (for example in a cutscene) that evolve without any activity on their part, as if in the third person. This analysis clearly undermines any simple argument about players' 'identification' with on-screen characters – and hence, we would argue, simplistic assumptions about the effects of computer games.

In chapter 4, we explored the ludic elements of *Baldur's Gate* in more detail. We began by considering the character-generation process that is characteristic of most RPGs. We traced how players construct their on-screen protagonists from a range of variables relating to gender, 'race', alignment, abilities and so on; and how other options for character definition or development appear during the process of play. Here, again, there is interplay between elements that are more or less fixed or restricted and those that provide scope for negotiation or exploration. Some of these elements are primarily ludic (for example, to do with particular statistical attributes), while others appear to be primarily representational (to do with physical appearance) – although many character attributes have implications in both dimensions.

Our analysis went on to consider two modes of play that could be said to underpin the pleasures of computer gaming. *Immersion* refers to the sensation of 'being transported' by a text or an experience. In the case of isometric RPGs such as *Baldur's Gate*, we argue that this immersion is not primarily perceptual, to the extent that it monopolizes the senses of the user (as is typically the case in a movie theatre, for example). Rather, it relies more on a form of psychological immersion, which creates a sense of effortless absorption in the world of the game. By the gradual delivery of large amounts of interconnecting information, the game is able to beguile the player.

In combination with immersion, playing *Baldur's Gate* involves *engagement*, where the player is forced to adopt a more deliberate,

reflective stance – for example, when processing new 'story' information, solving problems or planning strategy. As Douglas and
Hargadon (2001) suggest, players will move between these two attentive states when absorbed in the game, at some points responding in a
localized way to immediate on-screen events and, at others, mentally
'stepping back' to pause and reconsider options. Both states utilize
ludic and representational aspects of the game. Immersion and
engagement are not mutually exclusive, nor is one state 'better' or
more desirable than the other. On the contrary, the oscillation
between them is central to the game's generation of *flow*. Flow is the
player's feeling of being 'in the zone', a highly satisfying and engrossing sensation that is triggered in part by the player's motion between
immersed and engaged states.

Our analysis of *Baldur's Gate* shows how the ludic and representational dimensions of the game interact to create the pleasures of play:
the two elements weave together to offer the player an ever-shifting
range of options and forms of participation. Of course, players may
choose to play the game in many different ways, for example, ignoring
much of the narrative and choosing to rely on immediate reactions
rather than carefully considered strategies. Yet the rules of the game
clearly reward certain modes of participation rather than others.
While games depend upon activity on the part of the player, they are
far from giving players absolute control over the events that can be
produced. Constraints, and the subversion that such constraints
inevitably invite (via 'cheats' and walkthroughs), are intrinsic to playing games with rules (as opposed to 'just playing'); and it would be
quite wrong to see such restrictions and rules as necessarily negative.

Traversing game space

By definition, narrative analysis is centrally concerned with time. Yet
the experience of space – of traversing, discovering and exploring
space – is equally central to computer games. In chapter 5 we introduced this issue by means of analysis of two similar but contrasting
games from different genres, the RPG *Planescape Torment* and the
action-adventure game *Silent Hill*. One of the key differences between
the games is in their spatial organization. *Silent Hill* is structured more
as a maze: the player proceeds to particular locations in a predetermined sequence, and progress depends upon successfully solving
puzzles or overcoming obstacles at each stage. The player is under pressure to keep moving, simply in order to survive. By contrast, *Planescape
Torment* is structured more like a rhizome: although progress is conditional, the player may spin off into deviations and side-paths at many

points. There is less pressure of time, as the player is free to roam and simply observe the detail of the game world.

These two different spatial structures invite different ways of traversing the game space. The more open structure of *Planescape Torment* provides an experience that is more dynamic, in the sense that it appears to offer more options to the player, and less determined, in that it allows a more significant role for chance. It also provides greater flexibility in terms of how the player can gain access to the game world and move across it. By contrast, on all these dimensions, *Silent Hill* is more structured and predetermined. Again, these are not evaluative terms – we would not argue that more conditionally structured games are inherently less interesting. In each case, the games under consideration are utilizing the navigational structures that serve their purposes.

These different spatial structures are accessed by the player through an avatar. As discussed in chapter 4, isometric RPGs rely more heavily on psychological immersion. By contrast, the mobile camera and 3-D perspectives of *Silent Hill* are able to evoke perceptual or physical immersion. These differences, we argue, are implicated in the player's relations with the different avatars and, by extension, with the perils and attractions of the game world.

This analysis further illustrates the importance of the ludic dimension in terms of defining game genres and gaming experiences. In some respects, the basic scenarios of the two games (their representational dimensions) are quite similar. Yet the experience of playing the games is very different. In each case, the emotional power of the game is a result of the particular relationship between its representational content and its gameplay.

Dynamics of play

Our analysis of *Final Fantasy VII* adopts a rather different theoretical approach, drawn primarily from social semiotics, yet it also develops our account of the relationships between the ludic and representational dimensions of games.

Chapter 6 focused on the role of the avatar, proposing two different ways of understanding Cloud Strife, the game's protagonist-hero. In terms of the game's representational dimension, Cloud can be seen as a 'heavy hero', with forbears in oral folk culture, Japanese manga epics and American comic books. From this perspective, we would see the hero as a simple, formulaic construction, whose qualities are manifested not in psychological introspection but in agonistic physical conflict. However, unlike the heroes of these older narratives, we also play the role of Cloud: he is a 'digital dummy', who is manipulated and controlled by the player, albeit within the terms of the game system. These two contrasting perspectives again reflect the differences between the representational and the ludic dimensions of the text. On the one hand, we have the text as an object to be read, and the player as an audience; while, on the other hand, we have the text as a process, and the player as a performer.

From a semiotic perspective, these contrasting orientations are also apparent in the visual and verbal 'grammar' of the game. Cloud as 'heavy hero' is presented in the third person, the 'he' who acts in the narrative; while in his role as 'digital dummy', he acts in the second person, as the 'you' who performs in the game. In terms of linguistic mood, the former is *indicative* – it describes or offers us the world; while the latter is *imperative* – it makes demands on us to respond and to act. These differences are also apparent multimodally, in the visual design – the shift from the isometric perspective in which we explore the world of *Final Fantasy* to the 3-D of the battle scenes – and in the music, with the shift from the contemplative mode of gameplay to the upbeat, stirring music of the battle scenes.

Here, again, it is possible for players to move between these different orientations; and these movements may be apparent in the linguistic structure of their accounts of play. It is certainly possible for individual players to choose one orientation in preference to another; but we would argue that much of the pleasure of the game derives from the ability to shift between them.

Some of these differences were apparent in our analysis of the various forms of fan production in chapter 7. Here we distinguish between three different forms of 'fan work', exploring how they rework or re-present the original text, and the different social motivations and interests that are at stake in doing so. Here again, evidence for these differences can be found in the linguistic structures that are employed, and in the different modes (visual, verbal) that are in play.

Thus, the walkthrough we discuss is based almost exclusively on the game system, and pays little heed to the representational dimension; and this is manifested in its use of the second-person imperative. In some respects, it is technical and dispassionate, but the author also reveals a more intense investment, both in the play itself and in his own role as 'expert' fan. In contrast, the fan fiction and poetry focus on the representational dimension, tending to draw from the cutscenes (which advance or fill in the narrative) rather than the interactive elements of the game itself. Meanwhile, the 'slash' art we describe goes beyond the world of the game, articulating aspects that are arguably implied but not directly stated in the original text. The focus here is very strongly on the representational dimension, although in the form of objectified images rather than narrative.

The different modes (writing, visual images) and genres (walk-through, fiction, poetry) employed by fans provide different opportunities for their interpretive activity. For example, writing (particularly poetry) allows fans to express emotional responses directly that may only be implied in the original text, while images place a central emphasis on visual beauty – and, in this case, explicit eroticism – that is only fleetingly experienced in the game itself.

Our account of *Final Fantasy VII* thus offers a different theoretical 'take' – and some new analytical tools – with which to explore the relationships between ludic and representational dimensions of games, both at the point of play and in subsequent 'fan work'.

Going online

The emergence of online games poses new questions for game analysis. In our analysis of *Anarchy Online* we focused particularly on the question of motivation, briefly raised in relation to *Final Fantasy*. Why do players engage with the game in the ways that they do, and what does this tell us about their broader social purposes?

In line with our previous analyses, we argued that there are motivations relating to both the representational and the ludic dimensions of the game. *Representational* motivations involve the manipulation of visual imagery, the construction of characters and the generation of narrative, as well as elements of performance. Thus, we consider how players' constructions of their avatar may reflect aspects of their own lives, or their aspirations and fantasies, and how different modes of play (for example, the style of committed 'Role Players' as opposed to regular players) reflect different social motivations. *Ludic* motivations relate more directly to the activity of play, and hence to areas such as competition, rules and objectives. Here we consider how players learn to manipulate their avatars and understand the economies of the game, and we suggest that the game provides a 'restricted language' that enables them to generate sequences of actions.

In addition to these familiar motivations, we identified a third, which is particularly pertinent to online gaming: that of *communal* motivation. Here we are referring to the ways in which players interact with each other, forming teams, teaching and learning, and regulating their own and each other's participation. Like the other motivations, this is a multimodal phenomenon: it is reflected both in the visual appearance and performance of the avatar, and in the live chat that is generated in parallel with the on-screen action.

Here again, it is important to recognize that these different motivations overlap and interact: players shift from one mode of play to another, sometimes in role and sometimes out of it, sometimes focused on competition and at others on the visual refinements of the game world. The pleasures of gaming derive partly from the diversity and flexibility of the motivations that it can engage.

The social life of gaming

These communal or social aspects of gaming were explored in more detail in chapters 9 and 10, which adopted a broadly social-psychological approach to analysing play. In chapter 9 we offered an account of the social interaction that surrounds the act of play itself, through an account of four boys playing the action adventure game *Soul Reaver*.

Our analysis here focused on two main issues. First, we looked at the different *roles* that players adopt in collaborative play. We identified the boys in our study as the Novice, the Owner, the Expert and so on – and of course it would be possible to extend or to develop such categories in different ways in relation to different instances. The key purpose of such labels, however, is that they draw attention to the different social positions and social motivations that are at stake in gameplay, and the ways in which gaming can be seen as a kind of social performance.

Secondly, we looked at the dimension of *learning*, and the different theories of learning that might be applied to collaborative gaming. Here, having found instances of 'scaffolding' as players supported each other, we offered a broader analysis of how players gradually gain access to a 'community of practice'. We found that the Expert in our group participated, not always effectively, by attempting to take control of the game and model effective strategies for the other players, while the other players were able to focus on different aspects of the game, and hence to make effective contributions that went beyond what the Expert could provide. In this context, the ludic dimensions of the game were to the fore, and narrative or representational dimensions were not explicitly addressed; and, in this sense, the analysis here complements the approaches developed in previous chapters.

Chapter 10 addressed the question of *agency* by means of a further case study of players' engagement with the game *Abe's Oddysee* and its sequels. This analysis explicitly focuses on an implicit theme in the book as a whole: to what extent is gaming 'interactive' or merely 'reactive', and to what extent do players have power or control over the experience?

In our analysis of the *Oddworld* message boards, we identified three types of agency, drawing on Albert Bandura's (2001) typology. *Personal* agency refers to the ways in which players deal with unintended outcomes, devise new pleasures in the 'margins' of the game and adapt their approach in the light of new information. However, the focus here is not just on the ludic dimension: it also relates to players' interpretation of the story and themes of the game, and its broader political implications. *Proxy* agency refers to the ways in which players assist each other, both in developing strategies for play (for example, via the use of walkthroughs and exchanging advice) and in interpreting the backstory. Here, again, proxy agency works across both ludic and representational dimensions. Finally, *collective* agency refers to the ways in which fans create and sustain community, in this case particularly by means of fan production (drawing and creative writing). There are complex processes of teaching and learning happening here, as fans share expertise and encourage each other's creative efforts; and the community effectively comes to regulate itself in the interests of supporting its members.

As we argue here and in earlier chapters, players do have a considerable degree of power to determine the nature of the play experience, and the meanings and pleasures it affords. However, this power is bounded by the constraints of the game system and of the representational possibilities of the game: *activity* on the part of players – or even of the most creative fans – should not be confused with *agency*, that is, the power to define the dominant parameters for cultural production.

Making games, making meanings

Our two final chapters took a broader approach, and began to engage with questions about the production and circulation of games. In chapter 11 we examined the extent to which the theoretical considerations we outlined in the course of this book relate to the design and creation of computer games. We explored this question by means of a case study of the production of *The Thing*, a horror action adventure game based on the John Carpenter film. Despite the developer's commitment to remaining faithful to the film, the move from movie to computer game involved shifts in the structuring of time, space and interaction that alter their meaning.

Working with *The Thing*'s lead programmer, Diarmid Campbell, and a game scriptwriter/producer, Katie Ellwood, we investigated questions of genre and adaptation. First, we looked at the wider relationship between horror in films and in games. We went on to examine the relationship between the film and the game in terms of the adaptation of content (narrative, setting). It was noted that themes from the film are not merely replicated in the game, but are converted to game mechanics. Thus, elements such as the environment, team dynamics, trust, infection or the monster, all of which feature in the film, become ludic variables in the game.

Through discussion with Campbell and Ellwood, and a review of these factors in relation to the development of *The Thing*, it became apparent that the mutuality and interconnectedness of the ludic and the representational dimensions were of central concern to the game's designers. The game's characters, for example, are given personalities, in the hope that the player will be more likely to have an emotional response to a teammate's survival or demise. For the developers of *The Thing*, representational factors (storytelling, characterization, atmosphere) were not merely decorative or cosmetic but also functional. These elements work to intensify the player's involvement in the game, and thus they are complicit in the creation of compelling, engrossing play experiences. On the other hand, even cutscenes, arguably the least ludic and least interactive of game features, fulfil a ludic agenda. They communicate information of strategic necessity and counterbalance the player's intense concentration (localized on single incidents, or particular confrontations, for instance), pulling them back to the mission as a whole, the wider game world, or contextualizing the immediate task within an overarching narrative – and thus render activities, challenges and accomplishments meaningful.

Finally, chapter 12 turned to the complex question of gender and games. Our account of this issue pointed out the need to integrate different levels of analysis – looking not just at the game 'text' and the activity of the player, but also at the games industry, and the ways in which games are produced, marketed and distributed.

At the level of the text, it is certainly possible to analyse the ways in which gender is (or is not) represented, in a variety of ways. We can use relatively traditional forms of content analysis to consider the presence or absence of male and female characters, and the roles that they perform. We can also look more qualitatively at the images of males and females, and the visual characteristics they display. Yet we also need to consider the ludic dimensions of games – their rule systems, and the different forms of activity and choice they permit. At least in the case of the RPG genre – which has been the main focus of our analysis in this book – the positions that are available to players (and the demands and invitations that are made to them) are often multiple and diverse.

When we look beyond this, to analyse the nature of play itself, the potential for choice and diversity multiplies even further. As we have shown, players may engage with games in very different ways, emphasizing very different aspects of the game world, and manifesting very different styles of play. These differences depend in part on the social context of play and the social experiences the player brings to the game – which are themselves structured in terms of characteristics such as gender, as well as social class, age, sexuality and ethnicity (among other factors). This potential diversity somewhat belies the essentializing arguments that are often made about male and female preferences or styles of play.

However, this analysis would not be complete without some account of the role of the games industry. As we indicate, meanings and assumptions relating to gender are apparent at every level of the process of design, production, marketing and circulation of games, as well as in the various 'secondary texts' that surround the games themselves, both those generated by the industry (such as games magazines) and by players themselves (both around and – in the case of online games – within the games themselves). As we suggest, it is at this level that there has been a self-fulfilling process whereby games have become 'gendered' – although we also argue that there may be signs of change in this respect.

While this chapter has a specific focus on gender, the multifaceted approach we adopt here is one that we feel needs to be developed in future work on games in general. As we argue, it is in analysing the *interaction between* these three elements – industry, text and audience – that we can begin to understand the complex ways in which the meanings of games are defined and produced.

Insert coin to continue

We did not set out to address all aspects of computer games in this book. A more comprehensive analysis would need to take a fuller account of the role of the game industry, and of the wider 'gaming culture' generated by marketing, retailing, magazines and online resources of many kinds; and it would also need to situate gameplay more firmly in the context of everyday life and social interaction. We have deliberately focused on game texts, and on the interactions between the game and the player; and in doing so, we have also chosen to focus on a limited range of game genres. It is certainly debatable whether the approaches we have outlined would be relevant to other types of games; but we hope to have provided a set of analytical tools and concepts that could be applied more broadly.

The study of computer games is still at an early stage of development, and there are many areas and issues that remain to be explored. We urgently need more sustained, in-depth analysis of specific games and gaming experiences, not least to counter the easy generalizations about games that circulate within popular – and indeed some academic – debates. We hope to have provided at least a starting point for such analysis, and some pointers as to how it might be achieved.

Notes

Chapter 1   Studying Computer Games

1 See <www.theesa.com>.
2 See *White Paper: Computer and Video Games* (August 2003) at <www.elspa.org.uk>.
3 <http://www.digiplay.org.uk/facts.php>.
4 From DFC Intelligence at <www.dfcint.com>.
5 According to X-tribes Silvers research, reported in the *Guardian* newspaper 13 December 2003.
6 The Entertainment and Leisure Software Publishers Association, press release dated 1 September 2004. <www.elspa.co.uk>.
7 See the debate following Katz's article at <www.slashdot.org/features>.
8 See <www.digiplay.org.uk/timeline.php>.

Chapter 2   Defining Game Genres

1 Game programming is also rule-bound, but a discussion of this would require a greater knowledge of programming than we possess.
2 Here, and in all quotations from fan writing in subsequent chapters, we reproduce the original language verbatim.
3 Role Play (and Roll Play) Games have continued to evolve since the 1970s – for an account of drama and performance orientated Live Action Role Play (LARP) see Salen and Zimmerman, 2003: 21.
4 One of the most comprehensive accounts of these table-top RPGs is Gary Fine's *Shared Fantasy: Role-playing Games as Social Worlds* (1983). Over the course of a year (in the late seventies, in Minneapolis, USA) the author attended, observed and participated in gaming sessions at a community centre, in private homes, and at gaming conventions.
5 For details about *Adventure*, go to <http://jerz.setonhill.edu/if/canon/Adventure.htm>. Text-based games and RPGs are still played online. Discworld MUD, for instance, is a multiplayer text-based online game based on the fantasy novels of Terry Pratchett. <http://discworld.atuin. net/lpc/>.
6 Developed by Gary Gygax and David Arneson, and first published by Tactical Studies Rules, or TSR, in the early 1970s.
7 Toriyama was the artist of the original *Dragonball Z* comic, as well as the character designer for the 1993 arcade game of the same name (1993, publisher Banpresto).

Chapter 3   Games and Narrative

1 See Eskelinen (2004) for a response to Jenkins's paper.
2 The term 'ludic', introduced in chapter 1, refers to those parts of *Baldur's Gate* that make it a game.
3 For Chatman, narrators and narratees are optional (1978: 51), but not all narratologists would agree. Plus, in some cases the narratee and narrator might be implied, rather than overt.
4 See Juul (2001) and Eskelinen (2001) for a full discussion of these points.

Chapter 4   Play and Pleasure

1 More precisely, the game is based on *Advanced Dungeons & Dragons*, 3rd edition rules (Wizards of the Coast, 2000). *Baldur's Gate* can be played on a limited network, with up to six other players, but here the focus remains on the game as it presents itself to a single player.
2 There is the option to load an image of the player's own if desired.
3 One player insisted in interviews that characters were tools, and that how they look is of no importance. Yet this same player later abandoned a character he was using, purely on the basis of unsightly facial hair (a black handlebar moustache). The moustache was irritating in two ways: for one, it was easily and playfully attached to the avatar's face, yet impossible to remove; for another, it was so large that it was impossible to ignore. The game was *Neverwinter Nights* (2002). A player was seen to construct a team for another RPG (*Icewind Dale*, 2000) that was led by a human but otherwise was composed of halflings and gnomes. This team was later abandoned because the player said that 'it looked like a school outing'. These are both examples of ludic and representational factors combining, with unpredictable results.
4 These are often called 'Non-Player Characters', despite the fact that their actions are under the player's control. The distinction is that, rather than being constructed by the player, these potential teammates are generated by the game, and arrive during the course of play, 'in character', and offer to join the protagonist's quest.
5 Post submitted by Ninja Master Booje to a discussion about Digital Women at <www.womengamers.com> on 21 February 2001.
6 The look or role or biography of an avatar is no indication of how they will act. In *Baldur's Gate: Dark Alliance*, the characters are hardened, adventuring types. Their first task was to cleanse the monster rodents from beneath a city. I witnessed one play session where players discovered that the avatars were wearing very little under their removable armour. So, instead of crushing vermin, the avatars ran around in underpants and helmets and jumped up and down in puddles, while the players laughed hysterically and sang pseudo-Viking songs about bath-time.
7 Marie-Laure Ryan (2003) has discussed additional forms of immersion, including spatial, temporal and emotional.
8 It is worth considering the inverse as well: if the player dislikes the game's narrative themes, if the 'story' is too confusing, or if gameplay is too easy or too difficult, it will be disengaging and non-immersive.
9 The community discussion group at Bioware's website, from which this quote is taken, was still active at the time of writing. It provides examples of players of *Baldur's Gate* and *Baldur's Gate II* resorting (sometimes in obvious

frustration) to external assistance. This message was posted by Syiss, 11 November 02: see <http://forums.bioware.com/viewforum.html?forum=19>.

Chapter 5   Space, Navigation and Affect

1 See Krzywinska (2002) for an analysis of horror and horror games.
2 Additionally, both *Planescape Torment* and *Baldur's Gate II: Shadows of Amn* featured in *PCZone's* list of the best ever RPGs (July 2002, 'The PCZone A List').
3 Quoted from a review by a Zombie Girl, at *Zombie Girls Net*, online at <http://www.zombiegirls.net/other/silenthill.html>.
4 Aarseth proposed the term 'ergodic' to refer to texts where 'nontrivial effort is required to allow the reader to traverse the text' (Aarseth 1997: 1).
5 *Silent Hill* and *Planescape Torment* employ different styles of immersion; this, I would argue, is likely to alter the manner in which they incorporate or invite engagement, plus it will alter the role played by ludic and representational aspects in the evoking of either state.
6 Freud associates the reassuring double with narcissism. Kristeva (1989) has described the narcissist as a subject expelled from the realm of the maternal but resisting the Oedipal orders, or 'law' on offer. This yearning after an alternative state chimes with the inventive, elaborative tendencies of fantasy in general, including *Planescape Torment*.

Chapter 6   Playing Roles

1 According to *UK Playstation Magazine*, November 1997.
2 Except in the case of Livingstone and Jackson's *Fighting Fantasy* adventure game books, which were in many ways precursors of Role-Playing Games, and especially of text-based online games, or MUDs.
3 Halliday cites the choices available in the bidding process in contract bridge as an instance of a 'restricted language' (Halliday, 1989). We return to this idea in chapter 8.

Chapter 8   Motivation and Online Gaming

1 <www.anarchyonline.com>.
2 <http://www.anarchy-online.com/content/game/story/episodes/>.
3 In other online computer games, players can manipulate the 'skins' of their avatars or create modifications of one form or another, but because of the kind of server utilized by *Anarchy Online* this game does not lend itself to this kind of intervention. For more on skins and MODS, see Anne-Marie Schleiner's website <www.opensorcery.net>.
4 We have changed this avatar's name.

Chapter 11   Film, Adaptation and Computer Games

1 The magazine was *Astounding Science Fiction* (1997: Bilson).
2 The game was published by Black Label Games/Vivendi Universal Games.
3 We interviewed Katie Ellwood and Diarmid Campbell first in person, and again by email. Both then responded to an early draft of this chapter, and their comments were incorporated. Katie was co-writer and assistant producer of

The Getaway (2002) and the writer/narrative producer of *Getaway: Black Monday* (2005).

4 The abject is fascinating and repellent. It shapes 'the struggle each subject must wage during the entire length of his personal history in order to become separate, that is to say, to become a speaking subject' (Kristeva, 1982: 94). Accordingly, many cultures have developed taboos and rituals in relation to phenomena (such as bodily fluids) that transgress the borders of self, of separateness.

5 Critics of *The Thing* (film) read the special effects as 'excessive' – as detrimental to the film's narration. This is another case of perceived excess being associated with low cultural status. For a summary of the critical reception of *The Thing*, see Billson (1997).

6 To call the tone of this walkthrough 'cautionary', does not contradict our earlier description of walkthroughs as 'imperative' in mood. The cautionary technically belongs to the monitory mood in language, which expresses warning, so it is close to the imperative; and the second and third sentences in this quote from the walkthrough are actually in the imperative.

7 See also Don Carson's 'Environmental Storytelling: Creating Immersive 3-D Worlds Using Lessons Learned from the Theme Park Industry', in *Gamasutra*, March 2000, accessed December 2004, online at <http://www.gamasutra.com/features/20000301/carson_01.htm>. For more on space, journeys and games, see Fuller and Jenkins' 'Nintendo and New World Travel Writing: A Dialogue', in Steven G. Jones (ed.), *Cybersociety: Computer-Mediated Communication and Community* (Thousand Oaks: Sage Publications, 1995), 57–72.

8 Actually, there have been women scientists working in Antarctic since the late 1960s. Prior to this, research facilities were controlled by the US military, who refused to allow women into the region. According to a 2002 newspaper report, men outnumber women in the area by two to one, but it is unusual to see a research team without a female member. See a report by Kristen Hutchinson, in *The Antarctic Sun* newspaper, 9 November 2003, accessed December 2004, online at: <http://www.polar.org/antsun/oldissues2003–2004/Sun110903/womenCrackTheIceBarriers.htm>.

Chapter 12   Games and Gender

1 Interview with author, April 2003.

2 See H. Kennedy (2005) for more on women *Quake* players.

3 Of course, the computer games industry is hardly alone in having a 'gender gap'.

4 There are male dissidents within the industry. In one incident a programmer working on a helicopter simulation game managed to replace the 'token female bimbos in bikinis with boy bimbos in bikinis' (Schleiner 1999: 5). Unfortunately, bikini boys began to appear more often than anticipated, which led to the programmer losing his job.

5 This might not be choice, of course. At least one of the players wanted considerably more access than she was able to secure.

Games Cited

Computer game citations are based on game credits listed at <www.allgame.com> and <www.mobygames.com> (accessed August 2005).

Advanced Dungeons & Dragons (2000) (non-computer game) Published by Wizards of the Coast.

Anarchy Online (2001) Developer: Funcom; Publisher: Funcom.

Baldur's Gate (1998) Developer: BioWare Corporation; Publisher: Black Isle Studios/Interplay.

Baldur's Gate II: Shadows of Amn (2000) Developer: BioWare Corporation; Publisher: Interplay.

Baldur's Gate: Dark Alliance (2001) Developer: Snowblind Studios; Publisher: Interplay Productions Inc.

Dance Dance Revolution (2001) Developer: Konami; Publisher: Konami.

Dragon Ball Z (1993) Developer: Banpresto; Publisher: Banpresto.

Dragon Quest (1986) Developer: Enix Corporation; Publisher: Enix Corporation.

Dungeons & Dragons (1974) (non-computer game) Developer: Gygax and Arneson; Publisher: TSR Hobbies Inc.

Enter the Matrix (2003) Developer: Shiny Entertainment; Publisher: Atari Inc.

EverQuest (1998) Developer: Verant Interactive; Publisher: 989 Studios.

EverQuest II (2004) Developer: Sony Online Entertainment; Publisher: Sony Online Entertainment.

Evolva (2000) Developer: Computer Artworks Ltd; Publisher: 14 Degrees East.

Final Fantasy VII (1997) Developer: Square Soft; Publisher: Square Soft.

Final Fantasy X (2001) Developer: Square Co. Ltd; Publisher: Square Electronic Arts LLC.

Final Fantasy XI (2003) Developer: Square Co. Ltd; Publisher: Square Electronic Arts LLC.

Getaway, The (2002) Developer: SCEE; Publisher: SCEE.

Getaway 2: Black Monday (2004) Developer: SCEE; Publisher: SCEE.

Gran Turismo 4 (2004) Developer: Polyphony Digital; Publisher: SCEA Inc.

Halo 2 (2004) Developer: Bungie Software; Publisher: Microsoft Games.

Icewind Dale (2000) Developer: BioWare Corporation; Publisher: Black Isle Studios.

Ico (2001) Developer: SCEA, Inc. (Japan); Publisher: SCEA, Inc.

Lineage: The Blood Pledge (2001) Developer: NCsoft Corporation Ltd; Publisher: NC Interactive.

Mafia (2002) Developer: Illusion Softworks; Publisher: Take 2 Interactive Inc.

Neverwinter Nights (2002) Developer: BioWare Corporation; Publisher: Atari Interactive, Inc.

Oddworld: Abe's Oddysee (1997) Developer: Oddworld Inhabitants; Publisher: GT Interactive Software.

Oddworld: Abe's Exoddus (1998) Developer: Oddworld Inhabitants; Publisher: GT Interactive Software.

Oddworld: Munch's Oddysee (2001) Developer: Oddworld Inhabitants; Publisher: GT Interactive Software.

Planescape Torment (1999) Developer: Black Isle Studios; Publisher: Interplay Productions, Inc.

Primal (2003) Developer: SCEE Cambridge Studios; Publisher: SCEA, Inc.

Quake (1996) Developer: id Software, Inc.; Publisher: id Software, Inc.

Samba de Amigo (2000) Developer: Sonic Team; Publisher: Sega.

Silent Hill (1996) Developer: Konami Computer Entertainment Kobe; Publisher: Konami UK Ltd.

Silent Hill 4: The Room (2004) Developer: Konami TYO Ltd; Publisher: Konami of America, Inc.

Sim City (1989) Developer: Maxis; Publisher: Maxis.

Sims (2000) Developer: Maxis; Publisher: Electronic Arts.

SingStar (2004) Developer: SCEE Studio London; Publisher: SCEE.

Soul Reaver: Legacy of Kain (1999) Developer: Crystal Dynamics, Inc.; Publisher: Eidos Interactive.

Star Wars (1983) Developer: Dev Atari, Inc.; Publisher: Atari, Inc.

Tetris (1988) Developer: Atari Games; Publisher: Atari Games.

The Thing (2002) Developer: Computer Artworks Ltd; Publisher: Black Label Games.

Tomb Raider (1996) Developer: Core Design Ltd; Publisher: Eidos Interactive.

References

Aarseth, E. (1997) *Cybertext; Perspectives on Ergodic Literature*, Baltimore: John Hopkins University Press.

Aarseth, E. (2001) 'Computer Game Studies, Year One', *Game Studies 1*; online at <www.gamestudies.org>.

Aarseth, E., Smedstad, S. M. and Sunnana, L. (2003) *A Multi-Dimensional Typology of Games*, paper presented at the Level Up; Digital Games Research Conference, Utrecht.

Adelman, C. (1992) 'Play as a Quest for Vocation', *Journal of Curriculum Studies* 22(2): 139–51.

Allison, A. (2000) 'A Challenge to Hollywood? Japanese Character Goods Hit the US', *Japanese Studies* 20(1): 67–88.

Anderson, P. (1980) *Arguments within English Marxism*, London: Verso.

AOL (2004) <http://media.aoltimewarner.com/media/cb_press_view.cfm?release_num=55253774>.

Aristotle (1961) *Poetics*, transl. S. H. Butcher, New York: Hill and Wang.

Bakhtin, M. (1968) *Rabelais and His World*, transl. Hélène Iswolsky, Cambridge, Mass.: MIT Press.

Bakhtin, M. M. and Holquist, M. (1981) *The Dialogic Imagination: Four Essays*, Austin: University of Texas Press.

Bandura, A. (2001) 'Social Cognitive Theory: An Agentic Perspective', *Annual Review of Psychology* 52: 1–26.

Barthes, R. (1973) *Mythologies*, transl. Annette Lavers, New York: Hill and Wang.

Beato, G. (1997, April 1997) 'Computer Games for Girls is No Longer an Oxymoron', *Wired*: 101–6; online at <http://www.wired.com/wired/archive/5.04/es_girlgames.html>.

Billson, A. (1997) *The Thing*, London: BFI Publishing.

Boal, A., McBride, C. A. and McBride, M. O. L. (1979) *Theater of the Oppressed*, London: Pluto Press.

Bonnafont, G. (1992) 'Video Games and the Child', paper presented at *Myths and Realities of Play*, London.

Borgh, K. and Dickson, W. P. (1986) 'Peer Status and Self-perception among Early Elementary School Children: The Case of Rejected Children', in P. F. Campbell and G. G. Fein (eds), *Young Children and Microcomputers*, Englewood Cliffs, NJ: Erlbaum.

Bratman, Michael E. (1999) *Faces of Intention: Selected Essays on Intention and Agency*, Cambridge: Cambridge University Press.

Bryce, J. and Rutter, J. (2001) *In the Game – In the Flow: Presence in Public Computer Gaming*, paper presented at the Computer Games and Digital Textualities, IT University of Copenhagen; online at <www.digiplay.org.uk>.

Bryce, J. and Rutter, J. (2002) *Killing Like a Girl: Gendered Gaming and Girl Gamers' Visability*, paper presented at the Computer Games and Digital Cultures, Tampere, Finland; online at <http://www.digiplay.org.uk/media/ cgdc.pdf>.

Bryce, J. and Rutter, J. (2003) 'The Gendering of Computer Gaming: Experience and Space', in S. Fleming and I. Jones (eds), *Leisure Culture: Investigations in Sport, Media and Technology*, Eastbourne: Leisure Studies Association, 3–22; online at <http://les1.man.ac.uk/cric/Jason_Rutter/papers/LSA.pdf>.

Bub (2002) 'Console Roleplaying Games Part 1: The Early Years', *Gamespy Website* <http://archive.gamespy.com/articles/april02/crpg1>.

Buckingham, D. (1993) 'Just Playing Games', *English and Media Magazine* 28: 21–5.

Buckingham, D. (2000) *After the Death of Childhood: Growing Up in the Age of Electronic Media*, Cambridge: Polity.

Buckingham, D. (2002) 'The Electronic Generation? Children and New Media', in L. Lievrouw and S. Livingstone (eds), *The Handbook of New Media: Social Shaping and Consequences of ICT* London: Sage, 77–89.

Buckingham, D. and Scanlon, M. (2003) *Education, Entertainment and Learning in the Home*, Buckingham: Open University Press.

Burn, A. (2003) 'Poets, Skaters and Avatars: Performance, Identity and New Media', *English Teaching: Practice and Critique* 2: 6–21.

Burn, A. and Parker, D. (2001) 'Making Your Mark: Digital Inscription and Animation, a New Visual Semiotic', *Education, Communication, Information* 1(2): 79.

Butler, J. (1990) *Gender Trouble*, New York: Routledge.

Caillois, R. (1958/1979) *Man, Play and Games*, New York: Schocken Books.

Cardwell, S. (2004) 'The Hidden Gamer – the Female Audience for Online "Casual" Games', presentation at Women in Games Conference, Portsmouth, UK, June 2004.

Carr, D. (2005 in press) 'Contexts, Gaming Pleasures and Gendered Preference', *Simulation and Gaming* 36/4 (December), symposium issue on video game theory.

Carr, D. (2006 in press) 'The Rules of the Game, the Burden of Narrative: *Enter the Matrix*', in S. Gillis (ed.), *The Matrix: Cyberpunk Reloaded*, London: Wallflower Press.

Carson, D. (2000) 'Environmental Storytelling: Creating Immersive 3D Worlds Using Lessons Learned from the Theme Park Industry', *Gamasutra*, online at <http://www.gamasutra.com/features/20000301/carson_01.htm>.

Casas, F. (2001) 'Video Games: Between Parents and Children', in I. Hutchby and J. Moran-Ellis (eds), *Children, Technology and Culture*, London: Falmer, 32–47.

Casewell, R. (2003) 'Letter to the Editor', *Edge* 122, Bath, UK: Future Publishing Ltd.

Cassell, J. (2000) 'Storytelling as a Nexus of Change in the Relationship between Gender and Technology: A Feminist Approach to Software Design', in J. Cassell and H. Jenkins (eds), *From Barbie to Mortal Combat: Gender and Computer Games*, Cambridge, Mass.: MIT Press, 298–327.

Cassell, J. and Jenkins, H. (2000) *From Barbie to Mortal Combat: Gender and Computer Games*. Cambridge, Mass.: MIT Press.

Chatman, S. (1978) *Story and Discourse: Narrative Structure in Fiction and Film*, Ithaca, N.Y.: Cornell University Press.

Clover, C. J. (1992) *Men, Women and Chainsaws; Gender in the Modern Horror Film*, Princeton: Princeton University Press.

Copier, M. (2003) 'The Other Game Researcher', paper presented at the Level Up; Digital Games Research Conference, Utrecht.

Creed, B. (1990) '*Alien* and the Monstrous-Feminine', in A. Kuhn (ed.), *Alien Zone; Cultural Theory and Contemporary Science Fiction Cinema*, London: Verso, 128–44.

Crogan, P. (2000) 'Things Analogue and Digital', *Senses of Cinema 5*, online at <www.sensesofcinema.com>.

Crogan, P. (2004) 'The Game Thing: Ludology and Other Theory Games', *Media International Australia incorporating Culture and Policy* 110: 10–18.

Csikszentmihalyi, M. (2002) *Flow; The Classic Work on How to Achieve Happiness*, 2nd edn, London: Rider.

de Castell, S. and Bryson, M. (2000) 'Retooling Play: Dystopia, Dysphoria and Difference', in J. Cassell and H. Jenkins (eds), *From Barbie to Mortal Combat: Gender and Computer Games*, Cambridge, Mass.: MIT Press, 232–61.

Deleuze, G. and Guattari, F. (1988) *A Thousand Plateaus: Capitalism and Schizophrenia*, London: Althone.

Diniz-Sanches, J. (2003) 'Editorial; the Girl Issue', *Edge* 3 (March), Bath: Future Publishing Ltd.

Douglas, J. Y. and Hargadon, A. (2000) *The Pleasure Principle: Immersion, Engagement, Flow*, paper presented at the 2000 Hypertext Conference, San Antonio, TX; online at <http://faculty.gsm.ucdavis.edu/~hargadon/Research/Hargadon_ACM_PlePri00.pdf>.

Douglas, J. Y. and Hargadon, A. (2001) 'The Pleasures of Immersion and Engagement: Schemas, Scripts and the Fifth Business', *Digital Creativity* 12: 153–66.

Dove, S. (2004) 'Top Ten Booth Babe Pick-up Lines', *G4 VideogameTV* website; online at <http://www.g4tv.com/e32005/features/50/Top_Ten_Booth_Babe_Pickup_Lines.html>.

Durkin, K. (1995) *Computer Games: Their Effects on Young People. A Review*, Sydney: Office of Film and Literature Classification.

Dyer, R. (1997) *White*, London: Routledge.

Ermi, L. and Mayra, F. (2003) 'Power and Control of Games: Children as the Actors of Game Cultures', paper presented at the Level Up; Digital Games Research Conference, Utrecht.

Eskelinen, M. (2001) 'The Gaming Situation', *Game Studies*, 1 at <www.game-studies.org>.

Eskelinen, M. (2004) 'From Markku Eskelinen's Online Response', in N. Wardrip-Fruin and P. Harrigan (eds), *First Person; New Media as Story, Performance, and Game*, Cambridge, Mass.: MIT Press, 120–1.

Eskelinen, M. and Tronstad, R. (2003) 'Video games and configurative performances', in M. J. P. Wolf and B. Perron (eds), *The Video Game Theory Reader*, London: Routledge, 195–220.

Faceless (2000) 'Review of *Baldur's Gate*', *Mobygames.com*, online at <http://www.mobygames.com/game/view_review/reviewerId,523/gameId,712/platformId,3/>.

Fein, G. G., Campbell, P. F. and Schwartz, S. S. (1987) 'Microcomputers in the

Preschool: Effects on Social Participation and Cognitive Play', *Journal of Applied Developmental Psychology* 15: 197–208.

Feinstein, K. (1999) Interviewed in 'Towards a Definition of Videogames', *Electronic Conservancy*, online at <www.videotopia.com/errata1.htm>.

Feuerstein, R. (1979) *Dynamic Assessment of Retarded Performers*, Baltimore, Md: University Park Press.

Fine, G. (1983) *Shared Fantasy: Role-Playing Games as Social Worlds*, Chicago and London: University of Chicago Press.

Fisher, S. (1995) 'The Amusement Arcade as a Social Space for Adolescents: An Empirical Study', *Journal of Adolescence* 18: 71–86.

Frasca, G. (2003) *Ludologists Love Stories, Too: Notes from a Debate That Never Took Place*, paper presented at the Level Up; Digital Games Research Conference, Utrecht.

Freud, S. (2003) *The Uncanny*, transl. D. McLinton, London: Penguin Books.

Friedman, T. (1999) 'The Semiotics of *Sim City*'. *First Monday*, 4, online at <http://www.firstmonday.org/issues/issue4_4/index.html>.

Fuller, M. and Jenkins, H. (1995) 'Nintendo and New World Travel Writing: A Dialogue', pp. 57–72 in S. G. Jones (ed.), *Cybersociety: Computer-Mediated Communication and Community*, Thousand Oaks: Sage Publications.

Gansmo, H., Nordli, H. and Sørensen, K. (2003) 'The Gender Game. A Study of Norwegian Computer Game Designers', NTNU/SIGIS Report <http://www.sigis-ist.org>.

Gee, J. P. (2003) *What Video Games have to Teach Us about Learning and Literacy*, Basingstoke: Palgrave Macmillan.

Genette, G. (1980) *Narrative Discourse*, transl. J. E. Lewin, Oxford: Blackwell.

Giacquinta, J., Bauer, J. and Levin, J. (1993) *Beyond Technology's Promise: An Examination of Children's Educational Computing at Home*, Cambridge: Cambridge University Press.

Goldstein, J. (2001) *Does Playing Violent Video Games Cause Aggressive Behaviour?*, paper presented at the Playing By The Rules; The Cultural Policy Challenges Of Video Games, Chicago (26–27 October); online at <http://culturalpolicy.uchicago.edu/conf2001/agenda2.html>.

Goldstein, J. and Raessens, J. (eds) (2004) *Handbook of Computer Game Studies*, Cambridge, Mass.: MIT Press.

Gorriz, C. M. and Medina, C. (2000) 'Engaging with Girls with Computers through Software Games', *Communications of the ACM* 43: 42–9.

Graner-Ray, S. (2003) *Gender-Inclusive Game Design*, Highham, Mass.: Charles River Media.

Gray, A. (1992) *Video Playtime: The Gendering of a Leisure Technology*, London: Routledge.

Green, B. and Bigum, C. (1993) 'Aliens in the Classroom', *Australian Journal of Education* 37(2): 119–41.

Grodal, T. (2003) 'Stories for Eye, Ear, and Muscles: Video Games, Media and Embodied Experiences', in M. J. P. Wolf and B. Perron (eds), *Video Game Theory Reader*, New York and London: Routledge, 129–56.

Gunter, B. (1998) *The Effects of Video Games on Children: The Myth Unmasked*, Sheffield: Sheffield Academic Press.

Gurer, D. and Camp, T. (2002) 'An ACM-W Literature Review on Women in Computing', *SIGSCE Bulletin* 32: 121–7; online at <http://cs.wellesley.edu/~cs/docs/gurer-camp.pdf>.

Haines, L. (2004) *Women and Girls in the Games Industry*, Interim Report, Lizzie Haines Research/The Game Plan, Manchester, UK: Media Training Northwest; online at <http://66.102.9.104/search?q=cache:wAFjna6j68cJ:www.igda.org/women/MTNW_Women-in-Games_Sep04.pdf+lizzie+haines+girls+games&hl=en>.

Halliday, M. A. K. (1970) 'Relevant Models of Language', *Educational Review* 22: 26–37.

Halliday, M. A. K. (1985) *An Introduction to Functional Grammar*, London: Edward Arnold.

Halliday, M. A. K. (1989) *Spoken and Written Language*, 2nd edn, Oxford: Oxford University Press.

Herz, J. C. (1997) *Joystick Nation: How Video Games Ate Our Quarters, Won Our Hearts, and Rewired Our Minds*, Boston: Little, Brown.

Hodge, B. and Kress, G. (1988) *Social Semiotics*, Cambridge: Polity in association with Blackwell.

Hodge, R. and Tripp, D. (1986) *Children and Television*, Cambridge: Polity.

Holzman, L. (1995) 'Creating Developmental Learning Environments: A Vygotskian Practice', *School Psychology International* 16: 199–212.

hooks, b. (1992) *Black Looks: Race and Representation*, Boston: South End Press.

Hughes, F. P. (1999) *Children. Play, and Development*, London: Allyn and Bacon.

Huizinga, J. (1938/1955) *Homo Ludens: A Study of the Play Element in Culture*, Boston: Beacon Press.

Hultsman, W. (1992) 'Constraints to Activity Participation in Early Adolescence', *Journal of Early Adolescence* 12: 280–99.

Hutchinson, K. (2003) 'Women Come to Ice as Equals', *The Antarctic Sun* (November): 1; online at <http://www.polar.org/antsun/oldissues2003-2004/Sun110903/ womenCrackTheIceBarriers.htm>.

Innocente, E. (2002) 'Cloud's Strife', online at <www.rpgfan.com/fanfics/ffvii/cloud1.html>.

International Hobo (2003) *Demographic Game Design*, online at <http://www.ihobo.com/articles/>.

Iwamura, R. (1994) 'Letter from Japan: From Girls who Dress Up Like Boys to Trussed-up Porn Stars – Some of the Contemporary Heroines on the Japanese Screen', *Continuum: The Australian Journal of Media & Culture* 7: 109–30.

Izawa, E. (2000) 'The Romantic, Passionate Japanese in Anime: A Look at the Hidden Japanese Soul', in T. Craig (ed.) *Japan Pop! Inside the World of Japanese Popular Culture*, New York: ME Sharpe.

Jarvinen, A. (2003) 'Making and Breaking Games: A Typology of Rules', paper presented at the Level Up; Digital Games Research Conference, Utrecht.

Jarvinen, A., Helio, S. and Mayra, F. (2002) *Communication and Community in Digital Entertainment Services; Prestudy Research Report*, Tampere: University of Tampere Hypermedia Laboratory; online at <http://tampub. uta.fi/tup/951-44-5432-4.pdf>.

Jenkins, H. (1992) *Textual Poachers: Television Fans and Participatory Culture*, London: Routledge.

Jenkins, H. (1993) 'X Logic: Repositioning Nintendo in Children's Lives', *Quarterly Review of Film and Video* 14: 55–70.

Jenkins, H. (2000) 'Voices from the Combat Zone; Game Grrlz Talk Back', in J. Cassell and H. Jenkins (eds), *From Barbie to Mortal Combat: Gender and Computer Games*, Cambridge, Mass.: MIT Press, 328–41.

Jenkins, H (2004). 'Game Design as Narrative Architecture', in N. Wardrip-Fruin and P. Harrigan (eds), *First Person; New Media as Story, Performance, and Game*, Cambridge, Mass.: MIT Press, 118–30.

Jenkins, H. and Squire, K. (2002) 'The Art of Contested Spaces', in L. King (ed.), *Game On: The History and Culture of Video Games*, London: Lawrence King, 64–75.

Jessen, C. (1999) *Children's Computer Culture: Three Essays on Children and Computers*, Odense, Denmark: Odense University Press.

Juul, J. (2001) 'Games Telling Stories? A Brief Note on Games and Narratives', *Game Studies, 1*, online at <www.gamestudies.org>.

Juul, J. (2003) 'The Game, the Player, the World: Looking for a Heart of Gameness', paper presented at the Level Up; Digital Games Research Conference, Utrecht.

Karpov, Y. V. (1994) 'Vygotskian Approach to Instruction: The Problem of Learning and Transfer', unpublished manuscript, Vanderbilt University.

Katz, J. (2003) 'Up, Up, Down, Down', at <www.slashdot.org/features>.

Kennedy, H. W. (2005) 'Illegitimate, Monstrous and Out There: Female *Quake* Players and Inappropriate Pleasures', in J. Hollows and R. Moseley, *Feminism in Popular Culture*, London: Berg.

Kent, S. L. (2001) *The Ultimate History of Video Games*, New York: Prima Life.

Kerr, A. (2003) *Women Just Want to Have Fun: A Study of Adult Female Players of Digital Games*, paper presented at the Level Up: Digital Games Research Conference, Utrecht.

Kitkowski, A. (2002) 'Gaming in Japan: An Odyssee', *Places to Go, People to Be; The On-line Magazine for Roleplayers* 19.

Kline, S. (2003) 'Media Effects Redux or Reductive: A Reply to the St. Louis Court Brief', *Participations* 1(1), at <www.participations.org>.

Kline, S., Dyer-Witheford, N., de Peuter, G. (2003) *Digital Play: The Interaction of Technology, Culture and Marketing*, Montreal: McGill-Queens University Press.

Kouzlin, A. (1990) *Vygotsky's Psychology*, Cambridge, Mass.: Harvard University Press.

Kress, G. (2003) *Literacy in the New Media Age*, London: Routledge.

Kress, G. and van Leeuwen, T. (1996) *Reading Images: The Grammar of Visual Design*, London: Routledge.

Kress, G. and van Leeuwen, T. (2001) *Multimodal Discourse: The Modes and Media of Contemporary Communication*, London and New York: Arnold; Oxford University Press.

Kristeva, J. (1982) *Powers of Horror; An Essay in Abjection*, transl. L. S. Roudiez, New York: Columbia University Press.

Kristeva, J. (1989) *Black Sun; Depression and Melancholia*, transl. L. S. Roudiez, New York: Columbia University Press.

Krotoski, A. (2004) *Chicks and Joysticks: An Exploration of Women and Gaming*, London: Entertainment and Leisure Software Publishers Association (ELSPA); online at <http://www.elspa.com/about/pr/elspawhitepaper3.pdf>.

Krzywinska, T. (2002) 'Hands-on Horror', in T. Krzywinska and G. King (eds), *ScreenPlay*, London: Wallflower Press, 206–24.

Krzywinska, T. (2003) 'Playing Buffy: Remediation, Occulted Meta-game-physics and the Dynamics of Agency in the Videogame Version of *Buffy the Vampire Slayer*', in *Slayage* 8 (March 2003); online at <http://www.slayage.tv/essays/slayage8/Krzywinska.htm>.

Kücklich, J. (2003) 'Perspectives of Computer Game Philology', *Game Studies 3*, online at <www.gamestudies.org>.

Lanning, L. (2002) cited in W. Benedetti, *The Art of Gaming* at seattlepi.com. 12 March; online at <http://seattlepi.nwsource.com/lifestyle/61797_gameart. shtml>.

Laurel, B. (1991) *Computers as Theatre*, Menlo Park, Calif.: Addison Wesley.

Laurel, B. (1998) *Keynote Address: Technological Humanism and Values-Driven Design*, paper presented at the CHI-98, Los Angeles; online at <http:// www.tauzero.com/Brenda_Laurel/Recent_Talks/Technological_Humanism. html>.

Laurel, B. (1999) *Keynote Address: New Players, New Games*, paper presented at the GDC 99, San Jose; online at <http://www.tauzero.com/Brenda_Laurel/ Recent_Talks/Intro.html>.

Lave, J. and Wenger, E. (1991) *Situated Learning: Legitimate Peripheral Participation*, Cambridge: Cambridge University Press.

Lidz, C. S. (1995) 'Dynamic Assessment and the Legacy of L. S. Vygotsky', *School Psychology International* 16: 143–53.

Livingstone, S. and Bovill, M. (1999) *Young People, New Media*, report of the Research Project 'Children, Young People and the Changing Media Environment', London: London School of Economics.

Lombard, M. and Ditton, T. (1997) 'At the Heart of it All: The Concept of Presence', *Journal of Computer-Mediated Communication* 3; online at <http://www. ascusc.org/jcmc/vol3/issue2/>.

Lundgren, S. and Bjork, S. (2003) *Game Mechanics: Describing Computer-Augmented Games in Terms of Interaction*, paper presented at the Technologies for Interactive Digital Storytelling and Entertainment, Darmstadt, Germany; online at <http://www.tii.se/play/publications/2003/mechanics.pdf>.

McGonical, J. (2003) 'A Real Little Game: The Pinocchio Effect in Pervasive Play', in M. Copier and J. Raessens (eds), paper presented at Level Up: Digital Games Research Conference, Utrecht: University of Utrecht Press.

McLelland, M. (2000) 'Male Homosexuality and Popular Culture in Modern Japan', *Intersections* 3, January 2000; online at <http://www.sshe.murdoch. edu.au/intersections/issue3_contents.html>.

McMahan, A. (2003) 'Immersion, Engagement and Presence: A Method for Analyzing 3-D Video Games', in M. J. P. Wolf and B. Perron (eds), *The Video Game Theory Reader*, New York and London: Routledge, 67–87.

McMeeking, D. and Purkayastha, B. (1995) 'I Can't Have My Mom Running Me Everywhere: Adolescents, Leisure, and Accessibility', *Journal of Leisure Research* 27: 360–78.

Marr, A. J. (2001) 'In the Zone: A Biobehavioral Theory of the Flow Experience', *Athletic Insight: The Online Journal of Sport Psychology* 3; online at <http://www.athleticinsight.com>.

Mayra, F. (2003) 'Pac-man and the Ivory Tower', online at <www.igda.org/ columns/ivorytower>.

Megura, Kao (2000) *Final Fantasy 7 Walkthrough*, online at <http://www.the-spoiler. com/RPG/Square/Final.fantasy.7.html>.

Milles, I. (2003) 'Book Review of *Gender Inclusive Game Design* by Sheri Graner Ray', *iDevGames: The Macintosh Game Developer Community Website*, online at <http://www.idevgames.com/reviews/books/id55>.

Moby (2002) Moby's Editorial Forum, RPG Dreamers, online at <http:// www.rpgdreamer.com/editorial/mobyeditorial7.html>.

Morgan, Chris (2002) Walkthrough of *The Thing*, *Outpost 31*, accessed Jan 2005, online at <http://db.gamefaqs.com/console/ps2/file/thing.txt>.

Mortensen, T. (2002) 'Playing With Players: Potential Methodologies for MUDs', *Game Studies* 2, online at <www.gamestudies.org>.

Murray, J. (1997) *Hamlet on the Holodeck; The Future of Narrative in Cyberspace*, Cambridge, Mass.: MIT Press.

Murray, J. H. (2000) *Hamlet on the Holodeck; The Future of Narratives in Cyberspace*, 3rd edn, Cambridge, Mass.: MIT Press.

Myers, D. (1992) 'Time, Symbol Manipulation and Computer Games', *Play & Culture* 5: 441–57.

Neale, S. (1980) *Genre*, London: BFI.

Neale, S. (2000) *Genre and Hollywood*, London: Routledge.

Neale, S. (ed.) (2002) *Genre and Contemporary Hollywood*, London: Routledge.

Newman, J. (2002) 'The Myth of the Ergodic Videogame', *Game Studies* 2(1), online at <www.gamestudies.org>.

Ong, W. (2002) *Orality and Literacy: the Technologizing of the Word*, London: Routledge, online at <http://www.nwe.ufl.edu/~jdouglas/dc12303-Douglas.pdf>.

Orr Vered, K. (1998) 'Blue Group Boys Play *Incredible Machine*, Girls Play Hopscotch: Social Discourse and Gendered Play at the Computer', in J. Sefton-Green (ed.), *Digital Diversions: Youth Culture in the Age of Multimedia*, London: UCL Press, 43–61.

Pearce, C. (2002) 'Story as Play Space: Narrative in Games', in L. King (ed.), *Game On: The History and Culture of Video Games*, London: Lawrence King, 112–19.

Pearce, C. (2004) 'Towards a Game Theory of Game', in N. Wardrip-Fruin and P. Harrigan (eds), *First Person: New Media as Story, Performance, and Game*, Cambridge, Mass., and London: MIT Press, 143–53.

Pelletier, C. (2005, under review) 'The Uses of Literacy in Studying Computer Games; Comparing Students' Oral and Visual Representations of Games', *English Teaching: Practice and Critique* 4(1) (May, 2005); online at: <http://www.soe.waikato.ac.nz/english/ETPC/Current.html#forthcoming>.

Pelligrini, A. D. and Perlmutter, J. (1989) 'Classroom Contextual Effects on Children's Play', *Developmental Psychology* 25: 289–96.

Playstation 2: Special Edition, The Sex Issue 13 (May 2003), Bath, UK: Future Publishing Ltd.

Poole, S. (2000) *Trigger Happy: The Inner Life of Video Games*, London: Fourth Estate.

Poole, S. (2002) 'Character Forming', in L. King (ed.), *Game On: The History and Culture of Videogames*, London: Laurence King.

Propp, V. (1970) *Morphology of the Folktale*, Austin: University of Texas Press.

Radway, J. (1984) *Reading the Romance*, Chapel Hill, NC: University of North Carolina Press.

Rafaeli, S. (1998) 'Interactivity: From New Media to Communication', in R. P. Hawkins, J. M. Wiemann and S. Pingree (eds), *Sage Annual Review of Communication Research: Advancing Communication Science*, vol. 16, Beverly Hills, Calif.: Sage.

Ree, J. (1999) *I See a Voice: A Philosophical History of Language, Deafness and the Senses*, London: Harper Collins.

Rehak, B. (2003) 'Playing at Being: Psychoanalysis and the Avatar', in M. J. P. Wolf and B. Perron (eds), *The Video Game Theory Reader*, London: Routledge, 103–28.

Roberts, D. F. and Foehr, U. G. (2004) *Kids and Media in America*, Cambridge: Cambridge University Press.

Rockwell, G. (1999) 'Gore Galore: Literary Theory and Computer Games', *Computers and the Humanities*, online at <www.game-culture.com/articles.html>.

Ryan, M.-L. (1994) 'Immersion vs. Interactivity: Virtual Reality and Literary Theory', *Postmodern Culture* 5; online at <http://www.infomotions.com/serials/pmc/pmc-v5n1.shtml>.

Ryan, M.-L. (2003) *Narrative as Virtual Reality: Immersion and Interactivity in Literature and Electronic Media*, Baltimore and London: John Hopkins University Press.

St Louis Court Brief, The (2003) 'Debating Audience "Effects" in Public', *Participations* 1(1), online at <www.participations.org>.

Salen, K. and Zimmerman, E. (2003) 'This is Not a Game: Play in Cultural Environments', paper presented at the Level Up; Digital Games Research Conference, Utrecht.

Salen, K. and Zimmerman, E. (2004) *Rules of Play; Game Design Fundamentals*, Cambridge, Mass.: MIT Press.

Saussure de, F. (1916/1983) *Course in General Linguistics*, transl. Roy Harris, La Salle, Ill.: Open Court.

Schleiner, A.-M. (1998–2004) <www.opensorcery.net>.

Schleiner, A.-M. (1999) 'Parasitic Interventions: Game Patches and Hacker Art', online at <www.opensorcery.net>.

Schott, G. and Horrell, K. (2000) 'Girl Gamers and Their Relationship with the Gaming Culture', *Convergence* 6(4): 36–53.

Sellers, J. (2001) *Arcade Fever: The Fan's Guide to the Golden Age of Video Games*, New York: Running Press.

Smith, Andy (2002) *Drawing Dynamic Comics*, New York: Watson-Guptill Publications.

Spielmann, Y. and Mey, K. (2005) 'Call for Contributions: Special Issue of the Journal *Convergence*'; online at <http://convergence.luton.ac.uk/callforpapers/hybridity>.

Squire, K. (2002) 'Cultural Framing of Computer/Video Games', *Game Studies 2(1)*; online at <www.gamestudies.org>.

Stern, L. (1997) ' "I Think Sebastian, therefore . . . I Somersault": Film and The Uncanny', *Australian Humanities Review*, November 1997; online at <http://www.lib.latrobe.edu.au/AHR/archive/Issue-November-1997/stern2.html>.

Subrahmanyam, K. and Greenfield, P. M. (2000) 'Computer Games for Girls: What Makes Them Play?', in J. Cassell and H. Jenkins (eds), *From Barbie to Mortal Combat: Gender and Computer Games*, Cambridge, Mass.: MIT Press, 46–71.

Sutton-Smith, B. (1979) *Play and Learning*, London: Longmans.

Sutton-Smith, B. (1986) *Toys as Culture*, New York: Gardner Press.

Sutton-Smith, B. (1997) *The Ambiguity of Play*, Cambridge, Mass.: Harvard University Press.

Talmadge, W., Eric, B. and Paul, B. (2002) 'Creative Player Actions in FPS Online Video Games: Playing Counter-Strike', *Game Studies* 2, online at <www.gamestudies.org>.

Taylor, T. L. (2003) 'Multiple Pleasures: Women and Online Gaming', *Convergence: The Journal of Research into New Media Technologies* 9: 21–46.

Tobin, J. (1998) 'An American *Otaku* (or, a Boy's Virtual Life on the Net)', in J. Sefton-Green (ed.), *Digital Diversions: Youth Culture in the Age of Multimedia*, London: UCL Press, 106–27.

Tobin, J. (ed.) (2004) *Pikachu's Global Adventure: The Rise and Fall of Pokemon*, Durham, NC: Duke University Press.

Todorov, T. (1977) *The Poetics of Prose*, transl. R. Howard, Oxford: Blackwell.

Tolkien, J. R. R. (2002) *The Lord of the Rings and The Hobbit*, London: Collins Modern Classics.

Turkle, S. (1984) *The Second Self: Computers and the Human Spirit*, New York: Simon and Schuster.

Turner, J. (2001) 'Reasons for Liking Tolkien', *London Review of Books* 23 (November).

van Cleef, D. (1997) 'Review of *Final Fantasy 7*', *Games & Software Review* 2(3).

van Leeuwen, T. (1999) *Speech, Music, Sound*, Basingstoke: Palgrave Macmillan.

Volosinov, V. N. (1973) *Marxism and the Philosophy of Language*, transl. M. L. and I. R. Titunik, London and New York: Seminar Press.

Vygotsky, L. S. (1978) *Mind in Society: The Development of Higher Psychological Processes*, Cambridge, Mass.: Harvard University Press.

Waine, M. (2001) 'The Evolution of Console RPGs', *PS* 2 (October): 98–103.

Walkerdine, V. (2004) 'Remember Not to Die: Young Girls and Video Games', *Papers: Explorations into Children's Literature* 14, 28–37.

Werry, C. (1996) 'Linguistic and Interactional Features of Internet Relay Chat', in S. C. Herring (ed.), *Computer-mediated Communication: Linguistic, Social and Cross-cultural Perspectives*, Amsterdam and Philadelphia: John Benjamins, 47–63.

Williams, L. (1999) 'Film Bodies: Gender, Genre and Excess', in L. Baudy and M. Cohen (eds), *Film Theory and Criticism*, 5th edn, New York and Oxford: Oxford University Press, 701–15.

Wolf, M. J. P. (2002) *The Medium of the Video Game*, Austin: University of Texas Press.

Wolf, M. J. P. (2003) 'Abstraction in the Video Game', in M. J. P. Wolf and B. Perron (eds), *The Video Game Theory Reader*, London: Routledge, 47–66.

Wolf, M. J. P. and Perron, B. (2003a) 'Introduction', in M. J. P. Wolf and B. Perron (eds), *The Video Game Theory Reader*, London: Routledge, 1–24.

Wolf, M. J. P. and Perron, B. (eds) (2003b) *The Video Game Theory Reader*, London: Routledge.

Wood, D. (1994) *How Children Think and Learn*, Oxford: Blackwell.

Wood, D. and Wood, H. (1996) 'Vygotsky, Tutoring and Learning', *Oxford Review of Education* 22(1): 5–16.

Wood, D., Bruner, J. S. and Ross, G. (1976) 'The Role of Tutoring in Problem Solving', *Journal of Child Psychology and Psychiatry* 17: 89–100.

Wood, R. (1997) 'An Introduction to the Modern American Horror Film', in B. Ashley (ed.), *Reading Popular Narrative; A Source Book*, London and Washington: Leicester University Press, 189–92.

Woodcock, B. S. (2003) *An Analysis of MMOG Subscription Growth*, online at <http://pw1.netcom.com/~sirbruce/Subscriptions.html>.

Wright, J. and Samaras, A. (1986) 'Play and Mastery', in P. F. Campbell and G. G. Fein (eds), *Young Children and Microcomputers*, Englewood Cliffs, NJ: Erlbaum.

Zarabatny, L., Hartmann, D. and Rankin, D. (1990) 'The Psychological Functions of Preadolescent Peer Activities', *Child Development*, 61: 1067–80.

Ziajka, A. (1983) 'Microcomputers in Early Childhood Education? A First Look', *Young Children* 38: 61–7.
Zimmerman, E. (2002) 'Do Independent Games Exist?', in L. King (ed.), *Game On: The History and Culture of Video Games*, London: Lawrence King, 120–9.

Index